SELLING
ONLINE

Canada's Bestselling Guide to Becoming a Successful E-Commerce Merchant

JIM CARROLL AND
RICK BROADHEAD

WILEY
wiley.com

John Wiley & Sons Canada Ltd
22 Worcester Road
Etobicoke, Ontario
M9W 1L1

National Library of Canada Cataloguing in Publication Data

Carroll, Jim, 1959–
    Selling online : Canada's best-selling guide to beginning a successful e-commerce merchant / Jim Carroll, Rick Broadhead. — Rev. and updated.

Includes index.
ISBN 1-55335-019-7

1. Internet marketing.   I. Broadhead, Rick   II. Title.

HF5548.32.C37 2002   658.8'4   C2002-903680-1

Production Credits
Cover and text design: Kyle Gell Design
Author photos: Ray Boudreau (Jim Carroll), Wolf Kutnahorsksy (Rick Broadhead)

Printed in Canada

10 9 8 7 6 5 4 3 2 1

CONTENTS

ACKNOWLEDGEMENTS

First and foremost, we would like to thank Susan McKeown and her team at Visa Canada for their enthusiastic support of this book. The first edition of *Selling Online* was released in Canada in 1999 and followed by regional editions in the United States, Germany, and Russia. None of this would have been possible without the generous assistance of Visa Canada and other regional Visa organizations around the world. The initial idea for this book was conceptualized in Canada and we're extremely grateful to Susan for believing in this project from day one.

This book also wouldn't be possible without the support of our publisher, John Wiley & Sons Canada. Thanks to Robert Harris for championing this project, to Susan Girvan for coordinating production, and to our editor, Valerie Ahwee, for her editorial work on the manuscript.

Our work is supported by the assistance of many technology and Internet companies. We would like to acknowledge Osama Arafat at Q9 Networks for Web site hosting; Mark Jeftovic at EasyDNS for DNS services; Anthony Bamford and the gang at Media Planet for fabulous Web design assistance; Ian Barker at Infomart for access to Infomart Special Edition; and Tibor Shanto at Dow Jones Interactive for access to the Dow Jones Interactive service.

Finally, the process of writing a book is always made easier by the unwavering support of our families. Rick would like to thank his parents, as well as his sister Kristin and her husband Lionel. Jim would like to thank Christa for her motivation and encouragement through some of the more challenging aspects of this project. And also, thanks to Thomas and Willie for teaching the real meaning of life beyond technology.

ABOUT THE AUTHORS

Jim Carroll, FCA, is an internationally recognized expert on the "wired world" and the Internet, and a popular media authority, keynote speaker, and business consultant.

He is author of the critically acclaimed book *Surviving the Information Age*, a motivational work that encourages people to cope with the future, as well as co-author of the popular books *Get a (Digital) Life: An Internet Reality Check, Selling Online: How to be a Successful E-Commerce Merchant*, and *Lightbulbs to Yottabits: How to Profit by Understanding the Internet of the Future*.

In his presentations and workshops, Jim helps executives, staff, and organizations comprehend the impact of digital change, determine the strategies necessary to take them forward, and the action steps they must follow to survive and thrive in the wired world. He provides concrete guidance and direction on issues as diverse as business strategies, workplace issues, personal goals, business plans, and corporate direction.

Jim has spoken to tens of thousands of people as a conference opening or closing keynote speaker, and has also provided workshops and management strategy sessions for some of North America's leading organizations. He is recognized for his motivational style—humorous, engaging, challenging, yet thought provoking.

His clients include companies such as American Express, Taiwan Semiconductor Manufacturing Company, Visa, Cleveland World Trade Center, Electronic Transaction Association, Blue Cross/Blue Shield of Florida, KPMG, Monsanto, Deloitte & Touche, Nortel Networks, JD Edwards, American Academy of Ophthalmologists, World Congress of Association Executives, IBM, and countless others.

He is a frequent media commentator and pundit, with over 3,000 radio, print, Web, and TV interviews to his credit. He has also hosted a variety of audio/radio programs through the years that have gained an international reputation.

Jim writes on a regular basis for the media. His popular weekly "e-biz/ Digital Survivor" column in the *Globe and Mail* gained a widespread international following for its perspectives on the impact of technology, the

Internet, and e-commerce. He also writes for many other publications, including *Digital Marketing, CA Magazine,* and many, many more. An award-winning columnist, he was named as "one of 50 international journalists to know" by the *Online Journalism Review.* His columns are followed worldwide by many influential organizations.

A chartered accountant by profession, he has over twelve years of experience at the world's largest public accounting firm and a solid business and financial background in all major business, government, and industry sectors. He was recently named an FCA (Fellow of the Institute of Chartered Accountants of Ontario), an honour given to those who exhibit outstanding performance within their careers.

You can reach Jim by e-mail at **jcarroll@jimcarroll.com** or via his Web site, **www.jimcarroll.com**.

Rick Broadhead, MBA, is renowned as one of North America's leading e-business experts, industry analysts, and professional speakers. He is the co-author of a record-breaking thirty-two books about the Internet and e-business, including *Lightbulbs to Yottabits: How to Profit by Understanding the Internet of the Future* and *Get a (Digital) Life: An Internet Reality Check.* In 1994, Rick co-wrote the *Canadian Internet Handbook,* the first Canadian Internet book, which became a national number-one bestseller within weeks of its release.

Specializing in helping organizations to capitalize on the latest technology trends affecting their industries, Rick is a highly sought-after keynote speaker and consultant by industry and trade associations, small businesses, and Fortune 500 firms across North America. His clients have included organizations such as McDonald's, Rogers AT&T Wireless/AT&T Canada, the Canadian Real Estate Association, the Canadian Association of Chain Drugstores, Food and Consumer Product Manufacturers of Canada, Sun Microsystems, Scouts Canada, the Ontario Pharmacists' Association, Canada Post Corporation, the Association of Crafts and Creative Industries, Travelodge Hotels, Microsoft, the Government of the Northwest Territories, the Minnesota Office of Tourism, and Entel, one of the largest telecommunications companies in Chile.

Rick is also an experienced seminar leader in the field of executive development, having assisted executives and managers from hundreds of North American firms with their e-business strategies, including leading companies such as Kraft Foods, Ford Motor Company, Bayer, Sharp

Electronics, Royal Doulton, Polaroid, Motorola, Volkswagen, Sears, Xerox, Nestle, AT&T, and Coca-Cola.

As an Internet industry veteran and bestselling author, Rick Broadhead is regularly called on by both print and broadcast media for his analysis and commentary on events in the technology industry. Over the last six years, he has conducted hundreds of interviews with radio stations, television networks, magazines, daily and community newspapers, and industry publications from across North America.

In 1999, Rick partnered with United Media in New York, one of the largest newspaper syndicates and licensing companies in the United States, to create and launch e-Trivia, a nationally syndicated newspaper feature about technology.

Rick holds an MBA in marketing from York University's Schulich School of Business in Toronto, where he was awarded the George A. Edwards Marketing Medal for demonstrated excellence in marketing.

You can reach Rick by sending an e-mail to **rickb@rickbroadhead.com** or visit his World Wide Web site at **www.rickbroadhead.com**.

Contacting Us

We are always interested in hearing from our readers. We welcome your comments, criticisms, and suggestions, and we will use your feedback to improve future editions of this book. We do try to respond to all e-mail sent to us. If you're an e-commerce merchant in Canada, we'd love to hear from you! We're always looking for case studies and examples of successful Canadian companies to include in future editions of this book.

Contacting the Authors Directly

We would love to hear from you! Here is how to contact us on the Internet:

To reach:	Send e-mail to:
Both authors simultaneously	authors@handbook.com
Jim Carroll	jcarroll@jimcarroll.com
Rick Broadhead	rickb@rickbroadhead.com

Our World Wide Web Sites

The World Wide Web site for all our books is www.handbook.com. There you will find information about our most recent publications as well as ordering information.

We also invite you to visit our individual Web sites as well, where you will find information about our consulting and speaking activities as well as other background information on the both of us:

Jim Carroll's Web site: www.jimcarroll.com
Rick Broadhead's Web site: www.rickbroadhead.com

Two things to remember as you read through the book: inevitably some of the Web addresses listed in the book won't work. Web sites are constantly changing addresses and locations. In addition, Web sites often shut down altogether. This is a fact of life when it comes to the Internet. If you can't find a particular Web site, try to search for it within one of the popular search engines or Web directories. If that doesn't work, feel free to contact us by e-mail and we'll do our best to help you. Secondly, just as Web site addresses change so do the prices and services that we describe. Always contact the organization in question to get the latest pricing/services information.

1

Thinking Strategically and Realistically About Selling Online

"While the publicity and coverage of the dot-com world of retailing has diminished significantly, the importance of online retailing hasn't."

— *"The Values of Online Retailing Keep on Clicking,"*
DSN Retailing Today, March 25, 2002

This is a book about setting up a "store" or a "storefront" on the Internet. Selling products on the Internet is just one of many ways you can use the Internet in your business. In addition to being a selling tool, the Internet can also be used for marketing, customer support, cost containment, recruitment, procurement, communications, and a variety of other functions. Indeed, there is hardly an activity in the business world that doesn't cross paths with the Internet. Undeniably, selling online, also often referred to as "e-commerce," is one aspect of the Internet that gets a great deal of attention.

But can you actually sell things online? The fact that you bought this book reveals that you think so, but you might be discouraged by the early experiences of the "dot-com start-ups," many of which quickly went out of business following the dot-com boom of the late 1990s. Isn't that a signal that the idea of selling online is doomed? Not really. Although nearly everyone now agrees that online shopping will represent only a small percentage of retail sales well into the future, the small percentages often obscure the market potential. Think about this: even if Internet sales reach only 5 percent of total retail sales in a couple of years, that's still billions and billions of dollars that will be spent online.

Lots of small businesses have expanded their markets and found new sources of revenue by using the Internet during the last several years; some of those businesses are profiled in Chapter 8. Indeed, it is the small business entrepreneur, not the high-profile, publicity-hungry, overly greedy dot-com start-up, that is introducing many of the more exciting online services.

So while many early dot-com retailers might continue to struggle or have disappeared altogether, the fact remains that there is opportunity to be had online—if you are realistic about what you hope to accomplish, about your expectations, and about the degree of work that you will have to put into your online efforts.

This book is about how you—as a merchant—can use the Internet to reach new customers, service your existing customers in exciting ways, and sell your products globally.

e-fact

Of small business owners with Web sites, 58 percent say that their Web site has played an important role in the success of their small business.

Source: Homestead Technologies (www.homestead.com)

What You Need to Know Before You Begin

In this book, we'll help you understand the many different aspects of setting up a store on the Internet so you can sell your products and services worldwide. We'll discuss payment methods and security issues, review the most important components of an online store, help you market your online store and build brand loyalty, and bring you expert advice from companies that are already selling their products online. But before you immerse yourself in the exciting world of e-commerce, you need to have a full appreciation of three important issues:

- You need to have realistic expectations.
- Setting up an online store is a detailed process that involves five stages: planning, preparation, development, execution, and refinement.
- Selling online should be just one part of your overall Internet strategy.

Another important point is that this book is primarily focused on how to create an effective online store aimed at consumers (often referred to as B2C, or business-to-consumer, e-commerce). It does not examine in depth the issues associated with B2B, or business-to-business, e-commerce.

Yet B2B is an extremely important type of e-commerce and indeed will far surpass the levels of spending to be seen with B2C e-commerce. That's why (later in this chapter) we will examine some of the B2B issues that might also be part of your online strategy. Moreover, there is no doubt that B2B might greatly affect your retail store strategy as we discuss in the section "What About B2B?" Hence, while much of this book focuses on B2C commerce, many of the issues and strategies might be equally applicable to B2B commerce.

> Canadian Internet users check their e-mail more often than they brush their teeth.
>
> Source: AOL Canada (www.aol.ca) and RoperASW (www.roperasw.com)
>
> **e-fact**

Be Realistic About the Internet

What was the biggest problem on the Internet with what have now come to be known as the "dot-com years"? Inexperienced people with over-inflated expectations who created online stores with the belief that once they did the work, the dollars would roll in. Of course, for many of them, that did not happen. That's why we'd like to suggest that the most important thing you can do in your venture into the world of selling online is to take a serious look at your likelihood for success.

Before you begin thinking about setting up an online store, face some cold, hard facts about the reality of retail on the Internet:

- You might not succeed.
- You might create an online store only to find that no one is aware of it.
- You might fail to sell anything online.
- You might try to sell a product that no one is interested in purchasing.
- You might be destroyed by competition that is far more Internet-savvy and that has far deeper pockets than you.

- You might not be able to keep your inventory up-to-date, or you might have problems in filling the orders you do receive.

The fact is, your online store might come nowhere close to meeting your expectations—with disastrous results.

The Drumbeat of Internet Hype

One of the biggest dangers when developing an online store is not to succumb to Internet hype and develop unrealistic expectations of your online business. At the same time, it's important not to be dissuaded by all the negative hype about the Internet.

If you get caught up in the excessive promise of e-commerce from the early days, you could fall into the trap of believing that all you have to do is establish an online store, then sit back and wait for the riches of this modern-day gold rush to fall into your lap. Fortunately, the end of the dot-com era has helped many people to realize this was not true. When the market collapsed, people realized the online retail and dot-com start-ups were likely not the pots of gold at the end of the rainbow that had been promised by the Internet hype machine. The public and investors woke up to the fact that online sales for many vendors were less than exciting, and thus began the era of anti-hype—the idea that there was no opportunity to be had online, and that online shopping would always be a bust. This is probably as extreme a view as was the dot-com hysteria of years past.

The Hype Isn't Over—at Least in Terms of How "Easy" It Is

Yet even so, some of the hype about online shopping continues unabated. In addition, there continues to be an almost endless stream of stories about how easy it is to do business on the Internet. This is particularly true of sites that promise you can set up an online store in a "matter of minutes," a bizarre proposition if you think about it. After all, how many successful retailers do you know who can create a store in the "real world" in only a few minutes? As a result, many businesses are being led down the garden path when it comes to online retailing. They think that achieving online success is simple: just establish an online store with a few mouse clicks.

It's a major trap you should avoid. Don't delude yourself into thinking that online business is easy. If you plan on exploring the world of selling online and business on the Internet in general, be realistic about what it takes and what is involved. Those who have implemented successful strategies know that it involves a lot of money, plenty of hard work, real commitment, and a strong will. Even then the returns might be a long time in coming. Selling online isn't a game. It's a business.

> Two-thirds of companies in the United States say that their sales have increased as a result of using e-mail marketing.
>
> *Source: Direct Marketing Association (www.the-dma.org)*
>
> **e-fact**

Assess Your Likelihood of Success

Over the years, there have been many companies who rushed to peddle their wares over the Internet, yet many of these companies didn't have sound business plans, nor did they have any market research to guide them in their activities.

Before you decide to pursue the concept of an online store as a business strategy, you should carefully assess the viability of your idea. For example, you may have a product or service that people don't want to buy over the Internet. While there are many success stories of ventures selling books, music, and travel services over the Internet, there are also many stories of Internet ventures that haven't gone quite so well. Groceries? Lumber supplies? Lawn products? There are many who are skeptical about the likelihood that many people will buy such products online.

Survey several of your existing customers to see if they would consider buying your product or service electronically. This is an important bit of research to do. Clearly, an online store will be useless if the demographic you are trying to reach isn't hooked up to the Internet, or isn't willing to shop there.

There's a lot that could go wrong. You may end up investing a lot of money in an online store, only to realize that very few of your customers are ready to buy this way. You could spend a lot of time building a sophisticated Web site, then discover months later that traffic to it is dismal. Or you may be seduced by the sophisticated Internet and e-business technology you use and fritter away many precious hours that should have been spent elsewhere.

There is a real danger in getting caught up in an online store, particularly if you are already in business. You might find that in your effort to move online, you've neglected your regular business activities, so that your business is suddenly in a rather precarious position. That is why carefully assessing your plans is so important.

Why Do Online Retailers Fail?

- Unrealistic business models
- Low margins leading to losses
- Excessive spending on marketing
- Unrealistic expectations when it comes to online sales (companies failed to appreciate that consumers and businesses aren't going to change their shopping behaviour overnight)
- Failing to appreciate how expensive it is to set up an online store (it is not a low-overhead business model as people once thought; consumers still expect customer service, for example)
- Intense competition
- Lack of differentiation
- Lack of focus on the issues that really matter: profitability, gross margins, cash flow, quality of the business model, etc.
- Not appreciating the fact that the Internet is just another channel

How do you avoid failure? Follow the advice that we provide in this chapter and throughout this book. In particular, Chapter 8 is required reading for every company that wants to sell on the Internet. Thanks to our panel of twenty online retailers, you'll learn about some of the biggest pitfalls of online retailing.

Cautious Optimism Is the Best Rule

Don't misinterpret our comments of concern and caution. Don't think for a minute that the Internet and e-commerce aren't worthwhile. Indeed, getting online now is important: you will gain valuable experience with e-commerce and, over the long term, the Internet will play a major role in the global economy.

Like many people, we are big believers in the potential of e-commerce, but we firmly believe that as you get involved, you must recognize what you are up against.

That's why in preparing your Internet strategy, you should carefully assess its weaknesses. Where can your strategy go wrong? What are its potential vulnerabilities? What can you do to protect yourself from anticipated problems in your strategy? Where should you be aggressive, and where should you be cautious?

The Internet is littered with the broken dreams of many entrepreneurs. In most cases, those who fell for the hoopla failed to approach e-commerce with a careful, well-thought-out strategy that clearly assessed the risks and examined the potential for success of doing business in the wired world.

Consumers and businesses will spend over US $1 trillion shopping on the Internet in 2002.

Source: International Data Corporation (www.idc.com)

e-fact

This Is Serious Stuff

The Internet and e-commerce aren't a game. If you plan on taking your business to the Internet, you've got to approach this as a serious, important business initiative. You've got to plan, strategize, prepare, implement, execute, and follow up with the highest degree of professionalism and attention. You've got to think about issues like customer service and product fulfillment; otherwise you will condemn yourself to playing a game in which the likelihood of losing is extremely high. Setting up an online store is a business, and you should never forget that.

What Process Should You Follow?

As you go through the process of creating your online store, there are five main steps that you will go through. They are:

- Planning
- Preparation
- Development
- Execution
- Refinement

We discuss each of these steps below.

Step #1: Planning

Don't rush to create your online store. Instead, do your homework. Take the time to understand the opportunity that's before you, assess the risks, and figure out exactly what you hope to accomplish.

There are some key questions you need to ask yourself in the planning stage, many of which we cover below.

Twenty-Three Questions to Ask Yourself About Selling Online

1. *What are you trying to accomplish?* First and foremost, think about goals, goals, goals. Make sure that you clearly understand your goals, your mission, and your expectations before you set up your online store. What are you trying to achieve? What are your objectives? What do you expect to accomplish a year or two from now? Put your goals and dreams through a reality check and make sure they are realistic.

2. *Are you prepared to make the commitment?* Setting up an online store involves not only a financial commitment but a time commitment as well. If you want to be successful, you'll have to sacrifice a lot of personal time to get your online business up and running. Even after launch, the business will still demand a lot of your time. Make sure that you're prepared to stay committed to your online business venture.

3. *Do you have a backup plan?* In the event that your online business doesn't succeed, do you have a backup plan? Many people want to invest their life savings in an Internet venture, but they don't think about what they will do if their online business fails. Don't be foolish and throw all of your eggs into one basket. Don't assume that your online business will work. It may not. Think about what you're going to do if it doesn't succeed.

4. *Do you have a business plan?* It's important to put down your plans in writing so that you have a clear idea of where you are going and what you want to accomplish.

   A business plan is a written document that summarizes your business concept and your plans for your business. It includes an overview of the concept of your business, a market analysis, your sales and marketing strategy, financial projections, and an overview of how you intend to handle operational issues in your online store such as credit card security, customer support, shipping and fulfillment, and product returns.

   In the event that you need a loan from a financial institution in order to set up your online store, a business plan will be essential. A business plan is also crucial for a couple of other reasons. First, you're no doubt excited about the prospect of selling products on the Internet, but perhaps you're too excited. Too many people rush onto the Internet with ideas that aren't sound. Preparing a business plan will force you to think about every aspect of your online business: to set goals, determine the resources you need, and identify obstacles and challenges you will face daily. A business plan can help you see the "big picture," which will allow you to make business decisions more clearly and confidently. Going through this exercise will give you an opportunity to organize your thoughts more effectively. It will also make it easier for you to identify flaws in your strategy. And since a business plan will force you to test the assumptions you have about your business, it can make the difference between a business that succeeds and one that fails!

5. *What is the likelihood that your products will sell online?* Although we are strong believers that virtually any product can be sold over the Internet, not all products will sell well over the Internet. Don't go online blindly. Make sure you fully understand the buying habits and preferences of your target market. Is there an adequate customer base on the Internet for you to sell to? What is the feasibility of your idea?

6. *What are the online sales forecasts for the types of products you plan to sell?* You should ensure that you understand whether the product you hope to sell online actually sells online. To do so, visit your local library or use online databases like Electric Library Canada (www.elibrary.ca) to find articles and industry reports that project online sales in the industry that you want to enter. This will help you determine whether or not your idea is viable.

There are other useful resources that might help you assess your market, among them:
- NUA Internet Surveys (www.nua.com)
- eMarketer (www.emarketer.com)
- Shop.Org (www.shop.org)

You might also consider using online research from market research firms that specialize in the Internet industry, such as Jupiter Media Metrix (www.jmm.com) and Forrester Research (www.forrester.com). But caution is warranted, given that such reports are costly and may be too expensive for a small business.

7. *Are there potential sales channel conflicts that you need to be concerned with?* If your company manufactures products, and you currently sell these products through retail outlets other than your own, you need to talk with your retail partners before you launch your on-line store. Why? Retail stores may be sensitive to the fact that you are going to bypass them and sell your products directly to con-sumers and/or businesses on your Web site. In fact, "sensitive" may be the wrong word to use. The retailers who carry your prod-ucts may be downright angry if they learn that you're selling direct through the Internet, especially if you plan to undercut them on price. Of course, it's also possible that your retailers won't be upset by your plans. The only way to gauge their feelings is to let them know what you're doing and then see how they react.

Depending on your particular situation, losing the good rela-tionships that you have with retailers may not be something you want to risk. Have a discussion with your retail partners and brief them on your online plans. Based on their reaction, you may decide not to proceed. If they express concern, see if you can arrive at a compromise. For example, price may be a key issue. If you agree not to discount your products on your own Web site, the retailers may be much less resistant. Alternatively, you could work out an arrangement whereby the retailers get free advertisements on your Web site.

One way that some organizations have dealt with channel con-flict is to redirect any sales to their channel partners rather than trying to sell direct. This has been particularly true in the airline industry. For example, many airlines will sell tickets directly to customers, but they have also built into their Web sites the capa-bility for customers to choose to have tickets issued through their traditional travel agent, i.e., the channel partner of the airline. By building in this capability, the airlines are working hard to steer some business to their channel partners and thus assuage their concerns. The same type of capability could be built into your own site if you are a manufacturer—redirect any actual sales so that they are fulfilled by your channel partners. Finally, you might decide to sell only some and not all of your products online. This way, retailers get exclusivity on some products.

8. *What are the critical success factors for Internet-based sales in your industry?* Critical success factors are issues that can make the difference between the success and failure of your online store. Beyond basic critical success factors like customer service and return policies, which all online stores need to have, every industry has its own critical success factors that are crucial to online sales. For example, some products are more information-intensive than others. Selling books online is very different from selling cars. Customers who are shopping for a car will require a lot more information than customers who are shopping for books. If the products you are selling are high-involvement goods, and customers require a lot of information before making a purchase decision, you will need to take this into account when creating your online store.

   Also consider the issue of price. How critical will the prices of your products be? Some industries are more price-sensitive than others.

   Depending on your industry, shipping may be a critical success factor. For example, if you are selling chocolates, you will have to arrange for special shipping containers so customers will receive your chocolates in good condition. Failure to address that issue could spell the end of your online efforts.

   You also need to think about the types of people you are targeting. For example, are you trying to convert your existing customers over to an electronic order process, or are you predominantly focusing on new customers? The latter might imply a heavier concentration on marketing as a key success factor for your store.

   These are just a few examples of critical success factors that may affect your industry. There are many others. We suggest that you list all of the critical success factors you can think of for the products you intend to sell. Use this information as a basis for building your online business strategy.

9. *How will your online store differ from others on the Internet?* There are already tens of thousands of stores on the Internet. Have you thought about how you will differentiate your store from all the

others? Product selection? Product line? Price? Customer service and support? What unique value proposition will you offer your customers? Why should online shoppers shop at your online store instead of the others?

Your answers to these questions will be especially important if you intend to approach a financial institution for a loan or line of credit. Your likelihood of success will depend on how well you can differentiate your business from others in an already crowded on-line marketplace.

10. *Will you be focusing on a niche market?* Many people believe that one of the keys to success on the Internet is coming up with a business plan that targets a specific rather than a broad market. In other words, the more focused your product, the better the chances of success.

Rather than opening up an online bookstore that sells a variety of books, focus on a specific product category for books, such as travel books or hard-to-find books on some specialized topic. Needless to say, many of the major product categories will be dominated by big players with very deep pockets. There is still room for new players, but you may have a much better chance of success if you specialize in a particular niche of a larger market category.

11. *Are you prepared to deal with customer support issues?* Some organizations have discovered that once they put up an online store, they get flooded with customer support requests and are unprepared to deal with the volume of messages. Once you're in business, customers will begin inquiring about a wide range of issues, including shipping, returns and exchanges, order tracking, and, of course, your products. Make sure that you anticipate your customer support requests in advance and that you're prepared to meet them. For guidance on putting together a customer support strategy, see the customer service section of Chapter 3, "Tips for Building an Effective Online Store."

e-fact

The average Internet-using Canadian family spends over thirty-two hours online every week, and over 1,600 hours online per year.

Source: Ipsos-Reid (www.ipsos-reid.com)

12. *Do you have a fulfillment strategy?* Once you start getting orders, you must be prepared to package and ship products as quickly as possible. Not only that, but you need to be fully prepared to deal with returns and exchanges as well.

    Fulfillment and return issues have been some of the biggest problems that online retailers have encountered so far. Learn from other people's mistakes and work hard to avoid these problems in your own online initiatives.

    Make sure you work through how an order will flow from your Web site through to the packaging and shipping processes. Needless to say, you can't afford to have a disorganized fulfillment system; otherwise you'll quickly find yourself in over your head. We recommend that you create a flow chart of how an order will move through your store. This will help you visualize your order logistics.

    As you'll discover in Chapters 2 and 3, figuring out your shipping options can be an extremely complicated process. Make sure you thoroughly investigate the shipping options available through Canada Post and each of the major courier services.

13. *What are your core competencies?* Many organizations try to do everything themselves and end up overwhelmed. Even big retailers have made this mistake. Toys "R" Us, for example, tried to do its own fulfillment on the Internet until it realized fulfillment wasn't something it was good at.

    Toys "R" Us knew how to purchase and sell toys, but it wasn't an expert in packaging and shipping orders placed on the Internet. After a disastrous Christmas season selling on the Internet and getting fined by the U.S. Federal Trade Commission for misleading customers about delivery dates, Toys "R" Us partnered with another company to handle its fulfillment. Don't be afraid to outsource.

    As you read this book, you'll notice that running an online store requires skills in many different areas: customer service, Web site design, fulfillment, accounting, marketing, inventory management, etc. Identify those areas you're good at and those areas you're not good at. Don't try to do everything yourself. This is one of the most important lessons that a small business can learn.

14. *Are you ready to ensure that your "real world" and online store initiatives are in tune with one another?* If you already have a land-based retail

store, it's important to set up your online business so that your land-based store and your online store are in sync with each other from an accounting, inventory, and pricing perspective. You don't want to end up with two different accounting systems, two different inventory systems, etc. You also want to avoid situations where your online store tells customers that a product is in inventory when in fact the item is out of stock.

Your online store must also be in sync with your "real" store from a customer service perspective. Too many stores haven't integrated their online and offline operations nor trained their in-store staff to deal with questions about their Web site. There's also the case of people buying online and then wanting to return a product in person. The whole issue of channel integration is key for any business that wants to sell both online and through traditional retail channels. We discuss this in more depth in Chapter 3.

e-fact

Consumers around the world ordered more than 37.9 million products from Amazon.com during the 2001 holiday season!

Source: Amazon.com (www.amazon.com)

15. *Have you analyzed the competition?* A key part of building an online business is surveying the competitive landscape. Before you build your online store, make sure you spend time visiting Web sites that will compete with yours. In particular, get answers to the following questions:
    - Who are your competitors, both online and offline?
    - Of all the competitors you've identified, which ones have the largest market share?
    - What are your competitors doing to attract visitors to their online stores? Do they have affiliate programs? (For an explanation of affiliate programs, see Chapter 6.) Are they advertising in industry publications or on radio or television? Do they have an e-mail newsletter for their customers?
    - Are any of your competitors receiving either good or bad press coverage? Have they issued any press releases recently?
    - Do they have any strategic partnerships with online or offline firms?

- How does each competitor compare in terms of product selection, price, customer service, appearance (i.e., Web design), and reputation?
- What special features and/or services are your competitors offering?
- What are the strengths and weaknesses of each of your competitors?
- Are any of your land-based competitors not yet selling online? If the answer is yes, can you ascertain if or when they plan to launch their online stores?

Use all of this information to help you assess whether there is an opportunity in the market that is being missed by your competitors. For example, your analysis may reveal that there is a certain segment of the market that your competitors are not catering to. Alternatively, you may discover that customer service is severely lacking at your competitors' Web sites. These types of findings will help you build a strong business that builds on your competitors' weaknesses.

16. *What will it cost to sell your products online?* Selling products on the Internet involves a variety of costs. They include:
- Internet access fees
- Merchant account fees
- Credit card transaction fees
- Web hosting fees
- Domain name registration fees
- Online marketing expenses (e.g., affiliate programs, advertising, etc.)
- Professional service fees (e.g., e-commerce consultants, Web designers)

We discuss many of these costs throughout the book. Selling products online may be more expensive than you think! Make sure you itemize all of your potential costs and create a budget before you start to create an online store.

17. *How much revenue do you need to generate every month in order to break even?* Alternatively, figure out how many sales you need in a month (and the average dollar value of those sales) in order to break even.

Most small businesses ignore this important calculation in their planning. It's crucial to figure out these numbers before you set up your online store. You must take all your costs into account and calculate the gross margin you will earn on every sale (i.e., the difference between your selling price and what you paid for the product).

You may find that the final numbers are completely unattainable, which means that you will have to go back and re-examine your cost structure, your pricing, and perhaps your business models. Given the costs of Web hosting, domain names, real-time credit card processing, and your time, you may be surprised at how much revenue you have to bring in just to break even!

18. *Have you taken the time to learn from other online merchants?* One of the most valuable ways to learn about e-commerce and online retailing is to talk to people who are already selling online. Don't be afraid to call people (even complete strangers!) who are selling their products on the Internet. You'll find that many people are more than willing to share their experiences with you. As a first step, we suggest you consider subscribing to the I-Sales discussion list, an electronic mailing list dedicated to online sales issues. It's an excellent way to exchange information and gain valuable insights into online selling from people who are already doing it!

If you do sign up, be prepared for a lot of reading. Every day, you'll receive a "digest" of messages that have been posted to the list. If you can bear the high volume of messages, you'll find that the list is an excellent way to obtain lots of tips and online selling advice from other Internet users. You can subscribe to the I-Sales discussion list by visiting the I-Sales Web site at www.adventive.com. There is no cost to join.

e-fact

More than two-thirds of brick-and-mortar retailers judge their online success by the *wrong* metrics because they forget to take into account the *offline* sales that their Web sites generate.

Source: Jupiter Media Metrix (www.jmm.com)

19. *Have you identified Web sites that you like?* It is important to do some "best practices" research. Scour the Web to find sites of companies in your industry or area of work and study what they have done. Take a look at your competitors and other online stores in similar lines of business. Determine what you like and don't like within a

wide range of comparable Web sites. Consider adapting the best of what you see for your own online store.

As part of this process, you should also familiarize yourself with the elements of good and bad Web design. The Internet is littered with Web sites that just don't cut it. Many suffer from poor design, which is guaranteed to chase customers away as soon as they arrive. That is why you should take some time to understand Web design concepts. When examining your competitors' Web sites, also pay special attention to how their sites are designed. As we explain in Chapter 3, the design of your Web site will influence the perceptions that customers have about your business.

20. *How will you find your customers?* This is a crucial question for any business that intends to sell online. Where will your customers come from?

This is extremely important. After all, you can build a great store, but if your customers don't know it exists, then even the best Web design and product selection are rather useless. Hence, we address this question in more depth in Chapter 6, "Marketing Strategies for Your Online Store."

Make sure you avoid what has come to be known as the "The McDonald's Complex." Business consultant Pat Bishop explains it this way: "A majority of people who start a business, whether it be a brick and mortar store or an Internet business, assume that once they open, customers will flock in without any marketing or promotion. UNLESS YOU ARE McDONALD'S THIS WILL NOT HAPPEN." ("Build It and They Will Come Doesn't Work on Internet," *The Daily Oklahoman*, August 18, 2000). In other words, an online store won't magically attract customers. You will have to work hard to market your business and create your customer base.

21. *How soon can you be profitable?* You need to work out a time frame for your expectations and then determine if you can wait that long. Do you have the financing to see you through the inevitable early period in which you will likely be operating at a loss? How long can you last before things become desperate?

22. *Does your business model make sense?* One of the reasons Internet businesses fail is that they have bad business models. Several years ago, the business model was the last thing that people

considered, but now this is one of the first things you should ask yourself about.

Ask yourself if your expectations are reasonable. Do your plans make sense? Are they overly optimistic? It may be a good idea to hire a consultant or trusted adviser to review your plans and evaluate your projections and expectations to see if they are realistic and attainable.

Take the time to do a serious self-assessment—a reality check, as it were. And remember, you might be guilty of drinking your own wine. You may be so caught up in your plans that you won't realize some of your assumptions are overly optimistic. That's why you should get independent opinions from friends, family, business acquaintances, or Internet professionals.

23. *What features do you want in your online store?* Part of the planning process involves listing the design elements and functional features that you want to have on your Web site. In Chapter 3, "Tips for Building an Effective Online Store," we give you lots of advice in this area. You should also consult Chapters 6 and 7 to learn about some of the marketing and loyalty-building elements you can build into your online store. Identify some of the features and services that are important to you. Obviously, unless you have an unlimited amount of money to spend, you won't be able to do everything. However, you need to have some idea of what you want in order to move on to the next stage and get accurate price quotations from Web designers and online storefront services.

Step #2: Preparation

Once you've gone through the process that we outlined in the planning section above, you should be ready to map out your online store on paper.

Consider putting together a "site map," which is a representation of all the sections you want to have on your Web site. The site map should be accompanied by a list of features that you want to have in your online store. Keep in mind that your site map doesn't have to be fixed in stone. If you decide to work with a Web designer, you may want to modify the layout of your Web site based on his or her suggestions.

Once you have your site map in hand and a clear understanding of what you want your online store to look like, you're ready to get cost estimates from different storefront services, e-commerce developers/consultants, and/or Web design firms. The solution that you ultimately select will depend on how much money you are prepared to spend, whether you want to build the Web site yourself or have someone else do the work for you, and what types of features you want to build into your online store. In Chapter 2, you'll find an extensive discussion of the different options for creating your online store.

Fifty-nine percent of Canadian adults with a home Internet connection have purchased an item directly online.

Source: Ipsos-Reid (www.ipsos-reid.com)

e-fact

Step #3: Development

Once you've selected a company and/or service to help you build your online store, you're ready to move on to the development phase. Development involves actively building your online store using the software and professional services that you've chosen. As we discuss in Chapter 3, you'll also need to thoroughly test your online store before launch to make sure that it is functioning properly. Throughout this process, unless you're doing all the work yourself, you'll need to manage the activities of the companies you're working with.

Step #4: Execution

The execution phase occurs once your store is "live" on the Internet and ready to accept orders. After your store is up and running, you'll have to put in a lot of time and effort to ensure it is working correctly.

Make sure you understand just how much time it will take to keep your store running. Many people involved in online selling sit back and think the store will run itself, but that isn't true. You've got to keep prices updated, shipping rates correct, and stock levels properly indicated. These are just some of the details you will be monitoring on a regular basis.

Don't expect your store to operate perfectly once you have it up and running. The fact is things will go wrong—and sometimes you might not even know about it.

Consider what happened to the online store belonging to one of the authors of this book. The system that processes credit card orders on his online store suddenly stopped working one day, preventing customers from placing orders on his Web site. Customers who tried to place orders were greeted with an error message and were unable to continue. Only when a customer notified the author a few days later did he become aware of the problem! Had the customer not informed him about the difficulties she had placing an order on the site, he wouldn't have known that the online store was malfunctioning. As a result, he could have lost a substantial amount of business without even realizing it!

The fact is most customers who encounter a problem on an online store won't take the time to contact the owner of the store. They'll just shop somewhere else. Hence, you've got to monitor your store constantly to ensure it is in proper working order, which includes continually examining every aspect of your store. In this case, the author would only have known that there was a problem with the credit card process if he had gone through and tried to order a book himself. Does that mean that he should regularly check this aspect of his store by doing an actual test order? Perhaps.

Of course, the execution phase involves more than just monitoring your online store for problems. Execution implies all the things you need to do to ensure that your overall goal of selling online is functioning smoothly and properly. Execution means ensuring that customer support requests are taken care of, that returns are promptly cleared and credited to customer accounts, and that any rejected credit card transactions are quickly followed up. You should also run focus groups on your Web site on an ongoing basis to make sure it keeps pace with customers' expectations.

The competitive analysis that you did in the planning stage should continue once your store is completed. Constantly monitor your online competitors to see what they are up to.

e-fact

Forty percent of Canadian adults with access to the Internet regularly research products online.

Source: ComQUEST (www.comquest.ca)

Step #5: Refinement

The Internet is constantly changing. New technologies are being developed, new competitors are entering the market, customers' buying patterns are changing, and customers are becoming increasingly demanding. If you want to stay competitive, you'll have to constantly tinker with your strategy and change the look and/or features of your online store in response to changing market conditions. The Internet will be unlike any other industry you've ever worked in. Business moves at lightning speed on the Web. Just keeping up is half the battle.

What About B2B?

Of course, as you set up a store on the Internet, you're likely doing so as part of a B2C, or business-to-consumer, strategy. Yet today B2B is all the rage, and folks are discounting B2C. We believe that they are wrong. As we noted at the beginning of the chapter, while early Internet retail sales estimates were far too optimistic, the fact remains that there are some very good markets emerging online.

But what about B2B? Should you worry about it? That depends on who you are, what you do, and what is happening in your industry. First, recognize that much of what we talk about in this book might be equally applicable to a B2B strategy. If you typically sell to other businesses, your online store might work very well in supporting your business activities with them. Credit card payments are likely to be less important, however, so make sure that you provide for payments on account and other forms of payment.

Second, you might find yourself pressured to join a B2B Web site, or what is known as a vertical industry market. These are large e-biz sites established by buyers or sellers of products in particular industries, built with the intention of driving all business purchases in that industry through the site.

A third area in which B2B is taking off, often related to B2B sites, is e-procurement. The Internet is emerging as a tool by which companies streamline the way they conduct their purchasing process. You might find that some of your customers want you to get involved in their e-commerce procurement initiatives rather than your own online site. They won't want to do business with you through your Web site—they want you to do business their way.

Finally, as you take a look at your market, you might find that it is easier to join up and establish your product catalogue on a B2B Web site rather than building your own store. In the world of B2B, we are seeing the emergence of many sophisticated sites that allow you, as a retailer or product manufacturer, to create, in effect, a "store" within the B2B site. By doing so, you might find that you can access a far larger marketplace than if you to create your own store.

Whatever the case may be, as you consider your retail plans, take some time to understand the B2B initiatives that are going on in your industry or that might affect you, and determine how you might need to modify your activities accordingly.

Don't Forget Cost Savings Initiatives!

Last but not least, don't forget that e-commerce is not necessarily all about making money but also about saving money. Too many businesses have a one-track mind when it comes to the Internet and, in particular, e-commerce. They're constantly asking themselves how they can use the Internet to make money. But in addition to thinking about how the Internet can generate revenue for your business, you should also ask yourself how you can use the Internet to save money. For example, by sending an e-mail message, you can save the cost of a comparable long-distance telephone call, fax, or courier bill. Sending a document electronically rather than by courier means a potential cost savings of $12 or more! This can save you substantial sums of money.

A Web site is also an effective tool for reducing costs, particularly when used for customer support or marketing purposes. Even though there is a cost (often significant) to set up a Web site and maintain it, you will save money over the long term every time an existing or prospective customer or client downloads information such as a brochure from your Web site. A Web site can save you courier or mailing charges and can reduce your printing costs over time.

Always ask yourself how you can use your online strategy tool to save money in the way you do business.

Where Do We Go from Here?

In the remaining eight chapters we will walk you through all of the steps involved in setting up an online store on the Internet.

In Chapter 2, "Options for Building an Online Store," we describe some of the different methods that you can use to build an online store. They range from low-cost, do-it-yourself services to more expensive software solutions.

In Chapter 3, "Tips for Building an Effective Online Store," we offer advice on how to deal with important issues such as pricing, customer privacy, shipping, return policies, checkout procedures, and customer service. We also review the important elements of Web site design.

In Chapter 4, "Merchant Accounts and Online Payment Processing," we outline what's involved in getting a merchant account for your online store so you can process and authorize credit card transactions over the Internet.

In Chapter 5, "Online Security Issues and Credit Card Fraud," we explain the security risks that you will be exposed to on the Internet and we provide an extensive checklist of questions to help you assess the security of your online store. You'll also learn how to protect yourself from credit card fraud.

In Chapter 6, "Marketing Strategies for Your Online Store," we review a variety of different marketing vehicles for your online store, including permission marketing, affiliate programs, search engines and Web directories, and keyword-based advertising. We also discuss the importance of such issues as domain names and traditional advertising.

In Chapter 7, "Building Customer Loyalty in Your Online Store," we outline how you can use strategies like site registration, contests, personalization, online communities, and opt-in e-mail to build customer loyalty and increase repeat sales.

In Chapter 8, "131 Tips from Online Merchants in Canada and the United States," we've assembled a panel of online merchants to talk about best practices and critical success factors for online retailing. This is a chapter you won't want to miss!

Finally, in the Epilogue we close with some of our thoughts about the future of online retailing.

Let's move on!

2

Options for Building
an Online Store

*"After the dot-com crash, **profitable** Internet seems like an oxymoron. But many small businesses, with one eye on cost control and the other on customer service, are writing their bottom lines with black ink, not red."*

—"Small Online Businesses Turn Profit,"
Orange County Register, April 15, 2002

One of the most challenging aspects of building an online store is figuring out how to go about it. It can be a bewildering experience, given the wide range of different products and services that are available to you. As you venture forth, you'll discover a wealth of marketing literature from e-commerce companies, high-tech companies, and others involved in the Internet industry, each of which promises the best possible method of building an online store. You will come across many different "storefront" software programs that purport to give you everything you need to create your store. Look further, and you will see many different descriptions of the "ideal" components of an online store.

You can quickly become confused about where to start. Worse, you might choose to go in a certain direction, only to learn that you have made a serious mistake. Given the many different approaches to building your store, it is important to understand two areas clearly: the methods of building an online store, and the different features and capabilities that you might choose to build into your store. These are the two key topics that we address in this chapter.

Appreciating Your Expertise—and the Expertise of Others

As you will see in this chapter, there are many different ways to build an online store. These range from do-it-yourself software programs that walk you though a series of ready-made design templates, to complex software programs with a full range of features that can be implemented only by third-party organizations or individuals with a lot of technical expertise. Which solution you select depends on the answers to questions that you must ask yourself:

- How technically inclined are you?
- What is your budget?
- What types of products are you selling?
- How many products do you intend to carry?
- How quickly will you need to be able to expand your online store?
- Do you already have a retail store with its own financial and inventory systems that you want to integrate into your online store?
- What features and capabilities do you want your online store to have?
- Who are your competitors and what do their online stores look like? What features do their online stores have? Which features are desirable and which are not?
- What elements do you want within your store to make it the best possible store? Do you even know what those elements might be?

As you will learn in this chapter, what might have seemed like a simple undertaking can suddenly become quite complex. You are now wrestling with two major issues:

1. Do you have enough experience with online stores to know what features you should be including in your own online store? When researching online storefront solutions, do you even know what features and options you should be looking for?
2. Do you have the technical and design expertise—and the time—to build your online store yourself?

Chances are the answer is no to these questions. Indeed, that's probably why you bought this book. Let's put both of these issues into perspective.

e-fact

Sixty-six percent of online shoppers say that they do not have concerns about buying from foreign Web sites.

Source: WorldPay (www.worldpay.com)

Developing Your Expertise in Store Features and Elements

Regardless of how you go about creating your online store, you need to have some familiarity with the features and elements that make up a great online store. To help you develop your knowledge in this area, we will outline some of the common features and elements of storefront software programs later in this chapter. And in the next chapter, we'll examine a list of different features that you may want to consider for your online store.

But before you read those sections, it is important to develop your own opinions on what constitutes a great online store. You can do this by examining a variety of online stores, particularly those that involve your industry or marketplace, and by thinking about what works and what doesn't work. Hence, we believe a good starting point is to visit as many online stores as you can. This will give you invaluable information as you develop plans for your own online store.

What do you want to accomplish through such research? Let's use an example. Suppose you want to set up an online store to sell specialized craft supplies. In order to figure out what features should be part of your online store, you should research your competitors to see what they have done online. In addition, look at as many online stores as you can—both large and small—within the crafts industry. Broaden your review to gift shops and other types of online stores that are selling the same types of products that you intend to sell.

As you browse these online stores, keep track of the features and services they offer. Put yourself in the shoes of a typical customer. Carefully examine the design and layout of each Web site that you visit. What features do you like? What features don't you like? Is there anything that impresses you? Examine the purchasing process in depth. You might actually go so far as to place a few orders in some of the online stores to see how the ordering process works and to see how the products are packaged and delivered. Make careful notes about the strengths and weaknesses of each online store that you visit. This will be important information later when you begin determining which elements you would like for your own store.

This is critical research. Examining these stores gives you a good sense of what you should be doing, since you can see how well various approaches might work. It can also help you understand where your competitors are weak and how you might improve on these weaknesses.

Where can you find directories of online stores to look at? Fortunately, there are a number of places that have built and maintained directories of online retail sites in Canada. Perhaps one of the best, and the one that we refer to frequently, is the shopping listing at Canada.com, which features a nicely organized listing of over 1,100 Canadian online stores. You can access the listing by category (i.e., type of product sold) or alphabetically. You can find similar directories at the Canadian versions of major search engines such as Yahoo Canada (www.yahoo.ca), or check out RetailCanada.com (www.retailcanada.com). It's a massive directory organized by location and provides access to over 4,800 Canadian online stores. Specify your city or town, and you'll get a listing of the retailers or Web sites in Canada that you can use from your location. Another great source of links to retail sites in Canada is Sympatico's Shopping section (shopping.sympatico.ca).

Keep in mind that you don't have to limit your competitive analysis to Canadian companies in terms of finding features that you like. Because there are no borders on the Internet, customers can shop as easily at stores located in other countries as they can in Canada. Therefore, make sure you examine online stores in other countries as well. After all, your goal is to find out who is doing the best job of selling within your particular industry and emulate their "best practices." To venture beyond Canada, take a look at several Web directories that rate online stores for shoppers since they maintain lists of hundreds of online stores, such as BizRate.com (www.bizrate.com) and ePublicEye.com (www.epubliceye.com). You should also visit the online shopping areas of popular sites such as Yahoo! (shopping.yahoo.com) and America Online (www.aol.com/shopping).

When browsing through online store directories such as the ones we've mentioned, you'll come across a wide range of online stores, some of them built by small businesses and others built by large businesses with million-dollar budgets.

If you're a small business, you probably won't be able to afford an online store like Wal-Mart's (www.walmart.com) or RadioShack Canada's (www.radioshack.ca), but looking at these sites will give you a good idea of what's possible in an online store.

Learning About the Expertise of E-Commerce Developers and Consultants

Once you begin to look at different online stores on the Internet, you may be intimidated, from both a technical and design point of view, by the complexity of some of the online stores you come across. Fortunately, however, many of the storefront solutions that we will discuss in this chapter require very little, if any, technical knowledge on the part of the merchant. This is particularly true of the template-based services, which allow you to create a small-scale store with little effort. In fact, the technology has become so easy to use that even someone who hasn't used a computer before can set up an online store without much difficulty.

However, depending on your situation, it may not be appropriate for you to build your online store yourself. You might want to concentrate on starting or running your business and leave the technical and design issues to someone else. Not only that, but given that online store building is rapidly turning into a field that involves rather specialized expertise, you might quickly conclude that outside assistance is required with all aspects of building your online store, including creating a business plan. This is where an e-commerce developer/consultant might come in handy.

We should explain that the term "e-commerce developer/consultant" has a wide variety of possible meanings. We've used it as an umbrella term to include any firm that may provide services to help you with the process of establishing a site to sell products and services online. E-commerce developers and consultants include Internet service providers, graphic designers, strategic planners, database integrators, programmers, Internet security consultants, and a variety of other professions. Depending on the scale and scope of your online store, and how technically competent you are, you may want to hire an e-commerce developer or consultant to help you with the entire process of setting up your online store or just parts of it. And depending on the tasks you require help with, you may need to hire several different e-commerce consultants and development firms.

If you decide to go with one of the low-cost, do-it-yourself e-commerce storefront solutions that use templates, you might want professional help to customize the look of your site. As we point out later in the chapter, one of the disadvantages of using a do-it-yourself storefront program is that all the stores end up looking like they came out of a cookie cutter. Whether you need help in building and designing your online store, marketing it, adding special features (e.g., a gift registry), implementing security solutions, integrating existing inventory and customer databases into your online store, setting up customer relationship tools such as live chat services or personalization software, or doing anything else, there are literally hundreds or thousands of e-commerce developers and consultants across Canada and many more in the United States and beyond that can assist you. Here are just some of the organizations that could help you with different aspects of your online store:

- Many ISPs have established e-commerce divisions to help clients set up storefronts on the Internet, so you should take a look at national, local, or regional Internet service providers such as Victoria, B.C.-based Entirety Communications (www.entirety.ca), or Calgary-based Chinook Computers (www.chinook-computers.com). Some only offer packaged do-it-yourself e-commerce solutions and no consulting or design services (although they may have established partnerships or alliances with companies they can refer you to). Others may offer more comprehensive e-commerce services to small and/or large businesses. Check with the Internet service providers in your community to see what e-commerce services they offer.
- Canadian financial institutions such as TD Canada Trust (www.TDCanadatrust.com) and Scotiabank (www.scotiabank.ca) have specialized divisions that focus on electronic commerce, so it is worthwhile to check with your banking institution.
- Many Web hosting companies such as NetNation Canada (www.netnation.ca) and Ontario-based iNet Niagara (www.inet-niagara.com) or Radiant Communications (www.radiant.com) provide e-commerce hosting and/or design services, ranging from do-it-yourself solutions to custom storefront-building services.
- Web consulting firms that specialize in Web site creation, design, and strategy often have e-commerce services. Examples include Calgary-based Clarity (www.clarity.ca), Montreal-based

Clic.net (www.clic.net), or Saint John, N.B.-based Media Planet (www.mediaplanet.ca). Web consulting firms may also offer marketing services ranging from online media planning to online marketing campaigns. Some firms in this category may offer assistance with other areas of e-commerce such as logistics, fulfillment, and customer service.

- E-commerce solution providers such as 5Click.com (www.5click. com) can help you create an online store. There are many such firms across Canada that specialize in hosting e-commerce-enabled Web sites for small and medium-sized businesses.

- Graphic designers and Web design firms can help with the design of your Web site. There are literally hundreds of small and large graphic design firms across Canada that have expertise in designing Web pages. There are also many graphic designers with full-time jobs who do freelance work on the side, and who have some e-commerce/shopping cart experience, who may be able to help you with the graphic design of your site.

- Most telecommunications firms like Bell Canada (www.bell.ca) and Telus (www.telus.com) have e-commerce divisions with e-commerce offerings for small and large organizations.

- Specialist e-commerce developers/consultants that specialize in a particular area of e-commerce, such as personalization (see Chapter 7), online payment processing (see Chapter 4), security (see Chapter 5), or customer relationship management (see Chapter 3) can also help you with the creation and maintenance of your online store.

- In addition to the Web consulting firms we mentioned previously, there are lots of Internet and e-business consultants across Canada who have general Internet/e-commerce expertise or who have developed specialized expertise with certain e-commerce programs or storefront solutions. If you're operating on a small budget and simply want some professional input, you may want to hire someone on an hourly basis to advise you on setting up an online store.

This list just barely scratches the surface! As you can see, regardless of your needs, there is probably an organization out there that can meet them. Take some time to identify your needs and learn how these different organizations can help you.

Clearly, given the extensive list of companies, if you decide to hire an outside firm to help you with any aspect of your online store, it is important that you carefully assess the skills and experience of the organization in whatever job you're hiring them for. If possible, examine some of the work they have done for other clients. Ask for references. Talk to previous customers and ask the firm for examples of online stores or Web sites they have built or provided consultation for. If the company doesn't have a solid track record, and if you can't get any positive recommendations from previous or existing clients, you should look elsewhere. It's important to choose an organization that you're comfortable with.

How do you find e-commerce consultants and developers? In some cases, the Web site of the particular storefront solution you are considering might lead you to certain authorized resellers or consultants. Better yet, browse the Web for examples of small and large companies that are selling products online. If you see an online store that you like, you might notice a link to the company that built the site on their behalf. If not, contact the company directly and find out who developed their online store and/or what consultants they worked with.

Another way to locate experts to assist you is to talk to people in your community who are active in the Internet and e-commerce industry, or talk to local high-tech associations. In addition, read the technology section of your local newspaper to see if there are any e-commerce companies advertising their services there. You could also check the Yellow Pages or phone your local Chamber of Commerce. You may also want to post a message to the AIMS Canada message board. (AIMS, the Association of Internet Marketing and Sales, is a membership-based organization of Internet professionals from across Canada. Visit www.aimscanada.com for more information.)

Internet traffic will exceed voice traffic by more than eight times in 2005.

e-fact

Source: International Data Corporation (www.idc.com)

Approaches to Building an Online Store

There are four options when it comes to building an online store:
1. Use an entry-level browser-based storefront creation service.
2. Use stand-alone shopping cart software.

3. Use an online marketplace such as eBay or Amazon.com.
4. Use advanced e-commerce software.

The rest of this chapter is devoted to exploring each of these options in more detail. Before we discuss these methods though, let's put one other issue into perspective.

It is likely that you already have a Web site. If you do, and you create an online store using any of the above methods, it doesn't mean that you have to discard the rest of your Web site. Instead, you can simply add a link from the pages within your regular Web site to your store. You might notice that some of the e-commerce solutions we describe in the following sections specifically differentiate between solutions that can integrate into an existing site versus those that are used to create an entirely new site from scratch.

Of course, depending on the solution you choose, you might not have a consistent design between the rest of your site and your online store. If consistency in design is critical to you, then as you explore your options, make sure you determine how you can pursue the implementation of your store in such a way that it matches the look, feel, and design of your existing site.

Option #1:
Use Entry-Level Browser-Based Storefront Creation Services

Advantages
- Easy to use
- All tasks are handled from within your Web browser
- Your store can be updated from any Internet connection
- No need to install any software on your computer
- Fast set-up
- Little or no technical knowledge required
- No need to find a Web hosting company (the store is hosted on the storefront service's own Web site)
- No need to develop a separate Web site

Disadvantages
- Some services have limited flexibility in store design and layout
- Without additional programming or design work, your store may look similar to other stores created with the same product

- Customization may not be possible
- The user interface for some of these programs is awkward, slow, and/or clunky

Browser-based storefront creation services are the easiest services to use. They require very little technical knowledge and allow you to create your online store by filling out a series of templates or forms using your Web browser. Many of the popular browser-based packages have automated the set-up of your merchant account and online payment processing, two of the most important components of your online store (see Chapter 4 for an explanation of these components). This means it will be easy for you to accept credit cards on your Web site and process credit card transactions in real time.

Browser-based storefront creation services are popular with small businesses because they don't require you to install or configure any software on your computer. Your entire online store can be created using your Web browser. Setting up an online store using one of these services can be as easy as filling out a series of templates on the Web, selecting the layout you want for your online store, uploading (transferring) your company logos and product images from your computer to the service's Web servers, and answering a few questions. These services are typically very affordable for a small business. Pricing is usually on a monthly basis and ranges from under a hundred dollars a month to several hundred dollars per month.

Because browser-based storefront creation services are quite easy to use, many businesses can use them to build their online stores without much outside assistance. However, depending on your situation, you might decide to hire an e-commerce developer/consultant to help you design your store or add additional features to it. At a minimum, you may want to engage the services of a graphic designer to help you design logos or other graphical elements for your site.

Browser-based services are designed for businesses that want a quick and easy way to get an online store up and running with minimal hassle, but this ease of use comes at a price. If you need an extremely powerful program with lots of flexibility in design and layout, you may be disappointed. Browser-based storefront creation programs usually aren't sophisticated enough for businesses that need powerful marketing and merchandising capabilities and want maximum control over the appearance of their online store. That's why it's important to determine what you need in an online storefront solution before you select one to work with. You also need to think about how quickly you expect your online sales to grow and determine whether a browser-based program will be able to meet your needs as your business expands.

Where to Find Browser-Based Storefront Creation Services

A wide range of organizations offer browser-based storefront creation services.

You should first keep in mind that the nature of the offering from any one of the types of organizations described below could change at any time. It has been our experience that the e-commerce services provided by various companies change over time. We've seen one Canadian organization get into the business, then drop its service, only to start up another new service about a year later! Hence, you might find that the particular organization you choose to host your site no longer offers the service; or that an organization drastically changes its service; or that an organization you thought didn't offer a service suddenly does!

Having said that, where should you start? First, you could check with your existing financial institution. You might discover that they have partnered with a third-party e-commerce company to provide their clients with an all-in-one solution. For example, Scotiabank (www.scotiabank.com) has established ScotiaWeb store to help their clients with e-commerce storefronts, and TD Canada Trust (www.tdbank.ca) has established Online Mart, designed with the same objective (www.onlinemart.ca).

Other Canadian-based providers of browser-based storefront creation services include Yahoo! Canada (ca.store.yahoo.com), telecommunications companies such as TELUS (www.telus.com) and Bell Canada (www.bell.ca), and Microsoft Canada, through its bCentral Canada site (www.bcentral.ca). In addition, most regional and local Internet service providers and Web hosting companies across Canada offer online storefront solutions. As a starting point, check with some of the telecommunications companies, financial institutions, and Internet service providers that serve your community to see if they offer any e-commerce hosting services.

To help you with your research, we've listed a few examples of browser-based services in the table below. Sometimes you may find that a specific storefront program is available only through resellers, meaning that you need to sign up with a participating Web hosting company or Internet service provider in order to use the company's software. In most cases, you can visit the vendor's Web site and get a list of Internet service providers and Web hosting companies that sell the vendor's storefront software.

Examples of Browser-Based Storefront Creation Services in Canada

Vendor	*Web Site*
Bell Canada	www.bell.ca
Bank of Montreal/Royal Bank	www.moneris.com
Canada Post	www.canadapost.ca or www.canada-shops.com
DXShop	www.dxshop.com
5Click	www.5click.com
Microsoft Canada (bCentral)	www.bcentral.ca
NetNation	www.netnation.ca
Scotiabank, ScotiaWeb store	www.scotiawebstore.com
TD Canada Trust, Online Mart	www.onlinemart.ca
TELUS (BizEssentials e.Store)	www.telus.com
Yahoo! Canada Store	www.yahoo.ca or ca.store.yahoo.com

There are also a large number of U.S. and international-based services that you could use. However, you might find that many of them don't provide for Canadian currency transactions or Canadian merchant accounts (as discussed in Chapter 4). In addition, most U.S.-based services will require you to have a U.S. merchant account in order to use their services, which means you will need to have a U.S. bank account and billing address. Hence, it's not practical or possible for many Canadian merchants to use a U.S.-based storefront service.

Virtually all browser-based storefront creation services will walk you through six basic steps:

- Specifying the name and contact information for your online store
- Defining product categories and product information (product descriptions, prices, etc.)
- Choosing the layout and design of your online store
- Specifying tax and shipping information
- Specifying which credit cards you want to accept
- Setting up a merchant account and real-time credit card processing (see Chapter 4)

The manner in which you complete these steps varies from service to service, but often you will be able to build your online store by using a friendly "wizard" interface that makes it easy to get your store up and running quickly. We want to emphasize that not all browser-based storefront services are alike. They vary widely in their capabilities and functionality, which might affect your choice of service.

The features and options available to you will vary depending on which browser-based service you're using. For example, at some point during the set-up process, you'll be asked to choose a basic design and colour combination for your online store. Some storefront services will give you a lot of control over the colours, while others will require you to choose from a selection of pre-designed colour combinations. In addition, some browser-based storefront services have a very user-friendly interface while other services may be slow and awkward.

e-fact

Online consumers in Canada spent an average of $324 on online gifts during the 2001 holiday season.

Source: Ipsos-Reid (www.ipsos-reid.com)

If you're interested in using a browser-based storefront service, don't sign up for the first one you come across. There are lots of different browser-based products for you to choose from, so it's important to research your options carefully. In order to choose a browser-based storefront that best meets your needs, consider doing the following:

1. Compare the features of different browser-based services so that you fully understand the limitations and benefits of each service.

In the last section of this chapter, we'll provide a checklist of some of the features you should think about.

2. If possible, test-drive different storefront creation services. Some services offer trial periods so you can try out the service at no charge (or you can get your money back at the end of the trial period if you aren't satisfied).

3. If possible, get an online demo of the product. Some services provide an online tutorial that shows you how the store-building software works.

4. Inspect the user interface carefully. How easy is it to add/delete/ modify the products in your online store? Does the user interface look simple to use or does it appear cumbersome?

5. Create a checklist of the different features you are looking for in an online storefront and create a short list of storefront creation services that meet your requirements.

6. As part of your decision-making process, we highly recommend that you spend some time looking at online stores created using various browser-based storefront services. This will give you an idea of what the end product looks like. However, keep in mind that the appearance of a particular store may not reflect the full capabilities of the product that was used to create it. For each service you are considering, try to look at a wide variety of different storefronts created with it so that you see the different ways the service can be configured. Many browser-based storefront services have a "showcase" of sample stores created using their software on their respective Web sites. For example, on the Yahoo! Store site (shopping.yahoo.com/stores), you can look at hundreds of stores that were created using the Yahoo! Store software.

A Word of Caution

Although browser-based storefront creation programs are supposed to make setting up an online store easy, you may find yourself getting frustrated. We tested many browser-based storefront programs for this book and were horrified by some of them. For example, some of these programs have a user interface that is slow and/or cumbersome to use. The help screens didn't work on one of the services we tried, and on another, technical support wasn't available late at night when we needed it most. Perhaps most importantly, the final product of your efforts may shock you in terms of the design and functionality. That's why you should thoroughly research and test your options prior to making a commitment.

Browser-based storefront solutions are notable for their simplicity and ease of use. However, when it comes to creating appealing site designs, they often leave merchants disappointed. Many of the browser-based programs will create an online store that may look amateurish to you, or even downright ugly, but that's to be expected since most of these programs are designed for entry-level users. You need to appreciate that there is a trade-off when you use a browser-based storefront service. While you may get your online store up and running in a few hours or days, it might be unrealistic to expect the software to produce a magnificent-looking Web site design. For that, you will need to hire someone and be prepared to invest some additional money in your online store.

Fortunately, some browser-based programs give you a lot of control over the final design if you don't like the default designs that come with the software, so that you can avoid the cookie cutter effect that many browser-based storefront packages create. Hence, you might want to select a browser-based service that gives you control over the final design and layout of your site. Alternatively, if you want an online store that looks slick and cutting-edge, think about investing in a more expensive solution.

What Does It Cost?

Most of the browser-based storefront creation services cost anywhere from $30 to several hundred dollars per month, with extra fees for real-time credit card processing. Prices vary widely among different services, so it's wise to do your research. You might also find that there are several service options and prices within one service, usually depending on the number of items that you plan on selling.

As you undertake your research, you might find a few services that offer you a store for "free." We caution you against using such services for two reasons. First, you might find that there are still fees in the form of transaction processing charges, and that these might be higher than you might pay with a fee-based service. Second, many free storefront services disappeared during the dot-com shakeup in 2001 or shortly thereafter. Many individuals and businesses who had invested significant time in their storefront operations suddenly found their stores were no longer accessible and could not be easily recreated on another service. Remember this adage—you get what you pay for!

Almost a quarter of all Canadian adults bank online.

Source: NFO CFgroup (www.nfocfgroup.com)

e-fact

What If You Already Have an Existing Web Site or Need More Design Flexibility?

Most browser-based storefront creation programs include tools that allow you to design a complete online store, including the main entry pages for your online store as well as the shopping cart pages. The shopping cart is the e-commerce software that allows customers to select and then purchase the products they are interested in. The shopping cart program keeps track of the items a customer has selected until the customer is ready to check out. At this point, the software will collect shipping and billing information from the customer, automatically calculate the appropriate taxes and shipping charges, and allow the customer to choose a payment method, such as a cheque or credit card.

But what if you already have a Web site and just want to add online shopping capability to it? Many online merchants design their Web sites using their own software (or with the assistance of a graphic designer) and then simply link their Web sites to catalogues they create on a browser-based storefront service. This method allows you to have control over the appearance of your Web site while taking advantage of the powerful shopping cart features found in the browser-based storefront solutions. It's one way to get around the design restrictions of so many browser-based storefront programs.

If you want to design your Web site yourself, there are a lot of Web site-building programs that you can purchase. Some of the most popular include Microsoft's FrontPage (www.microsoft.com/frontpage), Macromedia's Dreamweaver (www.dreamweaver.com) and HomeSite (www.macromedia.com/software/homesite), and NetObjects' Fusion (www.netobjects.com).

If you're going to attempt to integrate a storefront program into an existing Web site, make sure you have at least some control over the design of the shopping cart pages so that the overall look of your Web site can be kept as consistent as possible, otherwise your Web site will appear disjointed and piecemeal. If it turns out that you don't have much flexibility in choosing your own design, you may want to consider one of the stand-alone shopping cart programs that we discuss in the next section.

Option #2:
Stand-Alone Shopping Cart Software

Advantages
- Store owner has complete control over store layout and design
- Perfect for individuals/firms who already have an existing Web site
- Store is hosted on your Web servers (or those of your Web hosting company)
- Highly customizable

Disadvantages
- Requires software installation and set-up
- Usually requires some technical knowledge and some familiarity with HTML
- Usually requires HTML programming and Web design work

If you want complete control over the layout and design of your online store, you may want to consider using one of the many stand-alone shopping cart software programs that are available today. These programs give you more flexibility with the design of your online store since you aren't limited to the design templates that come with a browser-based storefront solution. Some can be purchased in retail stores or downloaded from a Web site via the Internet. Others are available only through resellers.

With shopping cart software, it's expected that you have your own Web site, whether you have built it yourself or have hired a graphic designer or Web developer to do it. Your Web site is then integrated with the shopping cart program.

e-fact

Online retail spending in Canada will reach CAN $24 billion by 2006.

Source: Forrester Research (www.forrester.com)

There are usually two elements to stand-alone shopping cart software:

1. *Server software:* This software is run when someone is browsing through and shopping within your store.
2. *Design software:* This is the software that you use to design your store. You run it through either your Web browser by linking to the server software above, or by running a separate program in Windows that lets you design your store.

In some instances the server and design components are combined into one software package. In other cases they are separate modules.

Once you find a shopping cart program that you like, you have three choices:

1. You can install it yourself on your own Web site or server, which might be tough to do, since you might not have the expertise.
2. You can try to convince your ISP or Web hosting company to install it. That might be tough to do, since they might not want to install it as that would make them responsible for supporting it. *OR*
3. You can find an ISP/Web hosting company who has already installed that software (including the server and design elements).

We won't kid you. Setting up a shopping cart program and integrating it into a Web site is not as easy as using one of the browser-based storefront solutions that we described earlier in the chapter, especially if you encounter a situation in which you have to install the server portion of the program.

It can be a lot easier if you select the shopping cart software you want to use, and then find the ISP/Web hosting company that has preinstalled that software. For example, some ISPs have aligned themselves with particular shopping cart programs. In doing so, they have preinstalled the necessary server portions of the program on their computers and, if necessary, the design portion of the software. Visit NetNation Canada (www.netnation.ca), a Web hosting company that provides e-commerce hosting services, and you'll notice that they use the Miva Merchant Shopping Cart software program. They have installed both the design part of the program (which you can use to design your store) and the server portion of the software (which is run when someone accesses your store).

The best thing to do is check with the vendor of the shopping cart software you're interested in to see if there are any ISPs or Web hosting companies that have preinstalled it, otherwise, you will be in a situation in which you and your ISP (if it is willing) has to figure out how to install the shopping cart software you have chosen. For this installation, you may need to download the software via the Internet and be familiar with HTML. Even if you are familiar with HTML, you could still run into some problems while installing the software. For example, when one of the authors of this book was trying to install one of the popular shopping cart programs, he ran into some technical problems and had to get help from the company whose software he was using. Hence, one of the important considerations when choosing shopping cart software is the quality of technical support you will receive. Fortunately, some of the companies that sell shopping cart software may actually be willing to install their software for you if you run into difficulty installing it yourself. Ask whether this type of service is available before you purchase the software so you will not be surprised later if the software vendor isn't able to help you.

There are a variety of stand-alone shopping cart programs on the market with numerous different features and price tags. They range from free programs to more expensive software costing hundreds of dollars. Although you may be tempted to use one of the free shopping cart programs that are plentiful on the Internet, these programs often don't come with support, which means you're on your own if you run into technical problems. However, we encourage you to try them out and draw your own conclusions. When evaluating different shopping cart programs, keep in mind that you get what you pay for. A shopping cart program that costs $10 will probably be a lot less powerful than one that costs $400.

We've listed some of the more popular shopping cart programs in the table on the facing page. A good site for finding other shopping cart programs is the Shopping Cart and E-Commerce Guide at www.online-orders.net. This site contains an extensive list of both free and commercial shopping cart programs. Keep in mind that some of the solutions below allow you to purchase the software for installation on your own Web server, but they can also host your store for a regular monthly fee.

Using shopping cart software might have two big downsides if you aren't a computer whiz. First, as we have already mentioned, integrating a shopping cart program into your Web site can be a bit tricky if you don't have any technical knowledge. If you're not comfortable installing software and configuring computer codes, you might run into some difficulty in setting up the software.

Examples of Stand-Alone Shopping Cart Programs

Vendor/Product	Web Site
1ShoppingCart.com	www.1shoppingcart.com
Cart32	www.cart32.com
CartIt	www.cartit.com
MultiActive Software's ecBuilder	www.multiactive.com
Mercantec SoftCart	www.mercantec.com
Miva Merchant	www.miva.com
PDG Shopping Cart	www.pdgsoft.com
QuikStore	www.quikstore.com

Second, a stand-alone shopping cart program might not offer a complete storefront solution—many only provide the shopping cart. Unlike the browser-based storefront creation programs, a shopping cart program requires you to design a lot of the entry page items for your store, plus other sections within your site such as product support, technical support pages, marketing information, and other details.

In other words, many shopping cart programs won't help you build all the areas of your site—they are not an all-in-one solution. For example, some of the store elements that are automatically created for you with some of the browser-based storefront products, such as "Return Policy" and "Info" buttons, are not generated with most shopping cart programs.

Before choosing a shopping cart program, consider doing the following:

- Spend some time looking at online stores that use the shopping cart program you're considering. This will give you a feel for how the software works. Most shopping cart software vendors have links to sample online stores on their Web sites. Visit some of these stores and actually go through the process of placing items in your shopping cart so you can see what the customer interface looks like. You might even want to go so far as to e-mail some of the companies that are using the software to find out what their experiences have been.
- Carefully review the installation instructions and the skills required to set up the software so you'll know what you're in for.

Some shopping carts only require knowledge of HTML (the language used to build Web pages) while others may require more advanced programming knowledge. You might find that some of these companies provide information on their Web sites as to the skills required to use and set up their programs.

- Find out what type of technical support is available should you run into any problems. Is there an accompanying manual with the software that will walk you through the set-up process? How thorough is the technical/help documentation? Are there additional fees for technical support?
- Take time to review the list of features offered by the shopping cart software. Does it meet your needs? How do the features compare to other shopping cart programs on the market?
- See if a free trial of the software is available so you can play around with the software before making a commitment.
- Find out whether the shopping cart program allows you to make changes through your Web browser, or do you have to make the changes on your computer using a separate software program and then upload them to your Web hosting company's computer?
- Find out what credit card processing services are supported so you can accept credit card orders in real time. As a Canadian-based merchant, you'll want to make sure that you can use a Canadian-based credit card processor.

Once the shopping cart software has been installed on the appropriate computer, you can begin configuring it with information about your products. With many shopping cart programs, such as PDG Shopping Cart, you can do this through your Web browser. Once the PDG Shopping Cart software is installed, the installation instructions will direct you to a special address on your Web site where you'll be able to see the set-up screen for the software. In this way, using the shopping cart software program is very similar to the browser-based approach described above, except the actual store is located on your computer server.

Shopping cart programs can have extremely powerful features. For example, PDG Shopping Cart allows you to track inventory levels, send e-mail notification messages once an order has been received by your online store, and specify quantity discount rules. The latter feature means that you can configure the shopping cart software to give the customer a discount if the customer buys a minimum quantity of one of your products.

As noted earlier, because shopping cart programs vary widely in their capabilities and options, it's important to think about the features you want and research different shopping cart products before you make a final decision. If you've never set up an online store before, you probably don't know what features you want. That's why it's important to spend time on each shopping cart program's Web site to compare features and pricing information.

At this point, you may be wondering if you should use a browser-based storefront package like SoftCart or a shopping cart program like QuikStore or PDG Shopping Cart. The answer depends on your budget, your technical skills, and how much customization you require in your online store. If you are simply looking for a quick and easy way to start selling on the Internet with minimal hassle, you're probably better off with one of the browser-based storefront programs. On the other hand, if you already have a Web site and you're looking for a powerful, highly customizable shopping cart solution for your existing site, you can choose to purchase a stand-alone shopping cart program.

Over 60 percent of Canadian businesses have Web sites.

Source: Canadian Marketing Association (www.the-cma.org)/ IBM Canada (www.ibm.com/canada)

e-fact

Option #3:
Building an Online Store Within a Larger Online Marketplace

Advantages
- Large amount of visitor traffic
- Creation and maintenance of the storefront is easy and is handled through your Web browser
- Can be used to complement a stand-alone online store

Disadvantages
- You can't have your own domain name
- You must conform to the policies of the site you are using
- You may have to pay commissions on your sales

Instead of building an online store and putting it up on a Web site with its own unique domain name, you may want to consider building an online store and hosting it within eBay (www.ebay.ca) and/or Amazon.com (www.amazon.com), two of the largest e-commerce sites in the world. Both eBay and Amazon.com have programs that allow merchants to set up their own online stores within their own respective Web sites.

eBay Canada Stores

Many businesses have found success setting up storefronts on eBay (www.ebaystores.ca), the world's most popular online auction service. For a monthly subscription fee, eBay Canada allows you to set up an online storefront featuring your company logo, storefront search engine, customized product categories and colour schemes, store information, and policies. Using eBay's Store Builder program, you can set up and manage your storefront entirely through your Web browser. There's no need to download any software. If you have just a few items you want to sell on eBay, you can list the items individually without opening a storefront. This is the traditional way of selling on eBay and it is how most items are sold through the site. However, if you want to have your own branded presence on eBay where you can sell all your items in one place, you should definitely investigate an eBay Canada storefront. You can use your eBay Canada storefront as your primary online store or you can use it to complement an existing online store that you've set up outside of eBay. The choice is yours.

Tips for Selling on eBay Canada

- eBay Canada has a network of experienced eBay sellers who are ready to help you learn how to sell products on eBay. To find an assistant in your area, visit the eBay Trading Assistant Directory at pages.ebay.ca/tradingassistants.html.
- Qualified merchants who already have a Web site or online store may be able to use eBay Canada's Merchant Kit to aggregate and display their eBay auctions on their Web site, along with an eBay marketplace logo. The benefit of doing this is that customers can see all your eBay auctions when they visit your main Web page. Set-up is a snap since it only requires you to add one line of code to your Web site. For more information and links to other tools that can help you sell on eBay, visit eBay's Buying and Selling Tools Web page at pages.ebay.com/services/buyandsell/index.html.

- If you have a large business and intend to sell a lot of products on eBay, consider using one of eBay Canada's preferred solution providers (PSPs). These organizations can help you with logistics and auction management services as well as provide you with advanced software tools to help you with tasks such as payment processing and performance reporting. The cost of hiring a preferred solution provider involves a flat set-up fee as well as a commission on each sale. Contact eBay for further information.

Although you can't register your own domain name for your eBay storefront, eBay will assign you a unique Web address that you can promote in your advertising campaigns, on your business cards, etc. The Web address for your store will be www.ebaystores.ca/Storename in which "Storename" is the name of your store.

You can sell items on eBay using two different types of selling formats. The first is an auction format where you collect bids on your items and sell them to the highest bidders. If you would prefer to sell your merchandise in a more traditional way, eBay also supports "Buy It Now" and fixed price listings where you can sell items at fixed prices without any auctions.

The cost of selling products through eBay is very reasonable. In addition to the monthly storefront fee, eBay also charges both an "insertion fee" and a final value fee. The non-refundable listing fee for listing an item on eBay varies from $0.35 to $2.75 depending on the starting price of your item. The final value fee ranges from 5.25 percent to 1.50 percent and is based on the final sale price (or "final value") of your item. You can pay your eBay fees by credit card (on an automatic monthly basis) or by cheque or money order.

eBay isn't for everyone, but the advantage of selling on eBay is being associated with one of the most valuable brand names on the Internet. eBay draws millions of visitors to its Web site every month, and eBay Canada is one of the most visited online shopping destinations in Canada, so being part of eBay is like being a store in a busy shopping mall. For a small business, one of the biggest challenges in operating an online store is finding customers who want to buy your products. If your online storefront is part of the eBay Web site, it will be linked to all of your eBay listings and you will also be included in the eBay Stores Directory.

As of mid-2002, eBay Canada did not support online, real-time credit card processing. (See Chapter 4 for a discussion of real-time credit card processing.) It is the responsibility of the seller and the buyer to contact one another once a transaction has been completed. As the seller, you are responsible for collecting payment from the people who purchase from you through eBay. You can accept payment by credit card, but you will have to obtain the buyer's credit card information by fax, telephone, or mail and then process it manually yourself, either online or offline. You can also collect payment by money order, wire transfer, cheque, or through an online payment service such as PayPal (www.paypal.com). When you list an item on eBay, it is your responsibility to indicate what payment methods you will support, when payment is due, and what your shipping policies are. It is also your responsibility to fulfill the order once payment terms are met.

To learn more about setting up a storefront on eBay Canada, visit www.ebaystores.ca. For more information on how eBay works, we recommend you read the eBay Seller's Guide, which can be found at the following Web address: pages.ebay.ca/help/sellerguide/index.html.

An eBay Canada Small Business Success Story
By Mary Helen Amlin, Toyland Online, Bolton, Ontario

A few years ago, on the advice of a friend, I visited eBay.ca, registered, and started selling Disney videos as an additional source of income. Today, eBay.ca represents the majority of my household income.

After selling some initial items on eBay.ca, including two sentimental favourites, a Little Mermaid comforter and swimming Ariel doll, a friend of the family, who was actively selling on eBay.ca, suggested that my husband get involved in the business. At the time, my husband Greg was not interested. I was content listing five to six items each week, keeping track with e-mail folders and a lot of Post-It notes. That all changed in March 2001.

In December 2000, Greg's company offered him a job in Florida. Little did he know that when he turned it down, he was slated for dismissal. In March 2001, he came home early and dropped the bomb that he had been dismissed.

As Greg searched for another job, I did more and more work on eBay.ca. Greg helped by setting up a spreadsheet system for me to keep track of my listings. I immediately ramped up to fifty listings per week. As my business grew, I searched for additional products to sell. I met with many different vendors, and started to build a network of contacts in the toy industry. Initially many wholesalers didn't want to sell to me because I didn't have a traditional storefront. However, my persistence paid off, and I quickly built a network of vendors who sold to me on a regular basis. A few months later, I was listing nearly 100 items per week, and after downloading some auction assistance software, I was listing nearly 200 items per week.

After a year of unsuccessful job hunting, Greg and I made the decision that he would work on our eBay.ca toy business instead of returning to the traditional corporate environment.

Today, we are both committed to our burgeoning business. We have divided the workload; he coordinates shipping, and I write the listing descriptions and make phone calls. Even our kids get involved, although they get frustrated because they can't play with all of the toys!

Our next goal is to list 300 items per week. We are constantly on the hunt for brand-new quality items. eBay.ca has created a pure market environment. If the market doesn't like what you're selling, the silence around your listings is deafening.

Today, as a result of eBay.ca buyers who have helped our dreams come true, our mortgage is being paid, there is food on the table, and we have clear business goals for the next few years. I have never seen Greg so happy with work. Our dining room has replaced the traditional corporate boardroom, and when Greg goes to work each morning, our daughter tells him to drive safely as he descends the stairs to his at-home office.

Mary Helen Amlin can be reached at gka@gc-minis.com

Amazon.com zShops

Like eBay, Amazon.com has its own storefront program. Amazon.com's storefront program for high-volume sellers is called zShops (www.zshops. com). Merchants who sign up for zShops must pay a monthly subscription fee (which includes the right to list as many as 40,000 items) as well as a closing fee on each item sold, which varies depending on the final sale price. When a buyer pays with a credit card (Amazon.com calls this method Amazon Payments), you are also charged a per-item fee as well as a percentage of the total amount of the purchase. Amazon.com will immediately credit your account for the full payment amount and subtract their fees. Once every two weeks, any payments you have received will automatically be transferred to your chequing account. Your storefront will have a Web address of the form http://www.amazon.com/shops/nickname in which "nickname" is the name of your online store.

For low-volume sellers or sellers who don't need a branded storefront with its own unique Web address, Amazon.com offers another service called Amazon.com Marketplace. Amazon.com Marketplace is designed for merchants who want to sell the same items that Amazon.com is currently selling. Your items are listed alongside Amazon.com's current listing so that potential buyers will see them when browsing Amazon.com's own product listings. Because you are selling the same items that Amazon.com is selling, there are a few rules that you must follow. These rules are spelled out on Amazon.com's Web site:

> *Used items must be priced at or below Amazon.com's price for the same item. If your item is collectible—signed or out of print, for instance—you must set a price higher than the list price. If you're selling a new book, CD, cassette, video, or DVD, the price you set must be at or below the Amazon.com price. If you're selling new items in other product lines (including Computer & Video Games, Electronics, Tools & Hardware, Camera & Photo, Outdoor Living, and Kitchen & Housewares), you can set any price that you feel is fair. Please be aware, however, that listings for new items other than books, CDs, cassettes, videos, and DVDs will only appear on product information pages when that item is listed as out of stock by Amazon.com.*

Amazon.com collects a fee from you whenever an item sells through Amazon.com Marketplace. This fee is comprised of a small fixed charge plus a percentage of the sales price. There are no additional fees. The fee is deducted from the sale price and the balance of the proceeds go into your Amazon.com Marketplace account. Any funds in your account are automatically transferred to your bank account every fourteen days. There are no fees levied by Amazon.com in the event an item doesn't sell. When listing items through the Amazon.com Marketplace service, credit cards are the only method of payment allowed. Amazon.com also has an auction service, called Amazon.com Auctions, that allows sellers to sell items through online auctions. The cost of using Amazon.com Auctions includes a non-refundable per-item listing fee plus a closing fee based on the amount of the winning bid. The closing fee is charged only if your item sells. When a buyer pays by credit card, you are also charged a per-item fee as well as a percentage of the total amount of the purchase. As with Amazon.com Marketplace, proceeds from your sales minus any fees are transferred to your bank account every two weeks, as long as the purchase was made using a credit card.

At press time, Canadian implementation of Amazon.com zShops, Amazon.com Marketplace, and Amazon.com Auctions had not been launched. However, a Canadian Web site is now available at www. amazon.ca.

Option #4:
Advanced E-Commerce Software

Advantages
- Fully customizable
- Provides a complete storefront solution
- Is the most powerful e-commerce solution
- Often includes advanced features like Web site analysis and personalization
- Can often be tied into an organization's back-end systems

Disadvantages
- Need to install software
- May require programming expertise to set up and install
- May involve a long set-up process
- Bigger investment required: $1,000–$1 million+

The last option for building an online store is an advanced store-building software package. The "advanced" category includes low-end, mid-range, and high-end e-commerce packages. In most cases, the software will be physically delivered to you, but you may be able to download some of the low-end packages off the Internet. Pricing starts at around $1,000 and goes higher than $1 million.

On the low end of the price spectrum, there are packages such as AbleCommerce, which are suited for small businesses as well as large organizations. AbleCommerce uses a browser-based interface so that merchants can set up an online store without the need for any programming knowledge.

In the middle range, there are solutions such as IBM's WebSphere Commerce Suite or Microsoft Commerce Server. To give you an idea of how powerful some of these programs are, IBM's WebSphere Commerce Suite comes on several CD-ROMs. Although these programs are capable of just about anything, they are designed for large organizations with big budgets rather than small businesses.

Packages such as IBM's WebSphere are overkill for most small businesses and mom-and-pop storefronts. They're more appropriate for businesses with high-volume online stores that want a fully customized look and a wide range of reporting, analysis, and promotional tools. In particular, mid-range solutions are usually notable for their personalization features, relationship marketing tools, and cross-marketing capabilities, which are usually not available in the entry-level packages discussed above. For example, both IBM WebSphere and Microsoft Commerce Server allow merchants to personalize the content of Web pages based on a customer's demographic information or purchase history.

At the high end of the spectrum are packages like Blue Martini Software's Customer Interaction System and BroadVision's Retail Commerce Suite. These programs are designed for organizations with complex e-commerce needs. For example, businesses may want to develop a highly personalized e-commerce experience for their customers, tie their e-commerce operations into call centres, or integrate their Web sites with their warehouses or fulfillment operations. Blue Martini's software, for example, costs over $1 million and requires at least a couple of months to set up. It's the software that was used by Canadian Tire for the creation of their e-commerce site.

While a program like AbleCommerce won't require an army of Web developers, mid-range and high-end programs like WebSphere, Commerce Suite, and Customer Interaction Suite will almost certainly require expert computer programmers to build your online store, given the extensive range of options and capabilities of the software.

One of the benefits of using an advanced storefront package is that you won't outgrow it as quickly as you might outgrow one of the entry-level solutions. If you start off with one of the entry-level packages and your online store becomes really successful, your growing needs may be beyond the capabilities of the package you are using. Moving an e-commerce site over to an entirely new platform can be a lot of work. On the other hand, if you start off with a higher-end package that has lots of room to grow as your needs change, you can minimize disruptions to your online store down the road.

Examples of Advanced Storefront Solutions

Vendor/Product	Web Site
AbleCommerce	www.ablecommerce.com
Blue Martini Software Customer Interaction System	www.bluemartini.com
BroadVision's Retail Commerce Suite	www.broadvision.com
IBM WebSphere Commerce Suite	www.ibm.com/websphere
Intershop Communications' Enfinity	www.intershop.com
Microsoft Commerce Server	www.microsoft.com

Shoppers who use multiple channels (retail store, catalogue, Web site) spend 50 percent more and visit stores 70 percent more frequently than the average shopper.

Source: Shop.org (www.shop.org)

e-fact

What to Look for in an Online Store Solution

Now that we've reviewed the four basic options for setting up an online store, you need to think about the features you want to have in your on-line store so you can identify the solution that best meets your needs.

One of the most important considerations when choosing a storefront solution is to anticipate your future needs now so you won't have to con-tinually change your storefront software. As you begin selling online, you may discover that your existing storefront product is inadequate. That's to be expected as you expand your business and learn more about e-commerce, but it's quite a disruption to your business if you have to move your entire store over to a different software package to upgrade it. Imagine if you had to move your home every year or couple of years! Moving your online store can be quite a hassle and very time consuming, especially if you have hundreds of products in your inventory. If you think you may expand your product line or make significant changes to the features in your online store in the immediate future, make sure you choose a store-front solution that can meet your needs as you grow.

In the pages that follow, we provide you with a checklist of some of the different features you should be aware of as you research storefront solu-tions. By no means are we suggesting that the storefront package you ul-timately select should include every feature listed here. If you want one of the features below that is not included in a storefront package you are se-riously considering, contact the company and find out if the feature will be added to the product in the near future. It may turn out that the fea-ture does exist after all and you just didn't realize it! If the feature doesn't exist, find out whether it will be possible for you to hire a developer or pro-grammer to add the feature to your online store. If you're thinking of using a stand-alone shopping cart, some of the shopping cart software vendors may be willing to custom-program a feature for you if you're willing to pay for it. As we have noted several times in this chapter, many of the entry-level storefront packages limit the amount of customization you can do. If there is a feature that you absolutely must have and the storefront pack-age you're considering doesn't have it—and you can't add it yourself—you should consider using a different storefront package.

Affiliate Program Support

Does the storefront software have built-in support for affiliate programs? As you will see in Chapter 7, many online stores use affiliate programs to increase the number of visitors to their stores. An affiliate program in-volves signing up Web sites to promote your online store. In return, you pay affiliates a flat fee or a percentage of the final sale if they successfully refer a customer to your store. In order to keep track of all of the refer-rals and commissions, you need to monitor who is referring visitors to your store. Some storefront software packages have features that make it easier to manage affiliate programs. If you think you may start an affili-ate program in the future, you may want to look for storefront solutions that provide this type of support.

Auction Capabilities

With more and more Web sites offering online auctions, you may want to investigate whether the storefront solution you are considering supports online auction capabilities. Alternatively, find out whether your storefront service can be integrated with an auction site like eBay (www.ebay.ca).

> By 2005, consumers will spend twenty times more on the Internet when using a high-speed broadband connection than they do with traditional analogue dial-up modems.
>
> *Source: Gartner (www.gartner.com)*

e-fact

Back-End Integration

Can the store be integrated with your existing business systems? If you already have a retail business, you will probably want a storefront solution that can be integrated with your existing accounting, inventory, payment, and fulfillment systems; otherwise your retail systems will be out of step with your Internet systems and you could wind up with some significant logistical and financial challenges as a result. Ask yourself if it is important that your customers be able to determine, through your online store, whether a particular item is in stock. If that is a critical part of the sales process, then you will need a link from your store to your inventory system.

Capacity

Can the software handle heavy volumes? Does the site that will host your online store have a fast connection to the Internet? If you expect your store to attract a lot of customers every day, make sure the software can support those volumes. More importantly, make sure your Web hosting company has a fast connection to the Internet. You will quickly lose customers if your online store is sluggish and slow to navigate.

Cookie Support

Does the software allow you to keep track of your customers using cookies? Does the software support "persistent cookies"? These allow a customer to load up a shopping cart, leave your online store, and come back at a later time to pick up where he or she left off (this is called a "persistent shopping cart"—see Chapter 3). Can the software track your customers in other ways, using their IP addresses, for example?

Customer Registration

Does the storefront solution include customer registration capabilities and does it retain customer information once a customer has left your online store? Many online stores allow customers to register, which usually entitles them to special features such as access to special promotions (see Chapters 3 and 7 for more information on customer registration). Online registration also allows customers to store billing and/or shipping information on the site so they don't have to re-enter this information every time they make another purchase at your online store. Registration requires the customer to provide his or her name, e-mail address, and any other information the merchant requests. A registration feature is valuable because it allows a merchant to build a profile of its customers and this information can be used for marketing and promotional campaigns (provided that the customer has consented to this use).

Customization

To what degree can you customize the overall design and layout of the store? Ask the following questions:

- Does the service or software allow you to customize the appearance, layout, and look of the store, or are your choices limited?
- Can you control fonts, colours, and background colours and images? If the service uses design templates, how many can you choose from?
- Can you customize the messages displayed throughout the store and at checkout?
- Can you upload your own HTML pages to your online store, so that you can introduce other information, such as FAQs, support, and contact information?
- Can you customize product and category pages?
- What restrictions exist on customization?
- Are other customization possibilities available?

Data Export Capabilities

Can you export your sales data into a database, spreadsheet, or accounting program? If you plan to use a spreadsheet program or an accounting package like Intuit's QuickBooks to keep track of your online sales, find out if you can export data from your online store into the software program you are using.

Data Import Capabilities/Spreadsheet Support

Can you import an existing spreadsheet or database file into your online store? What spreadsheet and database formats does the store software support? For example, suppose your online store will carry a hundred different products and all of your product information is already in a database. Will you be able to import the database into your online store, or will you have to manually enter in the product information item by item?

Database Support

Will the software allow you to build a database-driven store so that your product information is created dynamically from a database? This may not be possible with entry-level storefront packages, but may be possible with some of the stand-alone shopping cart programs. Database support would definitely be a standard feature of all the mid- to high-range e-commerce solutions.

> Thirty-eight percent of online shoppers in Canada now have high-speed Internet access.
>
> *Source: Yankee Group (www.yankeegroup.com)*
>
> **e-fact**

Domain Name Registration

Can your online store have its own domain name? Find out if the storefront service you choose allows you to register a domain name for your online store (e.g., www.yourstorename.com). If so, what is the cost of registering the domain name and having it linked to your online store? Having a unique domain name for your online store gives it a more professional image and a simple address that customers can easily remember.

The whole issue of domain names can become quite complex. For example, if you can have your own domain name for your online store, why stop there? You might consider registering multiple domain names, all of which link to your store. That way, you've got multiple different addresses (i.e., based on product or trademark names) that lead customers to your store (see Chapter 6 for more information on domain names).

Electronic Mailing List Support

Does the storefront software come with its own mailing list capability? Some software programs have built-in features that allow you to manage a database of customer e-mail addresses so you can regularly send out promotional e-mail messages to targeted groups. Keep in mind that many people consider such unsolicited e-mail to be junk mail, so be careful how you use this feature. Some storefront solutions may impose a limit on the length of the e-mail messages you can send through the mailing list or on the number of customers you can add to the mailing list. Make sure you are aware of any such restrictions. Also find out whether it is possible to set up mailings to selected customers based on their demographic profiles, previous purchases, or other criteria.

E-Mail Acknowledgement to Customers

Find out if the storefront will allow you to send an e-mail acknowledgement to a customer once an order has been received by your online store. This type of e-mail acknowledgement system can be a very desirable feature since it assures customers their orders have been received. It can also save you time and money since it reduces the need for customers to contact you to find out the status of their orders. Therefore, check out the level of e-mail integration that is possible with the storefront solution that you choose. Also find out whether you can customize the content of the e-mail message that is sent to customers.

E-Mail Address Forwarding

Determine whether you can set up the storefront solution so that it forwards order information to different e-mail addresses. For example, suppose you want one copy of each online order to go to the owner of the company, a second copy to go to the sales department, and a third copy to go to the fulfillment department. Will the software do this?

e-fact

Nearly 4.8 million Canadian households will make consumer purchases over the Internet in 2004, up from 2.5 million in 2001.

Source: Yankee Group (www.yankeegroup.com)

Fraud Protection

What type of fraud-protection measures are available to you? Some storefront programs have built-in fraud-protection services that may be available for free or for an additional charge. Fraud is a serious issue and one that we discuss in more depth in Chapter 5, "Online Security Issues and Credit Card Fraud."

Help Files and Documentation

Does the software or service come with tutorials or online help files? Is the documentation comprehensive? Needless to say, make sure that any software or service you consider comes with adequate documentation and help files in the event that you need them.

Information Templates

Does the storefront solution give you templates so you can easily create your own shipping policies, privacy policies, and return policies and automatically add them to your Web site? Are there templates for adding basic contact information and background information about your company?

Integration with an Existing Web Site

Can the storefront software be integrated with an existing Web site? If you already have an investment in a Web site that you don't want to overhaul or subject to significant changes, then you should look for a storefront solution that can be easily integrated into your existing Web site.

Integration with Shipping Companies

What shipping options does the software support? Can the customer choose between Canada Post, United Parcel Service (UPS), and Federal Express (FedEx), or are only one or two of these options supported? Can you add your own courier companies? Also find out if the storefront software features any integration with the rate schedules of courier or shipping services. For example, some storefront products will automatically calculate the appropriate shipping cost for different carriers based on the weight of the products and the origin and destination of the shipment. Services like these will make it easier for you to calculate shipping costs for your customers.

Inventory Management

What inventory management features does the storefront software have? For example, find out whether the software will track inventory levels so it becomes an inventory management system. Will you and/or your customers be notified when you run out of stock of a particular item? If the stock of a product drops to zero, will the software automatically remove that item from the online store or inform customers (before they place an order) that the item is temporarily out of stock? Will you be notified if inventory runs low on any product in your online store?

Language and Currency Support

Will the storefront software support different currencies and different languages? If there is no built-in support for different languages and currencies, how difficult is it for you to add different currencies or languages to your online store, or is it even possible? For example, suppose you want to change all the menu buttons in your online store to another language. Can you do this? This will be an important consideration if you intend to attract a lot of international business or if your online store will cater to a specific country or demographic group where English is not the predominant language.

---

e-fact

Children are just as likely as adults to get frustrated with poorly designed Web sites.

Source: Nielsen Norman Group (www.nngroup.com)

Minimum Order Amount

Depending on the types of products you are selling and their prices, you may wish to set a minimum order amount. Some storefront software programs will allow you to do this. Customers who don't meet the minimum amount will not be allowed to check out of your online store until they increase the total amount of their order. This can be an important feature if you are selling low-priced items and want to generate a good profit margin on each order.

Multimedia Files

Does the storefront service allow you to add multimedia files to your online store? For example, are you able to include sound or video files or Shockwave animations? Can you upload files such as PowerPoint presentations or Adobe Acrobat documents?

Online Marketing Programs

Does the storefront solution you are considering offer any marketing programs to help you attract traffic to your online store? For example, does the company maintain an online shopping mall or directory of online stores to which you can add your site? Does it run any type of a banner exchange program so you can trade advertisements with other online stores? (For a discussion of banner ads, see Chapter 6, "Marketing Strategies for Your Online Store.")

Order Encryption/Encrypted E-Mail

What type of encryption software does the storefront software use to protect the transmission of online orders by the customer? Given current concerns in Canada and around the world regarding online credit card security, you will want to ensure that the storefront solution you are considering supports credit card encryption so that orders from your customers can be transmitted securely over the Internet. The most widely used type of encryption on the Internet is SSL (Secure Sockets Layer) encryption.

You should also check to see if the software supports e-mail encryption. When orders are e-mailed to you by the storefront software, you may want them to be encrypted so they can't be read by a hacker while in transit. One of the most popular e-mail encryption tools is Pretty Good Privacy (PGP). Some storefront software packages support PGP-encrypted e-mail.

Order Methods

What order methods does the storefront solution support? In addition to online ordering, you may also want to enable customers to place their orders by telephone, fax, or mail. Not all customers are comfortable with sending their credit card data and personal information over the Internet, so it's generally a good idea to build in other options.

Order Notification

Will the storefront solution notify you by e-mail and/or fax when a new order is received, or do you have to log onto the Web site to find out whether you have received any new orders? When comparing storefront solutions, find out what method the program uses to notify you when an order has been placed. In addition, consider how the order information is presented to you on the storefront software's Web site. For example, when you review orders on the Web site, are they easily accessible and presented in a user-friendly manner, or is it a cumbersome process to call up orders and examine them?

Order Tracking

Does the storefront software allow customers to check on the status of orders they have placed with you? This is a handy feature to have since customers can log onto your Web site after they have placed an order to find out whether their order has been shipped and/or processed. Some, but not all, storefront solutions provide this feature.

Packing Slips and Invoices

Does the storefront solution automatically generate packing slips and invoices? Are invoices automatically delivered to customers by e-mail? What do the invoices look like? Can you customize the packing slips and invoices to your specifications? Find out if the software or service will automate this type of paperwork for you. If you are doing a lot of transactions, this can save you a significant amount of time.

Payment Methods

What payment methods does the storefront solution support? You might want to establish a variety of payment methods for your online store, including credit cards, purchase orders, cheques, pre-established accounts, COD, and other options. Make sure that the solution you choose supports your requirements. Also find out whether you can create your own list of payment methods or whether you're restricted to what the software provides. Determine the credit cards you want to accept and make certain the storefront solution supports them. For example, not all storefront solutions will accept Discover, Diner's Club, and JCB.

Personalization Features and Customer Profiling

More and more storefront programs are implementing "one-to-one" marketing capabilities that enable a merchant to personalize product offers or Web pages for specific customers. While advanced personalization features are typically found only in the mid- or high-range storefront solutions, some entry-level packages do offer some personalization capability (see Chapter 7 for more information on personalization strategies). Because personalization capabilities can help you cross-sell and up-sell products to your customers, they are an important feature to think about when choosing a storefront solution. Investigate the following issues:

- Does the software come with cross-selling capabilities? Will the software allow you to cross-sell products to customers based on their initial selections? For example, some storefront products can be set up so that when a customer chooses a certain product, other similar products are recommended to the customer.

- Does the software make it possible for you to track a customer's shopping habits? As your customer base grows, you may want the ability to target your frequent customers with special offers based on their purchasing activity.

Men are more interested than women in shopping online.

Source: AT&T Broadband (www.attbroadband.com)

e-fact

Pricing Structure

How will you be charged for your online store? Make sure you understand the product's pricing structure and contract terms before making any commitments. Find out whether there is a minimum contract period for your online store or whether you can shut down the store at any time without financial penalty.

The charges you incur will depend on the type of storefront software you are using. With most browser-based storefront services, you are usually charged a one-time set-up fee and then a flat monthly fee, which increases with the number of products you are selling. The fee may also be based on how much disk space you use on their server and/or how much data transfer your online store generates. (Data transfer is a measure of how much information is being transferred from your Web site to the visitor's computer. In general, the more people visiting your site, the more data is being transferred.)

Under certain circumstances, some browser-based solutions may take a percentage of sales in addition to a monthly fee. Yahoo! Store, for instance, invites merchants to list their stores in Yahoo's shopping mall, called Yahoo! Shopping. Depending on your sales volume, Yahoo! may take a small percentage of your mall-derived sales.

If you decide to purchase shopping cart software or a mid/high-range software program instead of a browser-based solution, you simply purchase the software and then you own it. However, you will need to pay a monthly fee to a Web hosting company or Internet service provider so your online store can be placed on the Internet (unless you choose to run your own Web servers).

If you decide to process credit card transactions in real time, you will also incur various credit card processing fees. These are more fully discussed in Chapter 4.

Product Restrictions

Some storefront creation vendors will not allow you to sell certain products through their service. For example, if you intend to sell adult/sex products, you may find it difficult to find a storefront service that will accept you. If you plan on selling a product or service that would be considered explicit or high risk, make sure you clearly understand any rules or restrictions of the storefront service you are considering.

Quality of Appearance and Navigation

Does the software produce professional-looking online stores? What navigation aids are built into the software?

On the Internet, the look of your online store is crucial. A professional-looking store that is easy to navigate builds credibility, user satisfaction, and sales, while a store that is visually weak and hard to navigate scares off customers. If you are using a browser-based solution, make sure the end product looks professional. As recommended earlier, look at examples of stores created using the storefront programs you are evaluating. This will help you assess what your store will look like and determine whether the end product is professional or amateurish in appearance.

e-fact

The online market for paid subscriptions and content will quadruple to US $5.8 billion by 2006, from US $1.4 billion in 2002.

Source: Jupiter Media Metrix (www.jmm.com)

Real-Time Credit Card Processing

Will the storefront solution support real-time credit card processing so that your orders can be approved in real time over the Internet? What fees does the storefront solution charge for this service, and how do these fees compare to the fees charged by other storefront solutions?

Another important factor to consider is the bank or merchant account provider the storefront service is linked to. To accept credit cards in your online store, you will need a merchant account, and in order to process your credit card orders in real time, you will need to use real-time credit card processing. We discuss real-time credit card processing and merchant accounts in Chapter 4, "Merchant Accounts and Online Payment Processing."

Some storefront solutions may restrict you to a specific bank, merchant account provider, and/or payment processor, which will affect the credit card processing fees you will have to pay. Make sure you fully understand what restrictions, if any, exist regarding where you can obtain your merchant account or payment processing services. For example, can you obtain your merchant account or payment processing service from any organization, or are you restricted to using companies that have alliances with the storefront service? What fees does the storefront charge for setting you up with a merchant account and real-time credit card processing, and are they competitive?

Sales and Marketing Reports

What type of sales information does the storefront software give you? How detailed is that information? In addition to tracking sales activity on your Web site, you will also want to determine where your customers are coming from, what search engines they are using, and what keywords led them to your online store. Make sure you select a storefront package that generates useful sales and marketing reports. As the volume of orders in your store increases, you will begin to depend on these reports to identify best-selling and worst-selling products and to determine other sales and marketing trends in your online store. Find out if the software will answer questions such as:

- What are the top-selling products on your Web site?
- What products in your online store are generating the most revenue? The least revenue?
- Which pages on your site are generating the most visits? The least visits?
- Where are your customers coming from?
- What is the average revenue per order?
- How many orders are you receiving per day?

Also investigate the following issues:

- Are the reports strictly numerical or can you get graphical reports as well?

- Can you view orders by date and customer name as well as by product?
- What other options exist to sort/filter your orders?
- How frequently are the reports updated? Once a week? Once a day? Several times a day? In real time?

In order to get as much information as possible about how customers are using your Web site, you may need to supplement your storefront software's reporting capabilities with a Web site analysis tool such as WebTrends (www.webtrends.com), which will give you detailed reports that not only show where your visitors are coming from but what path they take through your Web site and where customers are abandoning your online store. Mid- to high-range storefront solutions often come with extremely powerful reporting capabilities. However, if you use an entry-level package, such as a shopping cart or browser-based storefront solution, you may find that you need to purchase a separate Web site analysis tool in order to gain a complete picture of how customers are using your Web site. In fact, many of the shopping cart products don't have any reporting capabilities at all! Most of the browser-based storefront solutions do have reporting capabilities, but some focus strictly on sales data, and won't give you an overview of where your customers are coming from or how they are using your Web site. For more information about Web site analysis tools, see Chapter 6, "Marketing Strategies for Your Online Store."

Sales and Promotions

Does the storefront solution allow you to implement sales and promotions? Merchandising products on the Internet isn't much different from merchandising them in the real world. From time to time, you will want to put certain items on sale or provide product discounts to your customers. Investigate such issues as:

- Does the storefront software make it easy for you to display new products prominently or highlight special promotions?
- Can customers redeem coupons on your online store?
- Does the software allow you to create and/or e-mail coupons to customers?

- How easy is it to put items on sale or reduce all the prices in your store by a certain percentage?
- Can you set up discounts that start and finish on certain dates/ times?
- Does the software make it easy for you to implement quantity discounts (e.g., buy three, get one free)?

By 2005, comparison shopping engines will influence US $25 billion worth of consumer spending on the Internet.

Source: Winterberry Group (www.winterberrygroup.com)

e-fact

Scalability/Inventory Restrictions

Some storefront solutions have a maximum number of products or product categories that you can have in your online store. Other storefront products may have different monthly fee levels depending on how many products you intend to have in your online store. Some packages may not impose a limit on the number of products or product categories that you can carry, but instead will have recommended maximums so that your online store doesn't slow down to the point where it's sluggish for you to update and slow for customers to use. Think about how many products you intend to carry and how many different product categories you will need to define. Make sure you find a storefront solution that can support your needs. If you think you will need to expand the number of products or categories that you carry, make sure that the storefront solution you are considering will be able to accommodate your needs as you grow. For example, if you want to expand the number of products that your store carries from a hundred to a thousand after the first year, will you have to switch to another storefront program? Also find out if there is a limit on how many different attributes (e.g., colour, size) you can assign to each product in your online store.

Search Capability

Does the storefront software allow you to build a searchable index of your product catalogue or your entire online store? When customers enter your online store, they may want to search your online store by keyword rather than browsing page by page through your site. Find out whether the storefront solution includes a search engine and whether you can customize the search results.

Search Engine Submission

Will the product submit your online store to some or all of the major search engines and Web directories? Once your online store is created, you'll want to submit it to each of the major search engines and Internet directories (we discuss this issue in Chapter 6). Find out if the storefront service you are considering includes this capability, or whether you have to do it yourself.

Security Holes

When doing your research, we recommend you investigate whether the storefront solution you are considering has experienced any security problems or security breaches. You should also try to get a feel for how seriously the company takes security issues. You can often get this information by talking to previous or existing customers or by talking to people who have some expertise in the field of Internet security. One survey, by a company called Internet Security Systems (www.iss.net), found that eleven popular shopping cart software programs had security vulnerabilities. Even worse, one-third of the companies didn't take corrective action to fix the security holes when they were notified of the problems. One of the identified security vulnerabilities allowed a hacker to access an online store and modify the store's prices! Another problem involved a shopping cart program that had left a default password in place, making it easy for hackers to access credit card numbers.

A separate investigation by a security services company called Cerberus Information Security/Atstake (www.atstake.com) discovered a popular shopping cart program contained a secret password that could allow a hacker to gain access to customer credit card information and other confidential information. The password was put in place by the software developer to allow technical support staff to remotely access the software if they needed to. However, most of the online store owners using the shopping cart software were unaware that the password even existed! Of even greater concern was the fact that hackers could have easily found the secret password since it was easily identifiable in the computer code used to create the software. Thankfully, when this story broke, the company in question quickly fixed the software.

These two events alone underscore the importance of investigating the security record of any storefront solution you intend to use. Obviously, most software vendors fix any explicit security holes once they are discovered, but if you follow the computer press, you are also aware that new security holes are found all the time. Hence, you should pay attention to this issue. You can read more about online security issues in Chapter 5, "Online Security Issues and Credit Card Fraud."

The percentage of Canadians accessing the Internet will grow to 80 percent by 2006.

Source: International Data Corporation (www.idc.com)

e-fact

Security Infrastructure

What type of measures has the storefront service taken to protect the orders your online store is receiving? Is the storefront service in compliance with the Visa top ten security rules that we list in Chapter 5? For example, are your customers' orders stored behind a firewall in an encrypted form so they can't be accessed and read by a hacker? See Chapter 5 for a list of some of the questions you should ask any storefront service you are considering.

Shipping and Delivery Options

What shipping options are supported? Will the software automatically calculate shipping costs for Canada Post and for different courier companies such as UPS and FedEx? In addition, can you customize shipping charges any way you want, or are you restricted in how you calculate shipping costs? These are two of the most important questions you can ask when choosing a storefront solution. As noted earlier in the chapter, this can be an extremely complex area. You will probably need the storefront software to support different shipping rates for different areas of the country and different parts of the world. In addition, you will probably need to charge different shipping rates depending upon the quantity and weight of the items a customer has ordered.

Before choosing a storefront solution, find out what options are available to calculate shipping charges. For example, can you calculate shipping charges by weight, geographic location, price, and quantity ordered, or are you restricted to only one or a couple of these methods? Can you assign a separate shipping cost to each item in your online store? If there are significant limitations on how you calculate shipping costs, it might be very difficult for you to manage your shipping costs or present attractive shipping alternatives to customers. For example, one package we looked at didn't allow merchants to customize shipping rates by country. This is exactly the type of problem you should watch out for if you intend to do a lot of international business.

Before you start shopping for storefront software, make sure you know how you intend to calculate shipping charges for your products. Once you've decided that, you can look for something that meets your requirements.

e-fact

By 2005, over 10 percent of consumer e-commerce in the United States will be done without a personal computer.

Source: Gartner (www.gartner.com)

Shopping Cart

All storefront solutions include a shopping cart. As noted earlier in the chapter, this is the component of your store that allows customers to select the items they want to purchase. It's one of the most important aspects of your online store. Because the shopping cart is the last part of your store the customer sees before checking out, it should be as comprehensive and user-friendly as possible.

Take some time to look at the different types of shopping carts that various online stores use in order to familiarize yourself with their features. Then, when comparing different storefront solutions, thoroughly investigate the shopping cart technology being used and ask the following questions:

- What type of functionality does the shopping cart provide?
- What properties/attributes can items in the shopping cart have (e.g., size, weight, colour, quantity)? Can you easily define your own attributes?
- Does the shopping cart always show the total value of the order, including taxes and shipping costs?
- How easy is it for customers to add or remove items from their shopping cart?

- How easy is it for customers to continue shopping once they've placed an item in their shopping cart?
- Is it easy for customers to change the quantity of items in their shopping cart? Is the total automatically recalculated?
- Can customers see a running summary of the items currently in their cart? Can they see this information while they are still shopping?

Software Interface/Ease of Use

If you're not a computer whiz but want to build your online store on your own, look for a storefront solution that is easy to use. Investigate the following issues:

- Are the software's features and commands well organized?
- Is the user interface intuitive?
- How easy is it to upload images to your online store?
- Is the interface easy to use or slow and clunky?
- How easy is it to add new products and categories? Can you add multiple products at once or do you have to add one product at a time?
- Does the software walk you through the process of setting up an online store or are you left to figure out the steps on your own?
- Does the software assume you have any technical knowledge?
- How useful are the help screens?
- How easy is it for you to make changes to your online store?

Taxation

Many provincial tax laws stipulate that you must collect sales tax for orders shipped to addresses in the province where your business is based. For this reason, make sure you choose a storefront solution that makes it easy for you to calculate taxes, when necessary, for the orders placed in your online store. Some storefront solutions maintain their own tax tables so you don't have to worry about charging the correct amount of sales tax. Depending on which province you operate out of, you may or may not be required to collect sales tax on the shipping cost as well as on the cost of the products.

Just like shipping costs, taxation can be an extremely complex issue. Contact your provincial government and make sure you thoroughly understand what taxes you are responsible for collecting in your online store and under what circumstances you must collect them. Only then can you begin to shop for a suitable storefront package. Once you understand your tax obligations, make sure the storefront package you select is capable of the level of customization you require. Investigate the following issues when evaluating different storefront solutions:

- How easy is it to define different tax levels for different provinces?
- Is the tax automatically determined by the storefront software or do you have to manually input the appropriate tax rates?
- If the storefront software maintains its own tax tables, how frequently are they updated?
- Does the storefront software allow you to distinguish between taxable and non-taxable products?
- Can you apply tax to shipping costs?

Technical Support

What type of technical support is available? Is telephone support available or just e-mail support? Regardless of which storefront solution you select, make sure quality technical support is available when you need it. If your online store stops working in the middle of the night, is there a twenty-four-hour technical support line that you can call for help, or are you on your own?

Thumbnail Images

A thumbnail image is a small version of a larger product image. Once you start working with your online store, you may want to create both large and small images of your products. For example, you may decide to use several thumbnail images on a single Web page so customers can see the selection in a particular product category at a glance. They can then see a larger image of any product by clicking on it. Does the storefront software support thumbnail images? Does the software allow you to create and/or upload thumbnail images easily? Some storefront solutions may create thumbnail images for you, while others will require you to create the thumbnail images yourself and then upload them to your online store.

WYSIWYG (What You See Is What You Get) Editing

Does the software allow you to see what your online store will look like before you publish it on the Internet? This is an important feature because it allows you to see the effect of changes to your online store as you make them. Without WYSIWYG editing, you would have to publish your store on the Internet every time you made a change in order to see whether it had the desired effect.

The Web will generate 32 percent of new car sales by 2006.

Source: Jupiter Media Metrix (www.jmm.com)

e-fact

It's Not an Easy Decision

By this point, you should have a better understanding of the various methods you can use to build your online store and the range of features available. As you have no doubt discovered by now, there are a lot of issues you need to consider.

The software solution you ultimately select doesn't have to include every feature or option that we've covered. Picking a good storefront solution usually involves making trade-offs. You may be hard pressed to find a storefront package that includes every feature you want in addition to ease of use and a high degree of customization. You need to prioritize the features that are most important to you and pick the storefront package that suits your budget as well as your current and future needs.

3

Tips for Building an
Effective Online Store

"The pressure to cut costs has become increasingly intense these days, but the need to keep customers happy never goes away."

—"Keep 'Em Happy—In a Down Economy, Retaining Customers and Building Loyalty Is More Vital Than Ever," *InformationWeek,*
January 28, 2002

It has been said that it is just as easy to lose customers on the Web as it is to attract them. This means that setting up a store on the Internet involves far more than just creating an attractive Web site to sell your products. It is all about exceeding expectations.

Consider the competitive aspect of the Internet. Regardless of what you sell, you will find yourself up against some stiff competition. The Internet is global, with the result that your competitors are no longer just the fellows down the street—you are now up against a variety of people and companies from around the world. This means that you will always be compared to the best, with the result that you will always have to strive to do better. The competitive nature of the Internet means that customers are unforgiving, always expecting the best deal and the best customer service.

The other important fact is that many customers on the Internet will expect the customer service you offer online to match or exceed that which you offer in the real world. Not only do consumers on the Internet feel empowered in a way that has not existed offline, they actually have been empowered. They can almost instantly compare your prices and service with other companies. They can quickly find out if previous customers have been satisfied with your company, and they can post their own complaints online if they are dissatisfied with your service or support. In short, the Internet has shifted the power in the buyer–seller relationship to the buyer. You cannot afford to slip up when it comes to your online store. Excellence in execution and delivery is a must. That is why one of the most important things you can do at this stage is understand some of the best practices in the execution and design of online stores.

In this chapter, we outline many of the important elements of a successful online store. We've conducted an exhaustive review of dozens of online stores and we've assembled a comprehensive checklist of all the components you need to think about.

The chapter reviews both the aesthetic and functional aspects of an online store. Some of the features and capabilities we discuss might require you to hire a programmer or Web designer in order to implement them within your online store. We want to emphasize that it is not practical or cost-effective for most online businesses to implement every feature we discuss in this chapter. However, if we had to design the perfect online store, these are the elements and features we would recommend.

Our discussion is organized into eleven sections covering the following topics:

- Credibility
- Product information
- Design and navigation
- Order information
- Shipping information
- Exchanges and returns
- Pricing
- Checkout procedures
- Customer service and support
- Channel integration
- Internationalization

Let's begin!

Tips for Building Credibility and Confidence in Your Online Store

How important is credibility on the Internet? Extremely. Given the many horrible experiences that customers have had shopping on the Internet in recent years, with problems ranging from late deliveries to unanswered e-mail messages, online shoppers are most likely to do business with those companies they know and trust. They will also avoid companies that have a notoriously poor record in customer service.

This underscores the importance of providing your customers with an online experience that will generate positive word of mouth. One of the biggest challenges for any online store is winning the trust of customers.

> **e-fact**
>
> Only 29 percent of Internet users say they trust Web sites that sell products or services.
>
> *Source: Consumer WebWatch (www.consumerwebwatch.com)*

Building credibility with your customers is particularly important considering the number of Internet businesses that have gone bankrupt or shut down in recent years. In addition, consumers may be wary—and legitimately so—of doing business with a Web site or company they have no experience with. If you are a small business that doesn't have a recognized brand name, most customers will not be familiar with your company and its reputation, and may therefore be reluctant to do business with you on the Web. When customers visit your Web site, they may be wondering whether it is a real, legitimate business. How do customers know your Web site won't vanish the following day along with their payment? In the pages that follow, we provide you with lots of ideas to build customer confidence in your online store and make shoppers less wary of doing business with you.

Invest in a Clean, Professional, Up-to-Date Design

Many of the online stores that rated highly during our research shared one important trait—they looked professional. They had a cutting-edge appearance, were obviously up-to-date, and used compelling design to lure us into the Web site.

Eighty-two percent of surveyed small office/home office (SOHO) businesses and 61 percent of surveyed small businesses say the Internet has increased the need for them to improve customer service.

Source: Cahners In-Stat Group (www.instat.com)

e-fact

The look of your store is vital when you're operating in an environment as competitive as the Internet. Customers will often decide whether or not to enter an online store based on the look of its front page. On the Internet, image isn't everything, but it is an important component of an online retail strategy.

In the previous chapter, we pointed out that one of the limitations of using browser-based services to create a storefront design is their lack of flexibility in design. If you have difficulty creating an eye-catching design yourself, you may want to invest in the services of a professional Web designer or e-commerce developer. Whether you use a browser-based service or high-end storefront software, getting help from a professional Web designer can give your online store a sharp appearance so it doesn't look passé or amateurish.

In effect, the front page of your online store is like the window display in a brick-and-mortar store. It lures the customer into the store. If the design of your online store is ineffective, it will likely discourage sales.

We're not suggesting that you spend tens of thousands of dollars designing your Web site. You don't have to. However, we want to point out the important role design can play in making your online store successful. Stores that look exciting and are full of lots of activity will be more effective in getting people past the front page, just as interesting window displays can lure people into retail stores. While this might not guarantee sales, it does go a long way toward turning browsers into buyers.

How do you know when it's time to overhaul the design and appearance of your online store? Spend some time browsing through other comparable online stores in Canada and the United States that sell the same products you do. Compare the design and features of these other online stores to yours. If your Web site looks amateurish or archaic in comparison to your competitors, then you know it's time to refresh the design of your Web site. If you're a small business, there's no point in trying to match what larger companies are doing on the Web, but at the same time, you want your Web site to look as modern and compelling as possible.

When designing your Web site, keep in mind the types of things that really bother customers. We've listed the top five pet peeves of online shoppers in the box below.

Top Five Online Shopping Frustrations of Online Shoppers
1. Pop-up boxes when visiting/shopping at a site (52%)
2. Banner advertisements (50%)
3. Congested Web pages (too many advertisements, images, or information) (35%)
4. Slow load times (26%)
5. Difficult to find a specific product (20%)

Source: Retail Forward (www.retailforward.com)

Regularly Update the Content on Your Web Site

Change the content on your home page as often as you would change the window display in a retail store. Coordinate your products with the seasons or specific holidays as often as possible. This keeps your Web site looking fresh and lets customers know that your online store is very much alive and in business. It doesn't take a lot of work to update your Web site with a little bit of current news. In fact, if the content on your Web site doesn't change from month to month, customers may begin to wonder whether your online store is still running.

Even simple modifications to your Web site can reinforce the fact that your Web site is being kept current. For example, consider placing a message at the top of your Web site to tell your visitors when your Web site was last updated. Change the date every two weeks or so to let visitors know your Web site is being maintained by someone. This may seem like a tiny detail, but it can be very reassuring to customers who want to know the Web site hasn't been abandoned.

There are many approaches to keeping your content fresh. A popular technique is to spotlight different products on your home page each month. Some storefront software programs allow you to highlight and feature new additions to your store easily so you can quickly and effectively give a high profile to new products. Whatever you choose to do, it is important that the content of your home page change constantly.

Make Sure Your Web Site Doesn't Go Down

When you operate a store on the Web, any downtime you experience can cripple your reputation—and your bottom line. By downtime, we mean any period of time that your online store is unavailable to your customers due to technical or other problems.

It isn't just your store that could go down—it could be the company that processes the credit card transactions on your store—and if this happens, you won't be able to accept credit card payments from your customers. One of the authors of this book once experienced a problem with his payment gateway that lasted an entire weekend; only when the payment gateway's staff returned to the office on Monday morning was his site fully operational once again.

How do you avoid these types of problems? When you are looking for a company to host your online store or process your credit card transactions, make sure you thoroughly investigate its reputation and track record. Find out what its policies are for support, whether support is reachable twenty-four hours a day, and what type of support is given outside normal business hours.

Also ask for references. E-mail people who currently use the company's hosting services and ask for feedback. Ask the company directly about its technical record. Follow the same procedure if you're thinking of using a browser-based storefront service.

One way to make sure your online store doesn't go down without your knowledge is to use a service like WatchDog (watchdog.mycomputer.com), which will constantly monitor your Web site and alert you via e-mail or text-based pager if it goes down for any reason. WatchDog costs between US $299 and US $999 a year, depending on how frequently you want it to check your Web site's availability. A service like this is certainly a good investment since it can help you identify technical problems with your Web site before you start to lose a lot of business!

If your online store does go down, more often than not the problem will be minor and you can get the site up and running quickly. But what happens if there is a serious computer problem and your online store provider loses all of your customer records and/or your entire online store due to a virus or other event? Hopefully this won't happen to you, but in case it does, make sure you have your entire online store backed up and stored offsite so you can recreate it if necessary.

Finally, make sure your online store can accommodate spikes in traffic. Find out how many credit card transactions your online store is capable of processing simultaneously and determine how many online shoppers your Web site can accommodate at any one time. Proper planning will help you avoid capacity problems and the lost business that usually results.

e-fact

Surfers who visit a Web site's customer service area account for only 39 percent of online shoppers, but this group accounts for 50 percent of total consumer online spending.

Source: Cyber Dialogue (www.cyberdialogue.com)

Provide Background Information on Your Company

Include a section at your online store where customers can evaluate your company and its track record. Regardless of how long your company has been in business, provide customers with information about your real-world facilities and locations, your street address (not just a P.O. box!), your telephone number, and an overview of your management team. A toll-free number is a good idea as well. If the company has been in business for many years, highlight this fact on your Web site. If your company is a relatively new organization without a strong track record, this section can still make a big difference.

In addition, provide details of your membership in local chambers of commerce or other business organizations. The more information you provide, the better. And it should be information that customers can verify if they want to.

e-fact

Delivery issues are the primary reason why customers contact online merchants.

Source: Jupiter Media Metrix (www.jmm.com)

Many online stores create an "About Us" section on their Web site to communicate information about their organization. This section usually provides information about the company, its management team, perhaps a message from the company president, press releases, and any other pertinent facts about the company that help to establish its real-world credibility. You could even include a picture of your store or office to show customers you are a real business! Background information such as this will definitely help put skeptical shoppers at ease!

Remember, on the Web customers have no way of knowing whether your company is credible unless you tell them! We've come across many online stores that don't have any background information on the business at all. Leaving this type of information off your Web site could drive visitors away.

Provide Customer Testimonials

Consider including on your Web site any testimonials or references from customers who have purchased products from you over the Internet and who have been happy with your service. Testimonials are both compelling and effective and can help boost the confidence of any shoppers who may be hesitant to do business with you. For an example of how effective this can be, visit the online store for The Worn Doorstep (www. worndoorstep.com).

Apply to Seal Programs

In addition to testimonials and including an "About Us" section on your site, consider applying to a seal program such as TRUSTe (www.truste.org) or BBBOnLine (www.bbbonline.org). These programs will give you a seal to place on your Web site if you meet their operating standards. TRUSTe is a program that oversees the privacy practices of Web sites, while BBBOnLine accredits Web sites for both privacy and reliability.

Use Merchant Rating Programs

Another way to build trust with online shoppers is to participate in merchant rating programs like BizRate.com (www.bizrate.com), which rate customer satisfaction with online stores. When online shoppers complete a purchase at a participating merchant, they are asked to complete a survey and rate their satisfaction with the merchant on issues such as product selection and customer support.

At any time, online shoppers can visit BizRate.com's Web site and review ratings from all of the participating online stores. Customers can look up ratings for individual merchants or they can browse through product categories to find the online store that has received the best ratings from customers.

Any online store can sign up for BizRate.com's customer ratings service and there is no cost to participate. Once you become a participating merchant, you are allowed to display the BizRate.com logo on your Web site and customers can click on it to see the ratings for your online store.

Why would you want to use such a service? By giving prospective shoppers access to your customer ratings, you demonstrate your organization's commitment to superior customer service. After all, if you provide excellent customer service, you should have no fear of making your ratings publicly available through a service like BizRate.com. Naturally, ratings from customers who have already made purchases from you can be a very effective tool in winning credibility and trust from new shoppers who may not be familiar with your name or reputation.

While BizRate.com is by far the most popular rating service for online stores, a number of other similar rating services exist, including ePublicEye.com (www.epubliceye.com), a ratings service targeted at small and mid-size online merchants.

---

e-fact

Brazil accounts for over half of all e-commerce revenues in Latin America.

Source: Boston Consulting Group (www.bcg.com)/Visa (www.visa.com)

Create a Privacy Policy

Many online shoppers are concerned about their privacy when they visit merchant Web sites. In fact, for many consumers, privacy is often a bigger concern on the Internet than security. For this reason, you should tell online shoppers how you intend to handle any personal information you collect from them on your site. For example, if a customer fills out a survey on your Web site or buys something from you, how do you intend to use the information that the customer gives you? There is also a great deal of concern that many companies collect private information online, often through the use of questionnaires, and then misuse it for various purposes, such as reselling it to other organizations. Misusing customer data in this way could be the kiss of death for your online store. People are very concerned about privacy online—and rightly so.

Online shoppers also worry that their personal information may be revealed or made accessible through a Web site, either on purpose or through error. To win the trust of online shoppers, you should prepare a privacy policy or customer information policy for your organization and post it on your Web site. The purpose of a privacy policy is to let customers know what types of information you collect from them and advise them of how you intend to use that information. Your privacy policy should also tell customers what they need to do to delete their personal information from your records if they so desire.

If you expect your Web site to attract children, it is a good idea to address this specifically—both in your privacy policy as well as on any forms or surveys you have on your Web site. Children's privacy on the Internet is a concern to many parents, and many organizations make sure this issue is sufficiently covered in their privacy policy.

Most Web sites fail to incorporate the minimum standards for usability, links, and privacy established by industry leaders and Web experts.

Source: Giga Information Group (www.gigaweb.com)

e-fact

The approach you take in your own privacy policy is entirely up to you and will depend on the types of products you sell and the kind of information you plan to collect from your customers. Privacy policies aren't really optional anymore—they're an essential part of doing business online.

If you need help writing your privacy policy, visit the Web site of TRUSTe (www.truste.com), a non-profit privacy initiative on the Internet. TRUSTe's site contains lots of resources about online privacy as well as a model privacy statement that will help you develop your own privacy policy. When developing your own privacy policy, take some time to visit the Web sites of other online stores to see what their privacy policies look like.

Sixty-five percent of Internet users say it is *very* important that a site display its privacy policy.

Source: Consumer WebWatch (www.consumerwebwatch.com)

e-fact

Explain What You've Done to Protect Your Customers

Many consumers remain paranoid about giving out their credit card numbers on the Internet. To ease their fears, make sure you describe, in nontechnical language, what measures you have taken to protect the transmission and storage of credit card data on your Web site. Customers will be more comfortable shopping on your Web site if you can assure them that any information they send you will be safe.

Guard Against Security Breaches

It's vital to prevent your Web site from accidental release or disclosure of private information from your customers. You need to make certain your Web site has no security problems or weaknesses that might allow someone, whether unintentionally or illegally, to gain access to any of your customer data through the Internet. If you were ever to have a security breach on your Web site, it could scare off potential customers and tarnish your organization's reputation.

If your online store is hosted by an Internet service provider or Web hosting service, find out what precautions it has taken to protect your store from any possible security problems. In Chapter 5, "Online Security Issues and Credit Card Fraud," we provide a list of some of the security-related questions you should ask the companies that will be supplying your online storefront software and hosting your online store on the Internet. (As we discussed in Chapter 2, the same company may or may not provide both services, depending on what type of solution you use to set up your online store.) As we explain in Chapter 5, many of the security problems on the Internet are due to human error, negligence, or storefront software that has security weaknesses.

An organization can do itself incalculable damage by making private information accessible online, intentionally or not, or by misusing any private information that it collects. Hence, you must work hard to ensure that those who visit your Web site, and hence your store, believe that their private information is safe with you and that you respect the private nature of the relationship.

One way to check the quality of the security on your Web site is to hire security experts or "ethical hackers" who review your Web site for any unplugged holes or potential security problems. Security experts can be hired through companies such as IBM (www.ibm.com) or Ernst and Young (www.ey.ca), but recognize that retaining such an expert is expensive and is usually only something that large organizations can afford.

Nearly all consumers who use Web-based customer service say that twenty-four-hour access is the top reason for doing so.

Source: Society of Consumer Affairs Professionals in Business (www.socap.org)

Tips for Displaying Product Information

Many merchants overlook the importance of providing good product information. The better the product information, the more likely an interested customer will make a purchase and the less likely it is the product will eventually be returned to you.

Provide Detailed Product Information

Don't stop at a simple one-line description of your products. Some of the most effective online stores we have seen provide product descriptions that are both comprehensive and compelling. In other words, an effective product description should be persuasive as well as descriptive. Remember that you're trying to sell the product! Give the customer reasons to purchase it. If necessary, hire a copywriter with a flair for the English language to write short paragraph-length descriptions of each of your products for your Web site. The copywriting should make the customer say, "Yeah, I need that!"

Provide Large Product Images

To minimize product returns and avoid disappointing your customers, give your customers the option to zoom in on product images or view enlarged pictures of the products you sell. This will allow them to see product details and features that may not be visible in smaller images.

Close-up product images are the Web site feature most likely to increase a shopper's likelihood of purchasing.

Source: PricewaterhouseCoopers (www.pwcglobal.com)

Provide Real-Time Inventory Information

There's nothing more disappointing than ordering a product on the Web and finding out afterwards that the product is on back order or out of stock. Unfortunately, many online stores don't provide their customers with real-time inventory information. This means that when an item sells out, the product continues to be displayed on the Web site as if it were still available, and customers continue to place orders, unaware that the product is no longer available.

---

e-fact

Online retailers will generate US $36 billion in revenue from the sale of gifts in 2005.

Source: Forrester Research (www.forrester.com)

To avoid disappointing and angering your customers, let them know right away if a product displayed on your Web site is out of stock or on back order. In Chapter 2, we explained that some online storefront solutions include inventory control features that will remove an item from your online store once you run out of stock. Other storefront packages will allow you to display an "out of stock" message when the supply of a product runs out. Take advantage of features like these—they will definitely save your customers a lot of grief.

Sell Well-Known Brand Names

Depending on the type of business you're in, carrying brand names that shoppers are familiar with may make them more likely to do business with you. Why? If you carry products and brand names that are relatively unknown, you may have a hard time building confidence in the products you sell.

If you carry well-known brand names that are backed by strong guarantees or warranties, make sure you communicate this information to your customers. This will help you build customer trust in your online store.

Use Holiday and Special Event Hints

If you sell products that make great gifts for Father's Day, Mother's Day, Valentine's Day, or any other holiday or special occasion, make sure you draw your customers' attention to these important dates as they approach. This can be accomplished with a simple graphic on your home page that mentions the special day.

For example, suppose it is two weeks before Father's Day. Shoppers on your Web site may not even be thinking about buying a Father's Day gift from your online store, but posting a reminder that the date is fast approaching may help to generate additional sales.

> As a result of research that Canadian shoppers do on the Internet, the Internet will influence CAN $59 billion in offline sales by 2006.
>
> *Source: Forrester Research (www.forrester.com)*

e-fact

Offer Panoramic Views

If you are selling products that can be difficult to visualize in a two-dimensional format, or if you're simply interested in making online shopping more exciting for your customers, you may want to consider allowing customers to view a 360-degree panoramic view of some or all of your products. Some people think that 3-D technology is gimmicky and won't do anything to increase online sales. However, it certainly makes online shopping more fun and exciting. Moreover, as online shoppers increasingly use high-speed Internet connections, 3-D images will make the whole online shopping experience more user-friendly for your customers.

Display Accurate Colour

According to market research by Cyber Dialogue (www.cyberdialogue.com), 60 percent of Internet shoppers do not trust the colours they see on their computer monitors. As a result, some 30 percent of Internet shoppers surveyed had decided not to purchase a product on the Internet because they were concerned that the true colour of the product was different from the colour they saw onscreen.

This is an important finding if you are thinking of selling any product over the Internet (such as clothes, furniture, fabrics, automobiles, etc.) in which colour is a significant factor in the purchase decision. The problem is a technical one, caused by differences in how computer monitors, Web browsers, computer operating systems, and software programs display colour. This means that pictures of products on your Web site will not look the same to all your customers. For example, a red sweater may appear orange to some of your customers, and varying shades of red to others.

Colour problems such as these can lead to customer dissatisfaction. They can also cause a high rate of returns. The Cyber Dialogue study found that almost 15 percent of shoppers had returned items because the colour of the actual product didn't match the colour displayed on the Web. To address this problem, some online retailers have implemented colour-correcting solutions from companies such as E-Color (www.ecolor.com) and Imation (www.verifi.net), which allow colours to be displayed accurately to online shoppers. These solutions can be expensive to implement, but they're worth checking out nonetheless.

Provide Sizing Information

You may not have heard the term "bracketing" before, but it's an issue that a number of online retailers have had to deal with. Bracketing is when an online shopper orders several different sizes of the same product with the intention of keeping only one size and returning the rest. This problem is normally associated with clothing purchases where customers aren't sure what size is appropriate. When purchasing from an online store, customers don't have the option of trying on clothing. So rather than running the risk that a garment will either be too large or too small, a customer will often order several different sizes of the same product. The customer will then keep the size that fits and return the rest to the retailer.

e-fact

Almost two-thirds of U.S. Internet users say that going online endangers their privacy.

Source: UCLA Center for Communication Policy (ccp.ucla.edu)

If you are selling clothing or clothing accessories on your online store or planning to do so in the near future, one way to cut down on bracketing is to offer sizing advice on your Web site so that customers can pick out the right sizes. Alternatively, you can use a service such as My Virtual Model Fit (www.myvirtualmodel.com), which can generate accurate size information for your customers. Keep in mind that offering this type of information on your Web site won't eliminate the bracketing problem entirely, but it can help to reduce product returns.

Cross-Sell Products

You should get in the habit of cross-selling products in your online store to increase sales. This means that wherever possible, product pages on your online store should feature accessories or complementary products that your customers may be interested in. Amazon.com (www.amazon.com), the popular online bookstore, does this quite effectively. Whenever a customer looks up a specific book on Amazon.com, similar books are always recommended to the customer.

The idea here is to up-sell customers. Eddie Bauer (www.eddiebauer.com) employs a similar strategy on its Web site. Customers looking at a specific piece of clothing can ask to see coordinating products by clicking on a link in the lower left-hand corner of the screen. It's an excellent strategy for increasing overall sales in your online store!

Offer Online Wish Lists

Online wish lists are a popular way to increase sales. An online wish list is like a wedding registry. It lets customers choose products from your online store that they are interested in receiving as a gift, perhaps for a birthday, for Christmas, or for any other special occasion. Customers can forward their wish lists to friends and family members, who can then log onto your Web site and purchase items on the list.

> Consumers are more satisfied making retail purchases online than they are shopping at traditional department and discount stores.
>
> Source: *American Customer Satisfaction Index (www.bus.umich.edu/ research/nqrc/acsi.html)*

e-fact

Offer Favourite Items Lists

A favourite items list allows an online shopper to save a list of the products he or she buys often. On subsequent visits to your online store, customers can easily add items to their shopping carts from their favourite items list without having to navigate through your entire Web site. You can see this technology in action on the Staples Web site (www.staples.com). It's a great way to make online shopping easier for your customers!

Tips for Better Site Design and Navigation

Make Your Web Site Easy to Navigate

Have you ever walked into a supermarket or drugstore and become frustrated when you couldn't find what you were looking for? Online shoppers often experience the same frustration if the Web site they are visiting is poorly organized with no helpful navigation aids.

The design and layout of your store must be simple and straightforward, yet rich in features to satisfy the needs of the customer. The best-designed stores provide customers with a site menu or navigation bar that is always on the screen, regardless of where the customer is on the site. This gives the customer one-click access to other areas of the online store, as well as any other areas of your Web site. The site menu also serves as a map, showing your customers where they are within the overall layout of your site so they won't get lost.

e-fact

Eighty-six percent of Internet users are in favour of "opt-in" privacy policies that require Internet companies to ask people for permission to use their personal information.

Source: Pew Internet and American Life Project (www.pewinternet.org)

e-fact

Fifty-four percent of Internet users have chosen to provide personal information in order to use a Web site.

Source: Pew Internet and American Life Project (www.pewinternet.org)

Offer Different Navigation Schemes

When designing your online store, think about the different ways customers might shop for the products you are offering. For example, if you are a florist, customers might shop for flowers by price, by occasion, or by product category. Or if you're a toy store, you could organize your products by category (e.g., action figures, dolls, games), by brand name (e.g., Fisher-Price, Lego, Nintendo), by character name (e.g., Pokémon, Winnie the Pooh), or by price range. The goal is to give customers different ways of finding products they are interested in purchasing.

The navigation methods you choose to implement on your online store will depend on the types of products you sell. You may want to consider organizing a focus group of potential customers to try to understand how they would prefer to search for products on your Web site. Alternatively, visit other online stores in your industry to get ideas on the different ways products can be grouped on your Web site.

Make It Possible for Customers to Search Your Online Store by Keyword

Even if you give your customers several different ways to browse your online store, there will always be some people who prefer to search for products by name or keyword. There will also be times when customers can't find what they are looking for (e.g., information on your return policy), and they'll want a way to do a quick search of your Web site.

We highly recommend that you include a search box on your Web site so customers can search for the information they're interested in. While some storefront software packages come with search capabilities, they may not be very powerful. If necessary, and if you can afford it, you can hire an e-commerce developer to add such search capabilities to your store if your online store software will allow you to. Alternatively, you could use an online search engine product like Atomz (www.atomz.com) to index the contents of your Web site.

Account for Misspelled Searches

What happens when a customer decides to use a search engine on your Web site but then spells a product name or a person's name incorrectly? Will your search engine still direct your customer to the right product or will it give the customer a "not found" message? Awareness of this problem led some retailers to set up their search engines to catch misspellings. By doing this, you can eliminate the lost sales that might result when customers misspell the products they're looking for and can't find them on your Web site.

> Two-thirds of female online shoppers say they would not make a major purchase without first researching it on the Internet.
>
> Source: International Data Corporation (www.idc.com)
>
> **e-fact**

Amazon.com (www.amazon.com) is a good example of a site that has implemented this type of capability effectively. For example, suppose a customer who is looking for a Barbra Streisand CD misspells her last name and types "Striesand" into the search box. Amazon.com has set up its search engine to recognize such misspellings. Even with the last name misspelled, Amazon.com will recognize that the customer is looking for music by Barbra Streisand and will display a list of Streisand CDs.

Adding this capability to your Web site isn't easy. A programmer must modify your search engine so that customers who misspell your product names are still directed to the proper Web pages on your site. Depending on the number of products you sell, this could be an expensive and time-consuming endeavour.

Use Drop-Down and Pop-Out Menus

One of the frustrations voiced by many online shoppers is the number of screens they often have to click through to get to the product they want. A good solution to this problem is to use a drop-down or pop-out menu that allows a customer to get to a desired area of your online store quickly. You can see an example of a drop-down menu on the Eddie Bauer online store (www.eddiebauer.com). Online shoppers only need to point their mouse at any of the product categories along the top of the site (e.g., "men's," "women's," "gear," etc.) and a drop-down menu automatically appears with a list of subcategories that the customer can click on.

A different type of drop-down menu can be seen on the Avon online store (shop.avon.com). Click on the down arrow beside "Shop by Category" and you'll see a list of product categories. Clicking on any of the choices will take you directly to the appropriate area of the Avon Web site.

A pop-out menu is similar to a drop-down menu except that instead of dropping down vertically, the menu pops out to the left or right.

The benefit of using drop-down and/or pop-out menus is that online shoppers can get to a specific area of your online store in one quick step without having to navigate through a series of Web pages. However, it's doable only if the online storefront solution you're using will allow this type of customization.

---

e-fact

The top priority for online gift buyers is that the gift arrives on time.

Source: Forrester Research (www.forrester.com)

Provide a Site Map

Another useful navigational tool is a site map, an index of all of the major sections and subsections of your site. Ideally, shoppers should be able to access the site map from anywhere on your online store.

A site map is an excellent resource in the event customers get lost or can't find what they're looking for. For a good example of a site map, look at the online store for RadioShack Canada (www.radioshack.ca). On the home page, click on the "Site Map" option at the bottom of the page. That will bring up a handy list of links to all of the major areas on the site.

Make Sure Your Web Site Loads Quickly

No matter how easy your site is to navigate, it will all be for naught if customers have to wait too long for your Web pages to load. Don't get carried away with a design that goes overboard in terms of layout and content. Specifically, don't fall prey to the temptation to overload your site with graphics, the latest and greatest programming feats, or other things that will bog it down and make it slow. We're not advising you to avoid graphics and animation on your home page, but make sure they don't adversely affect the performance of your Web site. Have family members and friends test your Web pages to see if they load quickly. If performance is slow, consider removing some of the graphics or use a service such as GIF Wizard (www.gifwizard.com) or NetMechanic's GIFbot (www.netmechanic.com), which will compress your graphics so they will load faster.

> Eighty-two percent of online shoppers say that shipping costs are paramount to their purchase decisions.
>
> *Source: Forrester Research (www.forrester.com)*
>
> **e-fact**

If your Web pages are slow, compressing your graphics may not be the only solution. Slow Web pages can also be due to poor Web site coding, the capacity of the server that is hosting your online store, the speed and congestion of the Internet connection used by your online store or Web hosting provider, the amount of content on your Web pages, or any combination of these problems. You need to take all these factors into account when you are trying to improve the performance of your online store. Depending on what type of storefront solution you are using, some of these issues may not be easy for you to control.

A good program to test how fast your Web pages load is NetMechanic's HTML Toolbox, which can be found on the NetMechanic Web site (www.netmechanic.com). Although the program costs a nominal amount per year, you can try out the service for free and even test out the speed of your competitors' online stores!

> Twenty-seven percent of Internet users say they have abandoned an online order because of privacy concerns.
>
> *Source: Cyber Dialogue/Fulcrum Analytics (www.cyberdialogue.com)*
>
> **e-fact**

Ensure Browser Compatibility

Although Microsoft's Internet Explorer browser is the most widely used browser on the Internet, many Internet users still use Netscape. The problem is that Netscape and Internet Explorer tend to display Web pages slightly differently. This means that when you design your online store, you should test it with both Web browsers to see how it looks. While a Web site may look perfect when viewed using Netscape, you may find misaligned columns or other problems when your site is viewed using Internet Explorer, or vice versa. These problems can usually be corrected by modifying the code on your Web pages. If this is beyond your capability, you may need to hire a Web developer to help you.

A great tool for identifying browser display problems is NetMechanic's Browser Photo (www.netmechanic.com).

Provide Easy Access to Shopping Cart Contents

One of the most crucial elements of any online store is the shopping cart, where customers can view the products they've ordered, add or delete items, and see the total amount of their purchase. As we mentioned in Chapter 2, shopping carts are included in all the major storefront solutions. Alternatively, you can purchase a stand-alone shopping cart program like QuikStore (www.quikstore.com) and integrate it into an existing Web site.

As customers browse through your store and order items, they often want to return to their shopping cart to review their order. Hence, it's important to design your store so they have easy access to their shopping carts from any area of your site. Fortunately, most of the basic shopping cart programs and storefront software packages make it possible for customers to view the contents of their shopping carts from anywhere on the Web site by clicking on a button such as "View Cart" or "Show Order." As a general rule, customers should always be only one click away from their shopping carts regardless of where they are in your store.

A good example of this strategy can be seen on the Wal-Mart Web site (www.walmart.com). Visit Wal-Mart's Web site and navigate to different areas of the site. Notice that as you move around the site, the navigation bar at the top of the site never changes or moves. Part of the navigation bar is a "Cart & Checkout" icon that always appears in the upper right-hand corner of the screen. At any time, customers can click on this icon to view the current contents of their shopping cart.

In addition to making the shopping cart easily accessible from anywhere on your Web site, you should also make it easy for customers to continue shopping on your site once they've added an item to their shopping cart. After an item has been added to their shopping cart, customers should be able to click on a button that says "continue shopping" (or something similar) if they want to continue browsing through your online store rather than checking out.

Fifty-three percent of online households have moved their furniture around to make the computer and the Internet more accessible.

Source: America Online (www.aol.com)

e-fact

As you evaluate different storefront solutions, take time to review the features that are built into the shopping cart. Also make sure you understand how the shopping cart will be integrated into your store. Can customers access the shopping cart from anywhere in the store? Can they move back and forth easily between the shopping cart and the rest of your store? Can products be easily added to and deleted from the shopping cart? Make sure the solution you choose gives you the layout and features you desire, or find out if the software will allow you to customize the shopping cart to meet your needs.

Use Running Totals

Online stores are beginning to realize that simply giving customers easy access to their shopping carts isn't enough. Customers want to be able to see what's in their shopping carts or, at the very least, a running total of their purchases, no matter where they are on the Web site. In other words, customers want to see a running total of their purchases on the screen *at all times.*

This feature allows customers to keep an eye on how much they're spending as items are added to their shopping cart. They don't have to return to their shopping cart to see this information, nor do they have to check out. The running total is always displayed on the screen.

Many online retailers have implemented this capability into their stores, including Restoration Hardware (www.restorationhardware.com). As customers navigate the online store and add items to their shopping cart, a current list of the selected items and the total amount of the purchase always appear along the left-hand side of the screen in an area called "Shopping Bag."

You'll find that your customers will appreciate having this information on the screen at all times because it avoids last-minute surprises at checkout. Unfortunately, this type of feature is not usually included in most of the entry-level storefront packages. If you like this idea, you'll probably have to hire someone to build this capability into your online store, provided that the online storefront package you are using allows customization.

Tips to Make It Easier for Customers to Order from You

Provide Step-by-Step Ordering Instructions

While it may seem obvious, don't assume that your customers know how to order a product on your Web site. Consider providing a step-by-step guide that walks customers through the process of placing an online order. For an example of such a guide, go to RadioShack Canada's Web site (www.radioshack.ca) and click on the "Help" menu option.

Provide Answers to Common Ordering Questions

Your customers will likely have lots of questions about ordering a product through your Web site. There are many issues to consider. Make sure your Web site provides answers to the following questions:

- *What forms of payment do you accept?* Do you accept only credit cards or will you accept other forms of payment as well?

e-fact

Revenues generated by selling online customer service software will grow to US $1.95 billion by 2004—more than a 1,000 percent increase from 1999.

Source: Datamonitor (www.datamonitor.com)

- *What name will appear beside the charge on the customer's credit card?* If the company name you use with the credit card companies is different from the company name you use on the Web, note this on your Web site, otherwise your customers will see a charge on their credit card statement from a name they don't recognize. This happens quite frequently because many organizations use parent companies or numbered companies for billing purposes but operate under an entirely different name on the Web. If a customer doesn't recognize a charge on his or her credit card statement, he or she will usually call up the bank and complain. This may lead to a chargeback, a situation that arises when a customer disputes an item that he or she has been billed for. (For more information on chargebacks, see Chapter 4, "Merchant Accounts and Online Payment Processing.") Chargebacks are not only inconvenient, they can cost you both time and money, so it's important to take as many precautions as you can to reduce the likelihood of chargebacks in your online store. One way to reduce chargebacks is to have your operating name and/or phone number appear beside the charge on the customer's credit card statement. Check with your financial institution or merchant account provider for details.

- *Do you accept orders from anywhere in the world?* Make sure you indicate whether you will accept international orders and, if so, from which countries. Also identify any countries that you do not ship to.
- *Can customers cancel their orders at any time?* Let your customers know whether it is possible for them to cancel an order once it has been placed, and whether any charges apply.

Offer Alternatives to Placing an Online Order

Many consumers remain terrified of sending their credit card numbers through the Internet. It is important that your online store respect these concerns. Many online retailers give customers the option of ordering by telephone, fax, or mail because they recognize that many online shoppers aren't comfortable paying by credit card. If you decide to accept orders by telephone, fax, or mail, make sure this information is well publicized on your Web site, especially in the ordering and checkout sections, so you won't lose customers who don't want to order online.

More than 60 percent of online consumers say if they are dissatisfied with a company's e-commerce site, they are less likely to purchase from the company's traditional store.

Source: Boston Consulting Group (www.bcg.com)

e-fact

Offer Instant Payment Services

While credit cards remain the most popular form of payment on the Internet, you may want to consider using an instant payment service such as PayPal (www.paypal.com) on your online store. PayPal is very popular because it allows online shoppers to send money to merchants quickly and easily, even if they don't have a credit card number handy. The benefit for merchants is that they can accept credit card payments without a merchant account. (For an explanation of merchant accounts, see Chapter 4, "Merchant Accounts and Online Payment Processing.")

PayPal is very easy to use for both consumers and businesses. Shoppers sign up for a PayPal account on the PayPal Web site by filling out an application form. They can use a credit card or deposit money into their account via electronic funds transfer. Whenever a shopper wants to send money to a merchant, he or she logs onto the PayPal Web site and fills out a form, specifying whom the money should go to and how much. The amount is automatically charged to the shopper's credit card or chequing account or deducted from his or her PayPal balance.

The merchant will receive an e-mail notification that a payment has been received. The merchant can log onto PayPal (or sign up for a new account if he or she doesn't already have one) and the money will immediately appear in the account balance. The funds can either be transferred to a bank account via electronic funds transfer, sent in the form of a cheque, or left in the account for his or her own PayPal payments.

To make it easy for customers to send you PayPal payments, you can add a PayPal button to your Web site. Online shoppers who want to pay you via PayPal simply click on the button to send you a payment. The payment is sent directly to your account, and your customer can return to your Web site.

PayPal is free for consumers to use, but businesses pay a fee to receive money via PayPal. Visit the PayPal Web site at www.paypal.com for the latest pricing information. We recommend that you investigate PayPal as an alternate form of payment on your online store. We also suggest you investigate a similar Canadian service called CertaPay (www. certapay.com).

e-fact

Nearly 80 percent of online consumers in the United States have heard of person-to-person (P2P) online payment services such as PayPal.

Source: GartnerGroup (www.gartner.com)

Provide Order and Shipping Acknowledgements

One frequently voiced complaint about ordering products on the Internet is the lack of communication from the merchant once an order has been placed. Indeed, placing an order on the Web can sometimes feel like sending a credit card number into a black hole. Unless a customer hears back from the merchant, how does he or she know that the order was received? In this respect, ordering a product on the Internet is like sending an important fax to someone. If you don't hear back from the person you sent the fax to, you begin to wonder if it actually arrived.

As an Internet merchant, it's important to acknowledge every order by e-mail and to stay in contact with the customer at various stages of the order and delivery process. When a customer places an order with you, make sure you send the customer an e-mail confirming that the order has been received. Once the order has been shipped, send the customer a second e-mail to confirm that the order is on its way. These confirmations are an important part of building a relationship of trust and credibility with your customers and are almost considered de rigueur for online stores.

Not only do these types of confirmations help you provide excellent service to your customers, they also eliminate the need for customers to e-mail you with questions such as "Did you receive my order?" and "Has my order been shipped?" Many of the storefront solutions we discussed in Chapter 2 allow you to send order and shipping acknowledgements to your customers.

Provide Online Order Tracking

In addition to providing e-mail confirmations, consider enabling your customers to track the status of their orders on your Web site. This is a really handy self-serve feature and reduces the need for customers to call or e-mail you with inquiries about the status of their orders.

Provide Order History Information

In addition to providing customers with the status of current orders, many online stores allow customers to access a listing of previous orders. Godiva's online store (www.godiva.com), for example, has an "Order History" section on its Web site that keeps track of all the purchases a customer has made. In order to limit access to this type of information, Godiva requires customers to register on the site and obtain a user name and password.

This type of service makes it easy for a customer to reorder a product. A customer who doesn't remember what he or she ordered can look up the information in the order history file. Although some products, like books, don't really lend themselves to repeat orders, gift products like flowers and chocolates do, and customers frequently forget what they ordered in the past. Order tracking also makes it easy for customers to look up details from past orders, such as a shipping address or the date an order was placed, without having to call or send an e-mail to your customer service department.

We should point out that implementing any type of registration system on your site and linking it to an order tracking system can be quite complicated. If this type of feature is important to you, make sure the storefront software solution you select can support registration and order history/tracking.

Offer Courier Tracking

Once an order has left your store or warehouse, it's in the hands of the postal service or courier company. As a service to your customers, consider giving them the ability to track their parcels on your Web site. For example, consider what REI has done on its online store (www.rei.com). When a customer places an order on REI.com, an e-mail acknowledgement and an order number is sent to the customer. Forty-eight hours after placing the order, the customer can access the order tracking page on the REI Web site and find out where the parcel is. Some online merchants simply direct their customers to the Web sites of the courier companies for parcel tracking. For example, Amazon.com sends customers a confirmation e-mail message when their orders are being shipped. At the bottom of the e-mail message is a tracking number for the courier company that is handling the delivery. Amazon.com has a section on its Web site with links to the Web sites of various courier companies so customers can track their own parcels.

But why steer customers to another Web site when you can keep them on your own site? Consider integrating the courier company's parcel tracking system into your own site. Contact the courier companies you work with for directions on how to do this. Placing the tracking forms directly on your Web site gives customers the convenience of tracking their shipments on your online store without having to go elsewhere to get the information.

Tips and Ideas for Shipping

Avoid the Temptation to Offer Free Shipping

We caution you to avoid the temptation of giving away free shipping or discounting shipping fees heavily. In their desperation to attract new customers, we've seen many online retailers waive or drastically lower their shipping charges, hoping that this will encourage more customers to buy online.

> More than any other reason, online purchasers return products simply because they are not what the consumer expected.
>
> *Source: PricewaterhouseCoopers (www.pwcglobal.com)*
>
> **e-fact**

Retailers often do this because the cost of shipping can sometimes be as much as the cost of the product being purchased, deterring many shoppers from buying online. However, before you offer your customers free or low-cost shipping, make sure you can afford it. Large online retailers can usually afford to subsidize the cost of shipping more easily than smaller retailers can. But regardless of your size, giving away shipping can cut into your profit margins substantially, and you could wind up with some serious financial problems. If you're thinking of giving away or discounting the cost of shipping, make sure your profit margins are high enough to support this practice. One strategy is to offer free shipping only if orders exceed a certain amount, such as $100.

Better yet, if you have one or more retail stores and you're worried that customers won't purchase online because of the high cost of shipping, give customers the option of ordering online and picking up the product in person at one of your stores, a strategy we discuss later in the chapter. Another option is to build the cost of shipping into the price of your products and then offer free or low-price shipping, given that many buyers online have come to expect free online shipping.

Provide Comprehensive Shipping Policies

Your online store should provide customers with a thorough description of shipping costs as well as the different shipping methods you offer (e.g., regular service, overnight delivery, two-day delivery, etc.). To avoid disappointing your customers, make sure you explain the normal delivery times for each method of shipping you offer. For example, if a customer chooses regular shipping, when is the earliest date the product would arrive? In addition, we recommend the following:

- Let customers know how long it usually takes for your organization to process the order once it's been received on your Web site.

Most customers are under the impression that if they place an order on your Web site for overnight delivery, the order will definitely arrive the next day. Some organizations find it takes at least a day to process the order and get it ready for shipping. For example, Godiva (www.godiva.com) has the following notice on its Web site: "All orders placed before 11:00 am (EST) will be processed that same day. If your order is placed after 11:00 am (EST), please allow 24 hours for processing." If you expect this to be the case in your organization, make sure customers are aware of this before they place their order; otherwise you may start receiving complaints from customers who didn't receive their orders when expected.

- If a customer elects to have an online order shipped to a home address, remind the customer that someone may have to be home to receive it. Many online shoppers get frustrated because their orders are delivered during the day when no one is home. After several unsuccessful delivery attempts, the delivery firm may end up returning the parcel to you. To avoid this problem, you might want to recommend that customers use their place of work as their shipping address so the courier company can deliver the order promptly.

- During busy holiday periods, make sure you post order deadlines on your Web site. Work closely with Canada Post and/or the courier companies to ensure that you are aware of cut-off times for getting orders delivered on time. If you expect to be overwhelmed with orders, make sure the deadlines you post will give you enough time to get all of the orders shipped on time.

- Give customers the option of purchasing insurance on shipments, especially if the products being shipped are valuable.

Discuss Import Duties and Brokerage Fees

If you plan to ship to customers in other countries, make sure you fully investigate whether any import duties or brokerage fees are likely to be levied on your products by the destination country. Many countries charge import duties and/or other taxes on products arriving from a foreign country. Usually the customer is notified of these charges at the time of delivery and payment is required before the customer is allowed to receive the product. If the shipment is being delivered by courier, the driver may request payment of the duties and fees before releasing the product. Import duties can be substantial if the product in question is expensive.

When customers are buying from your online store, they may mistakenly assume that the price they are paying includes everything, only to be shocked later when a courier arrives at their door demanding more money. While you have no control over the amount of import duties levied by another country, this type of surprise may be enough to deter customers from ordering from your store again. This is why it is extremely important to inform your customers that they may have to pay duties on the products they are ordering from you.

If you anticipate a lot of sales to specific countries, you should determine as closely as possible the level of duties that will be charged on a purchase and build this information into your store. Having said that, you should also ensure customers understand that the ultimate amount of duty cannot be determined exactly up front, and that they are responsible for whatever duties are charged. This will help avoid any misunderstandings.

Consider Charging Handling Fees

When figuring out the shipping rates for your online store, you may want to consider charging your customers an additional fee to cover your handling costs. Think about all the activities involved in preparing a product for shipping. You have to:

- purchase the packaging materials;
- enclose the appropriate paperwork (e.g., copy of the receipt);
- wrap and seal the package;
- complete and apply the appropriate labels and/or waybills;
- apply postage (if using Canada Post); and
- take the shipments to your local post office or courier depot and/or call the courier company to pick up your deliveries, if necessary.

That's a lot of work, isn't it? There's labour involved, as well as the cost of the packaging materials (boxes, packing tape, etc.). Many organizations offset these costs by building them into a handling fee, which can be added to your shipping cost to form a shipping and handling fee. Whether you want to do this depends on the types of products you are selling and what your competitors are doing.

Place "You're Not Too Late" Reminders on Your Web Site

If you sell products that customers may want to give as gifts for Father's Day, Mother's Day, Christmas, and so on, it's a good idea to place "You're not too late" banners on your Web site right up until the last possible shipping day. These let customers know they can still order products from your store in time for that special day. For example, shoppers who are on your site the week before Father's Day might assume they can't get a gift from your store delivered in time. Depending on what shipping methods you offer, it may be possible for shoppers to place their orders on the Friday before Father's Day and still receive the shipment in time, but shoppers won't know this unless you tell them! Because many people leave their shopping until the last minute, keep reminding them right up until your last shipping day that they can still order products in time for the special day.

Remember that many online shoppers are distrustful of online stores and may not feel confident ordering from you just days before a special occasion. Why? Because they don't think you can deliver the product on time. A simple statement on your Web site can boost confidence in your Web store and help you to close sales with last-minute shoppers whom you might have otherwise missed.

Fully Disclose Shipping Fees

Finally, when it comes to shipping, there should be no surprises. Make sure customers know exactly how much they will be charged for shipping before they input their credit card number into your Web site. Make your shipping fees highly conspicuous—don't bury them in a hard-to-find place on your Web site. To understand why this is important, think about how much people dislike car dealers. Many people who have bought a car complain that they encountered unknown or hidden sales charges at the last minute. Do the same thing on the Internet and you will foster the same sense of distrust.

Integrate Shipping Information Directly into Your Online Store

If you intend to use Canada Post to ship your products to customers, we highly recommend that you use Canada Post's Sell Online shipping module. It allows you to integrate exact shipping prices for all your products directly into your online store. Customers will be given a choice of several prices and different delivery methods (e.g., Priority Courier, XpressPost,

Regular Mail), and they can select the cost and delivery speed that best meets their needs. For further information about the Selling Online shipping module, visit www.canadapost.ca.

Tips for Handling Exchanges and Returns

Provide Comprehensive Exchange and Return Policies

The lack of clear refund policies and cancellation terms on e-commerce sites is a common problem on the Web. Needless to say, an exchange and return policy is an integral part of an online store. Customers will want an assurance that if they are not satisfied with their purchase, they can return the product for a credit or exchange. To keep your customers satisfied, we suggest you implement the following suggestions:

- Develop a clear, unambiguous policy regarding returns, exchanges, damaged products, and other problem purchases and post this policy on your Web site in a conspicuous place.
- Explain your cancellation policy. This policy should describe how customers can cancel their order, whether there is a time limit on cancellations, and whether a full refund will be issued (or whether there is a restocking charge), including shipping and/or other charges, in the event a customer cancels the order.
- Provide information on any warranties or guarantees on the products you sell.
- Make it easy for customers to find your return, cancellation, and exchange policies so they won't have to search high and low for them. In fact, many customers will look for these types of policies before they even consider buying a product from you. If your return policy isn't displayed, you may lose the sale altogether.
- Link to your return and exchange policy from the checkout area of your online store. A customer may decide to read your return policy at the last minute. If this information isn't immediately accessible and the customer has to leave the order page to go find it, the customer may not bother going back through the checkout process.

Create a Satisfaction Guarantee

To encourage customers to buy from your online store, consider establishing a satisfaction guarantee and publishing it on your Web site. A satisfaction guarantee lets customers know they can return any product to you if they are not 100 percent satisfied with it. Isn't a satisfaction guarantee the same thing as a return policy? Not at all. Think about it. Which has a greater impact on you—a section that says "Return Policy" or a section that says "Satisfaction Guarantee"? The guarantee should not replace your return policy but complement it.

Tips for Pricing Strategy

Create a Pricing Policy

Your Web site should clearly indicate what happens when there is a pricing error on your Web site or a discrepancy between an advertised price and a price on your Web site. There have been several high-profile cases of products accidentally listed on Web sites at several hundred dollars below the correct retail price. In some instances, retailers have chosen to honour the incorrect prices rather than upset their customers, sustaining losses of thousands of dollars as a result. Other companies affected by pricing glitches have cancelled the orders they received, only to endure the wrath of angry shoppers who felt they were misled. When a pricing glitch occurs on your Web site, you're really in a difficult predicament.

e-fact

Only 5 percent of Canadian Internet users are willing to pay a monthly or annual fee to access a news and information site.

Source: Ipsos-Reid (www.ipsos-reid.com)

To help you deal with these types of embarrassing situations, we recommend that you create a policy on pricing and typographical errors and publish it on your Web site. Pricing errors can happen very easily because of technical glitches or old prices that were inadvertently not updated, so you should be prepared. For an example of a pricing policy, visit the Help section of Amazon.com's Web site and look at the "Pricing and Availability" page.

Show Prices in American Dollars

When setting up your online store, you need to think about whether you want to display prices in U.S. dollars in addition to Canadian dollars. There are a number of online retailers in Canada that show prices in both American and Canadian dollars as a courtesy to American shoppers. For example, the online store for Uniquely Yours Bed and Bath (www.uniquelyours.com) allows shoppers to toggle between Canadian and U.S. prices.

For simplicity's sake, some online stores in Canada have decided to price all of their products exclusively in American dollars. (For an example of a Canadian company that does this, visit Binkley Toys at www. binkley-toys.com.) Doing this is somewhat risky, however, since it could drive away your Canadian customers. On the other hand, if you do most of your business internationally, all-American pricing may make sense.

Remind Americans About the Benefits of Shopping Canadian!

It's cheaper for Americans to shop online in Canada because of the favourable exchange rate. Make sure you point this out on your Web site! It will help attract American shoppers and let them know you are eager to do business with them. For an example of an online store that does a great job of selling itself to Americans, visit Toad Hall Toys (www.toadhalltoys.com) and click on the "Currency" icon on the left-hand side of the page.

Tips for Improving the Checkout Process

Create an Express Checkout Service

Some Web merchants, in an effort to speed up the checkout process and make online shopping more convenient for their customers, have implemented express checkout services so customers can store their shipping addresses, credit card data, and shipping preferences on the site. That way they don't have to re-enter this information each time they make a purchase. For an example of this practice, visit Gap's online store (www.gap.com).

Use Online Address Books

Consider giving your customers the ability to store the shipping addresses of their friends and relatives on your Web site. This makes it easier for online shoppers to send gifts to their friends and family members without having to type in their full addresses every time they place an online order on your site. For an example of this practice, visit Nordstrom's Web site (www.nordstrom.com).

It goes without saying that an online address book makes it easy for your customers to do business with you. Because this type of feature makes the checkout process faster and more convenient for your customers, it can also increase customer retention and customer loyalty.

Minimize Abandoned Shopping Carts

Web store veterans will tell you that one of the most frustrating problems with an online store is that many shoppers abandon their purchases before their order is completed. According to some studies, more than 60 percent of purchase attempts are abandoned in this way. The box below shows some of the most common reasons why an online shopper may start to shop on your Web site but then decide not to complete the purchase.

Top Ten Reasons Why Shoppers Abandon Online Purchases
(based on a survey of 719 online shoppers)

1. Shipping costs are too high (72%)
2. Customer is comparison shopping or browsing (61%)
3. Customer changed their mind (56%)
4. Customer decided to purchase the item(s) later (51%)
5. Total cost of items is too high (43%)
6. Checkout process is too long (41%)
7. Checkout requires too much personal information (35%)
8. Site requires registration before purchase (34%)
9. Site is unstable or unreliable (31%)
10. Checkout process is confusing (27%)

Source: Vividence (www.vividence.com)

To help you minimize the number of abandoned purchase attempts that occur on your online store, we've put together the following eight suggestions:

1. Allow customers to register on your Web site so their mailing address and credit card information are stored on your servers

(provided you have implemented adequate security measures). This speeds up the checkout process and allows customers to make future purchases without having to key in all of their personal information each time.

2. Make registration optional for those customers who don't want to register. As the Vividence study shows, many shoppers abandon online purchases because they are forced to register. If you insist that customers register before they make a purchase, explain the benefits of doing so and emphasize that customers only need to do this once.

3. Keep the checkout process clear, simple, and hassle-free. When a customer is ready to place an order, keep the number of questions to a minimum. Don't make the process overly complicated or time consuming and don't ask for an unnecessary amount of personal information.

4. Number the steps in the checkout process so customers know at each stage how many more steps they have to complete before they're done. Alternatively, display a graphic at each stage of the checkout process that illustrates how far along the customer is in the process and how many steps are left. Customers are less likely to get impatient and give up on a purchase if you tell them they're near the end.

5. Display your security guarantee, privacy policy, and return and exchange policy throughout the entire checkout process in order to build confidence.

6. Fully disclose the total cost of the purchase, as well as any and all shipping or handling charges, before the customer checks out of your online store. Show customers the total cost of their purchases before asking them to key in their credit card numbers.

7. Display a telephone number (or better yet, a toll-free number) that customers can call if they have any questions during checkout. Make sure this toll-free number appears throughout the checkout process. Alternatively, allow customers to chat "live" with a customer representative if they have any questions during the checkout phase. Products such as LivePerson (www.liveperson.com) provide this capability.

8. Don't force customers to download any special software programs or plug-ins in order to do business with you.

Use Persistent Shopping Carts

As noted previously, it's not uncommon for online shoppers to visit an online store, place a couple of items in their shopping cart, and then abandon the purchase altogether. If customers abandoned the purchase because they changed their minds about purchasing the item, they probably have no intention of coming back. However, often the customer gets pulled away from the computer unexpectedly in the middle of a purchase and has every intention of returning later. Unless your online store is using what is called a "persistent shopping cart," the items the customer placed in the shopping cart won't be saved, and the person will have to start shopping all over again. Facing the prospect of having to start shopping from scratch again, the customer may decide to forgo the purchase, leaving you without a sale.

Many online stores use persistent shopping carts so customers can place items in their shopping cart, turn off their computer, and then come back hours or days later and pick up where they left off. In the event customers abandon a purchase, but then forget to come back, the items will still be waiting in their shopping carts when they eventually return. Check with the storefront software you are using to see if persistent shopping carts are supported. Not only does this feature improve customer service, it keeps you from losing valuable sales!

Tips for Improving Customer Service and Support

It goes without saying that customer service has become the number one priority for online retailers. In fact, online retailers have lost billions of dollars in sales in recent years because of shoddy customer service. If you want to build a successful online business, you have to take customer service very seriously. Although many large online retailers have invested millions of dollars to improve the quality of customer service they offer online, there are many things you can do to improve customer service on your Web site without breaking the bank.

e-fact

The market for customer relationship management (CRM) products will reach US $16.8 billion by 2003.

Source: AMR Research (www.amrresearch.com)

Offer Telephone Support

Many online shoppers will want to make human contact with you to verify that you are real, or to resolve a complaint if they are unable to get answers to their questions on your Web site. Make sure you have enough knowledgeable people on staff to handle telephone calls from customers who are shopping on your Web site. In addition, think about installing a toll-free number so customers can call you without incurring long-distance charges. If you install a toll-free number, make sure it works across North America (not just in Canada), so that customers in the United States can reach you. In addition, include a direct-dial number on your Web site so customers in other parts of world can call you. We've come across many online stores where the only telephone number published is a toll-free number that works only from within Canada and/or the United States. Needless to say, international customers won't be able to call you if you do this.

Make It Easy for Customers to Find Your Contact Information

There is nothing more infuriating to an online shopper than not being able to find a telephone number, fax number, or mailing address on a store's Web site. In particular, one of the cardinal sins with an online store is not publishing a telephone number for your business. That is why you should make sure your online store provides clear, unambiguous contact information. It should list, at a minimum, the full name of the business including its legal name (if different from the online name), telephone number, mailing address, and fax number. Make sure your contact information is easily accessible from your Web site's home page—don't force customers to hunt for your telephone number and mailing address.

To make it easier for customers to get in touch with the right person, consider posting information on how to contact particular departments or people for various issues, such as product support, shipment tracking, returns, etc. While setting up different e-mail addresses for different functions can be a good idea, too many choices can also be a source of confusion for customers. A study of customer service on the Internet by New York–based Jupiter Media Metrix (www.jmm.com) uncovered one company that had eighteen different e-mail addresses for customer relations! Obviously, this situation is more frustrating than helpful for the customer. If you aren't dealing with huge volumes of e-mail, sometimes it's best to have a single e-mail address for all customer service inquiries.

Provide Feedback and Complaint Mechanisms

We certainly hope your customers won't need to contact you with a problem or complaint, but if they do, you should make it easy for them to get in touch with you. Let your customers know that you're committed to resolving their problems quickly and efficiently and invite them to contact you with any problems or concerns they may have. In addition, encourage customers to give you feedback on your Web site and your products. It goes without saying that customer feedback is extremely valuable to any merchant. As Lands' End (www.landsend.com) says on its Web site, "It's a rare Lands' End product that doesn't owe some improvement—or improvements—to customer feedback!" If you tell customers you're interested in getting their comments and feedback, they're more likely to contact you!

Respond to E-Mail Messages Promptly

While it's important for customers to be able to contact you by telephone, many customers prefer to use e-mail. The problem with e-mail is that many online stores get overwhelmed with messages from customers and they can't reply in a timely manner. You should be able to respond to every e-mail message your site receives within a maximum of twenty-four hours. If you can't provide that level of service, you should consider hiring more people or investigate ways to automate the routing of your messages and the responses customers receive. For some customers, twenty-four hours is too long to wait, so many online retailers are trying to respond to e-mail messages within two or three hours. Recognizing how critical e-mail response times are, Lands' End (www.landsend.com) has actually installed software that measures the length of time it takes the company to respond to every e-mail message it receives from customers.

Because many organizations don't reply to customer e-mail messages quickly, online shoppers may be skeptical about contacting your store by e-mail. As a result, you could be losing sales and not even realize it. To encourage customers to communicate with your store by e-mail, we recommend that you establish an e-mail policy and display it on your Web site. An e-mail policy is simply a pledge to reply to customers' questions within a certain time period.

If you promise to reply to customer e-mails within a certain time period, you'll find that customers will be more willing to contact you with their questions or concerns. However, make sure you can honour whatever deadlines you establish. If you tell customers you'll respond to their e-mail messages within twenty-four hours and then take forty-eight hours to reply, you'll quickly lose their trust and confidence.

Professionally Manage Your E-Mail

If you find yourself dealing with a really large volume of e-mail messages, you may want to explore an e-mail management solution from a company such as Kana Communications (www.kana.com) or eGain (www.egain.com). These companies sell e-mail management products to help online businesses deal with high volumes of e-mail. These products ensure that e-mail messages from your customers are intelligently and automatically forwarded to the right departments. In addition, e-mail management software often uses artificial intelligence technology to interpret a customer's e-mail message automatically and reply with the appropriate canned response. Keep in mind that these types of applications can be expensive and hence may be appropriate only if you are receiving hundreds of messages a day from your customers. Many online retailers have found it necessary to resort to such software both to improve customer service and to reduce the number of phone calls they receive. Another option is to outsource your e-mail management and hire a company to answer your e-mail messages for you, either on an ongoing basis or only on an overflow or after-hours basis.

Provide Answers to FAQs (Frequently Asked Questions)

One way to cut down on the volume of e-mail messages from your customers is to create a FAQ document and post it on your Web site. This document contains answers to the most common questions your customers ask. Once this document has been created, add a link to it from the section of your Web site that lists your e-mail addresses and contact information, and encourage customers to read it before contacting you.

In 2005, consumers will spend more than US $632 billion at brick-and-mortar stores as a result of research they've done online—more than three times the amount they will spend online!

Source: Jupiter Media Metrix (www.jmm.com)

e-fact

Create an Online Help and Customer Service Centre

As customers are browsing your Web site, they may have questions about ordering, shipping, return policies, security/privacy polices, or other matters. In an effort to help online shoppers get answers to their questions quickly, many online retailers include a "Help" or "Customer Service" button right at the top of their home page. Clicking on this button will lead customers to an online help centre or online customer service centre. Consider creating a similar area on your Web site and provide a link to it from every page on your site.

Include Reference Materials on Your Online Store

Wherever possible, include reference materials on your Web site to help your customers make an educated purchase decision. An excellent example of this strategy is outdoor equipment/apparel retailer REI (www.rei.com). Each section of its Web site contains links to informative articles that give shoppers advice on buying outdoor products. For example, the fishing section of REI's Web site contains helpful articles on how to choose fly reels and rods.

This type of helpful product information will make your customers more loyal to you and more inclined to use your online store. But perhaps more importantly, if you help customers choose the right products from your online store, it's less likely a customer will make the wrong choice and have to return an item. Product returns are costly and frustrating for both consumers and online merchants.

REI's Web site also contains a bulletin board where shoppers can ask each other for advice on topics related to the outdoors (e.g., hiking, climbing, cycling) and the products that REI.com sells. An online bulletin board is yet another way to support your customers and give them more confidence in the products they buy from you. You can also educate your customers by providing product tips, ask-an-expert features, product reviews, and informational articles. Think about adding some of these features to your Web site.

Offer Live Sales Assistance

Earlier in this chapter, we discussed the high incidence of consumers abandoning their purchases before completing an online transaction.

e-fact

Twenty-four percent of Internet users have provided fake names or personal information in order to avoid giving a Web site real information.

Source: Pew Internet and American Life Project (www.pewinternet.org)

Some online merchants hope they can reduce abandoned purchase attempts by giving customers a way to interact with a live person without having to pick up a telephone. Godiva (www.godiva.com) is one of many online stores that use this strategy. Godiva uses technology from a company called LivePerson (www.liveperson.com) to offer its customers live access to its customer service representatives. With this type of software, not only can customers type back and forth with a customer service agent, the agent can "push" Web pages to a customer's Web browser and guide them to specific areas of the site. For example, if a customer asked for a gift recommendation, the agent could bring up a specific product page on the customer's screen.

This technology adds a human touch to the often impersonal nature of online shopping. Not only does live-chat software improve customer satisfaction by giving your customers instant access to company representatives, it may also reduce the number of telephone calls and e-mail messages your company receives.

If you do decide to implement live-chat technology, make sure you regularly review the transcripts of chats with customers to identify the types of questions they are asking. You can then use this information to update the FAQs section on your Web site so other shoppers with the same questions won't need to contact you via live chat or on the telephone. If you regularly update your FAQs in this manner, you'll be able to reduce your customer service costs.

Depending on the vendor you select, live customer service software can cost upwards of several hundred dollars per month. This means that you'll need to weigh the costs and benefits of using this type of a service on your Web site.

Offer Voice Chat

While most online stores offering live sales assistance are doing so using text chat software, several merchants are offering voice chat as well so customers can actually talk with a customer service representative. The call is actually carried over the customer's Internet connection and the customer doesn't need to have an extra phone line available. In order for this to work, the customer needs to have a microphone attached to his or her computer, as well as speakers and a sound card. Most new computers come with these features, although many customers may not have the microphone attached to their computer when they visit your online store, so they may not be able to communicate with you in this way.

The other problem with voice chat is that the sound quality isn't always reliable. Because the call is being routed over the Internet, it's not as dependable as a regular phone line. Nevertheless, the quality of Internet-based phone calls is constantly improving and more retailers are experimenting with the technology. For an example of a retailer using live voice chat, visit the J. Crew Web site (www.jcrew.com). J. Crew uses a technology from a company called eStara (www.estara.com).

Although voice chat technology is still in its infancy, it's yet another way to offer excellent service to your customers.

Tips for Channel Integration

Invest in Effective Customer Relationship Management

You've no doubt heard the phrase "The left hand doesn't know what the right hand is doing." Well, it seems to be true of many organizations on the Web. The online part of the company doesn't interact well with the offline part of the company, resulting in poor service for customers.

Although it is not a major issue for small businesses, one of the biggest challenges for large companies selling online is effective customer relationship management, also known as CRM. Although you will come across many different definitions of customer relationship management, we define CRM as the process of seamlessly integrating all the various points of customer contact into a single database. For example, a customer may walk into an organization's retail store and ask about an e-mail inquiry that was submitted several days earlier, or a customer may call an organization on the telephone to follow up on a live-chat session that the person had on the organization's Web site.

e-fact

Consumers who visit a retailer's Web site and then buy from the retail store spend 33 percent more on an annual basis in the retail store compared to the retailer's typical store customers.

Source: J.C. Williams Group (www.jcwg.com), National Retail Federation (www.nrf.com), and BizRate.com (www.bizrate.com)

One of the authors of this book once called a hotel chain to try to cancel a hotel reservation he had made on the organization's Web site. The woman at the call centre who took his call didn't have access to the Web reservations database, so she had to transfer him to another customer service agent who dealt with the Internet bookings. The problem? The hotel hadn't yet combined all its databases, so customers had to deal with different customer service representatives depending on whether their reservation was made online or over the phone. Obviously, this can confuse and aggravate customers, who don't want to experience delays when they contact an organization to resolve an issue. It's important to remember that your customers don't see your online and offline operations as separate entities. Regardless of whether they contact you by e-mail, phone, or live chat, they expect the person at the other end to be able to help them.

> Seventy-four percent of online buyers in the United States have not viewed, created, or purchased from an online gift registry.
>
> *Source: Jupiter Media Metrix (www.jmm.com)*

e-fact

This presents a big problem for a business: how to ensure that every employee has a record of all the interactions a customer has had with the organization, regardless of which channel the customer used to contact the organization. In other words, every customer service representative should be able to access a history file of all the customer's dealings with the organization, including e-mail correspondence, transcripts of chat sessions, order history, etc. The goal is to have a 360-degree view of your customers. As you can imagine, pulling all this information together into a single database that all employees can access is an extremely expensive and complex undertaking, often costing millions of dollars, but the benefit is greater customer loyalty and better customer service.

Not surprisingly, integrating customer service systems has become a top priority for online retailers. There are literally hundreds of companies that specialize in this area, including firms like Siebel Systems (www.siebel.com) and E.piphany (www.epiphany.com). In addition, many of the companies that specialize in live-chat software and e-mail management software can also help you with CRM solutions.

Once you have synchronized all of your customer information databases so customer service representatives can see a customer's complete purchase history across all of your divisions (e.g., phone, Web, catalogue, retail stores), the marketing possibilities are enormous. For example, a customer service representative handling a live-chat request or responding to an e-mail could cross-sell products based on the types of purchases the customer has made in the past. In addition, once all of your databases are combined, it will be possible to analyze customer purchase behaviour and develop individualized marketing strategies and campaigns for each customer. Not only can this increase sales, it can improve customer service since customers will be offered highly personalized product recommendations. (For more information on the benefits of personalization technology, see Chapter 7, "Building Customer Loyalty in Your Online Store.")

If you are interested in learning more about the latest trends in the CRM industry, good sites to visit include RealMarket (www.realmarket.com) and CRMCommunity.com (www.crmcommunity.com).

Offer Synergy Between Your Online and Offline Operations

You may have come across the phrases "clicks and bricks" and "clicks and mortar." They refer to a strategy pursued by many organizations that have both an online store and a physical brick-and-mortar store.

In the early days of e-commerce, it was assumed that the Internet would cannibalize sales in traditional channels such as retail stores or catalogues. Many retailers were therefore hesitant to sell online, fearing it would take away business from their catalogues and/or brick-and-mortar stores. That fear proved unfounded and retailers have since discovered that operating multiple channels can actually improve overall business. Now that retailers have concluded consumers aren't going to stop shopping at brick-and-mortar stores or from catalogues, they're working on creating multichannel businesses and, at the same time, creating closer links among their Web sites, retail stores, and catalogue operations.

---

e-fact

Auction sales will reach 25 percent of online sales by 2006.

Source: Forrester Research (www.forrester.com)

Once you begin to serve customers through several channels, make sure your channels are seamlessly integrated so they reinforce one another. Also make sure your online brand is consistent with your real-world brand. Customer relationship management technology is a big part of a clicks-and-bricks strategy, but there are other aspects as well. For example, your customers may want to:

- buy a product online but return it to one of your retail stores;

- research a product in one of your retail stores but then buy it online;
- research a product in your catalogue but then buy it online;
- purchase a gift certificate in one of your retail stores but redeem it online;
- access your Web site from your retail stores; or
- order a product on your Web site and pick it up in person from one of your retail stores.

If you have one or more retail stores, think about ways in which you can offer greater synergy between your physical and online operations. RadioShack Canada (www.radioshack.ca), for example, allows visitors to its Web site to query the inventory of their local RadioShack store to see if a product is in stock.

Many online retailers that have catalogues have made it easy for customers to look up a product they saw in a catalogue and then buy it online. For example, Staples/Business Depot's Web site allows customers to add products to their online shopping carts by entering the appropriate catalogue numbers.

In an effort to give customers more choice as to when and how they shop, many retailers are beginning to introduce what Sam's Club (www.samsclub.com) calls a "click-and-pull" strategy, allowing customers to place an order online but pick it up in person. The idea is to use your Web site to pull customers into your retail stores. This strategy also allows consumers to enjoy the convenience of shopping on the Web without having to worry about delivery times or shipping charges, two of the most frequently voiced complaints about shopping on the Internet. Customers of Office Depot's online store (www.officedepot.com), for example, are given the choice of picking up their online order or having it delivered to their home or office. If the pickup option is selected, the Web site will automatically find the closest retail location that has the customer's desired item(s) in stock.

One final word of advice in this section: the Web is simply another channel for customers to use. It doesn't replace retail stores or catalogues—it complements them. In fact, many retailers have discovered that customers who use more than one channel spend more than those customers who only buy through a single channel. As customers are frequently using more than one channel to do business with online retailers and spending more as a result, you may want to consider creating a catalogue to complement your online store. If you operate in multiple channels, make sure you service your customers in a seamless, integrated way regardless of which channel they choose to use. The benefit of pursuing this type of tight integration between your online and offline channels is increased convenience and better service for your customers—and increased sales for you!

---

e-fact

Sixty percent of Internet shoppers bookmark an average of seven shopping sites.

Source: Cyber Dialogue/Fulcrum Analytics (www.cyberdialogue.com)

Offer Products Online That Customers Can't Find in Your Retail Store(s)

When online retailing was in its infancy, many brick-and-mortar retailers assumed that in order to be successful on the Web, their online stores had to carry everything their real-world stores offered. But not long after duplicating their real-world stores online, retailers quickly realized that selling certain products online simply wasn't profitable. For example, Wal-Mart (www.walmart.com) has stopped selling apparel online as well as low-margin items that were not practical to ship. Wal-Mart began selling high-margin items that sell well on the Web—products like cameras, computers, flowers, DVD players, and electronics. Wal-Mart realized its Web site was actually better used to sell products that customers couldn't easily buy in a Wal-Mart store. This was a complete reversal of the company's earlier thinking, but it's a more profitable strategy for Wal-Mart. While most people don't think of Wal-Mart when it comes to buying flowers and computers online, these are the types of products that sell well online, and Wal-Mart is a brand that most people trust, so the strategy makes sense. The point is to always think outside the box. If you have a retail store, don't think that the only products you can sell online are the products you sell in your physical store. Obviously, you don't want to get carried away either and start selling products that don't fit your brand and its image, but there's no point in selling products on your Web site that you're going to lose money on. Focus on those products that you can sell online profitably, and don't be afraid to experiment.

Tips for Internationalizing Your Web Site

Translate Your Web Pages

Although the majority of Internet users speak English as their first or second language, the number of non-English-speaking Internet users will continue to grow as the number of Internet users expand in Africa, South America, and Asia. China already has the second-largest number of home Internet users in the world, making it an important market for any on-line store that wants to expand its reach beyond North America. Even within North America, there are millions of people who don't speak English, yet most Web sites don't have content in languages other than English. These figures have important implications for any Canadian business that wants to sell its products to international markets or simply to domestic Internet users who don't speak English.

In order to make your products and/or services more appealing to non-English-speaking Internet users, both domestically and abroad, you should consider translating your entire Web site, or parts of it, into other lan-guages to help you reach your target market. If translating your entire Web site into one or more languages is beyond your financial means, con-sider offering just your ordering and shipping information in languages other than English.

Before translating your site into multiple languages, think about the consequences. If you start to offer product information in languages other than English, customers will start to expect product support in those lan-guages as well. In addition, customers will start to e-mail you in languages other than English. Then there's the issue of your invoices and other lit-erature that you send with the products you ship. You'll have to translate that material as well. In other words, you are creating a whole new set of responsibilities for your online store once you translate sections of your Web site. Make sure you are capable of coping with the consequences!

Only 18 percent of consumer e-commerce sites in the United States offer testimonials from customers.

Source: eMarketer (www.emarketer.com)

e-fact

A Final Word of Advice

In this chapter, we've provided you with dozens of tips and techniques to help you maximize the effectiveness of your online store, but even more important than our advice is what your customers think.

You should thoroughly test your online store before you make it avail-able to the public and you should also continue testing at regular inter-vals after the launch. Testing your store before it officially opens will help you identify potential problems and work all the kinks out of your site before "real" customers start to use it. You can do this by having a group of your friends and colleagues test your site and identify problems, features they don't like, and features they'd like to see. Also ask them to give you feedback on the layout and overall design and appearance of your store. What improvements would they suggest you make?

When you have your friends test your Web site, make you sure you ask them whether the information on your Web site is understandable. If you're trying to sell a complex product (e.g., insurance), don't use confusing language that may not be understood by the people you are trying to sell your products or services to! While this may seem like an obvious point, it's a mistake many organizations make. This is why it's important to have your Web site reviewed by people outside your organization who do not work in your industry. They can give you the kind of feedback you won't get if the only people who critique your Web site are people who work within your company or industry.

In addition, have your friends or colleagues place "test" orders on your Web site and get their feedback on the ordering process. Make note of glitches or unforeseen problems that crop up. You'll be amazed at how many useful ideas and suggestions this can generate. As suggested earlier in the chapter, have people view your Web site using both Microsoft Explorer and Netscape Navigator. You will want to ensure that your Web site looks the same regardless of which Web browser the customer is using.

Also have your friends test your Web site using different modem speeds. Although more and more consumers and businesses are using high-speed connections to the Internet, such as cable modems and ADSL/DSL modems, make sure your Web site can be used by those consumers who are still using dial-up Internet connections.

It's especially important to test your site after any major enhancements or redesigns. There are two reasons for this. First, you want to make sure your site enhancements are working properly. Second, you want to make sure your customers like the changes you've made. Unfortunately, it seems that few Web sites solicit feedback about their site redesigns. One study by Forrester Research (www.forrester.com) found that Fortune 1000 companies spend an average of US $1.5 million to US $2.1 million per year on site redesigns without knowing whether the redesign work makes their sites easier to use. Don't make this mistake with your online store. Thoroughly test all changes to your Web site and solicit feedback from your customers regularly.

One way to measure customer response to your online store is to hire a professional online market research firm such as Vividence (www.vividence.com) or SurveySite (www.surveysite.com) to help you evaluate your Web site. A firm such as SurveySite can randomly survey visitors to your Web site and ask for their opinions of your online store. They can also interview your customers to help you understand why shoppers may be leaving your Web site without making a purchase. Consider surveying your customers in this way to test new ideas and, most importantly, to ensure that your Web site is meeting the expectations of your customers.

The Twenty Biggest Customer Service Mistakes You Can Make on the Web

1. Not publishing a toll-free number that works within both the United States and Canada.
2. Not publishing a direct-dial number on your Web site so international visitors can contact you if the toll-free number doesn't work.
3. Not acknowledging a customer's order by e-mail.
4. Making it difficult for the customer to find the customer service section of your Web site.
5. Telling a customer a product is in stock when it isn't.
6. Failing to meet delivery dates posted on your Web site.
7. Not providing a list of frequently asked questions and their answers.
8. Not providing your staff with access to the information a customer has entered on your Web site.
9. Unfriendly customer service on the telephone.
10. Ignoring customer e-mail messages.
11. Answering a customer's e-mail inquiry with a canned response that doesn't adequately address the question being asked.
12. Not being able to track a customer's order or e-mail inquiry.
13. Poor site design.
14. Not providing staff with access to all the interactions that a customer has had with your organization.
15. Failing to disclose return policies, cancellation terms, shipping costs, and warranty information.
16. Not updating your Web site frequently.

17. Subjecting your customers to frequent service interruptions and technical glitches.
18. Sending your customers unsolicited e-mail messages.
19. Selling your customers' data to another organization without permission.
20. Having a slow Web site.

Source: Compiled by Rick Broadhead and Jim Carroll

4

Merchant Accounts and
Online Payment Processing

"Almost all goods and services bought on the Internet are paid for by old-fashioned credit- or charge-cards."

— *"The Personal Touch: Internet Payment Systems,"*
The Economist, August 5, 2000

Because the most common method of online payment is the credit card, this chapter is devoted to dealing with credit card payments. There are two fundamental elements to accepting credit cards on the Internet: (1) merchant accounts and (2) real-time credit card processing.

In the pages that follow, we'll explain, in simple terms, what's involved in setting up your online store so you can accept credit cards for purchases. We'll also show you what you need to do to process credit card transactions through your online store.

Merchant Accounts

In order to accept credit cards in your online store, you need to have a merchant account.

If your business does not already accept credit cards offline, you might not know what a merchant account is.

A merchant account is not a bank account but rather a special account that you set up in order to accept credit cards as a form of payment. The merchant account is used to process credit card payments from your customers and then deposit them into your business chequing account, minus any service and transaction fees. (We discuss the fees associated with merchant accounts later in the chapter.) Every month, you'll receive a statement from your bank or merchant account provider with a summary of all the transactions that were made in your online store.

Regardless of how an order is accepted—via a Web site, fax, mail, or telephone—if it is a credit card order, you will need a merchant account. You will need to get a separate merchant account for each credit card plan that you want to accept—Visa, MasterCard, American Express, etc. You will also need to get a separate merchant account for each type of currency you want to accept in your online store.

Most online stores accept Visa and MasterCard, and some accept other cards such as American Express and Diner's Club. The choice of which credit cards you want to accept in your online store will depend on your own circumstances, what you can afford, the profile of your customers, and the credit cards that you expect they are most likely to use.

Can You Sell on the Internet Without a Merchant Account?

Yes. For example, you could have customers pay by cheque or money order and send you payment by mail. However, since credit cards are the most widely used form of payment on the Internet, we recommend that you accept credit cards in your online store. Most of your customers will want to pay by credit card, so you'll be losing out on a lot of business if you don't accept them.

How Do You Get a Merchant Account?

You usually obtain a merchant account from organizations known as acquiring financial institutions. In Canada, most of the major banks act as acquiring financial institutions and will be able to establish a merchant account directly for you. (The one major exception is CIBC, which transferred its acquiring business to a company called Global Payments.) In addition, there are bank-affiliated organizations that also offer merchant accounts. For example, RBC Financial Group and the Bank of Montreal have created Moneris Solutions (www.moneris.ca), a company that specializes in credit card services in Canada.

Obtain your Visa merchant account from the bank that handles your business banking accounts, such as Royal Bank Financial Group (www.royalbank.com), TD Canada Trust (www.tdcanadatrust.com), Scotiabank (www.scotiabank.ca), Desjardins (www.desjardins.com), and Laurentian Bank of Canada (www.laurentianbank.com). In Canada, MasterCard is represented by the Bank of Montreal (www.bmo.com), Citibank Canada (www.citibank.ca), National Bank of Canada (www.nbc.ca), and most credit unions, so you must contact one of those organizations in order to get a MasterCard merchant account.

American Express, Discover, and Diner's Club are handled differently from Visa and MasterCard in that your merchant accounts are set up directly with those organizations.

If you decide to contact a bank to obtain a merchant account, make sure the bank knows that you plan on taking payment over the Internet in an online store. There are different types of merchant accounts and you will need to get one that allows you to accept credit card payments on the Internet. This is usually known as an Internet merchant account.

If you already accept credit cards in a retail store, you probably will not be able to use your existing merchant accounts in your online store. Most banks prefer merchants to establish a separate merchant account for use on the Internet.

The most common complaint among Internet users with regard to returns is having to pay for return postage.

Source: PricewaterhouseCoopers (www.pwcglobal.com)

e-fact

In addition to going directly to an acquiring financial institution to get a merchant account, another option is to go through an organization known as a merchant account provider or Internet payment service provider. These organizations have aligned themselves with particular financial institutions and can offer merchant account services. In Canada, examples include Beanstream, Internet Secure, and PSiGate. If you're having trouble getting your merchant account directly from a bank, try contacting one of these organizations. Unlike many banks, most Internet payment service providers do not require up-front security deposits. However, they often compensate for this by having a rolling reserve fund, which means each month they hold back a percentage of your sales for a certain number of months.

Other Sources of Merchant Accounts in Canada	
Beanstream	www.beanstream.com
Internet Secure	www.internetsecure.com
PSiGate	www.psigate.com

Many of the browser-based storefront solutions discussed in Chapter 2 have relationships with acquiring banks or Internet payment service providers and allow you to apply for a merchant account right on their Web sites.

We should point out that if you choose to set up your storefront using a browser-based storefront creation service, you may not have a choice as to where you obtain your merchant account. Many browser-based storefront creation services have partnered with a specific bank or Internet payment service provider and have integrated an online application directly into the set-up process so you won't have to contract for a merchant account on your own. When you are building your online store, you'll be given the opportunity to fill out an online application and apply for a merchant account immediately. In such cases, it is often mandatory that you obtain your merchant account from their partner organization. Even if you already have an existing Internet or regular merchant account, you may not be able to use it.

Merchant Account Resellers

Keep in mind that the Canadian situation for merchant accounts is quite different from the United States. In the United States, there are literally hundreds of merchant account resellers. As a Canadian merchant, you should restrict yourself to looking at offerings from Canadian financial institutions and Canadian Internet payment service providers or the particular organizations they have aligned themselves with. We highly recommend that you avoid the temptation of getting your merchant account from any organization that sends you unsolicited e-mail messages, as these organizations may be unreliable and unreputable.

What Will You Have to Pay for a Merchant Account?

There are a variety of fees you may have to pay in order to operate a merchant account. It is very important to understand all these fees before you sign a merchant account agreement.

The different charges you will often encounter include the following:

- Application/set-up fees
- Discount rate
- Transaction fees
- Monthly fees
- Equipment rental fees
- Fraud-screening fees
- Chargeback fees
- Holdbacks and rolling reserve funds
- Escrow accounts
- Other fees

Each of these is discussed below.

Application/Set-up Fees

You may be charged a fee for setting up the merchant account. The exact amount of the fee can vary from one organization to the next. If your application for a merchant account is denied, you usually do not have to pay the set-up fee.

Discount Rate

The discount rate is a fixed percentage taken from every transaction you process in your online store. Typically, the discount rate ranges from 2 to 4 percent. For example, suppose you sell a product for $20.00 on your Web site. If the discount rate that applies to this particular sale is 3.25 percent, you would receive $19.35 on the sale and your bank or merchant account provider would keep $0.65 (3.25 percent of $20.00). On a $40.00 sale, the bank or merchant account provider would keep $1.30 (3.25 percent of $40.00) and you would receive $38.70.

You should be aware that discount rates vary among banks and credit card plans. For example, American Express usually has a different discount rate from MasterCard or Visa. The discount rate for an Internet merchant account is typically higher than the discount rate for a merchant with a retail store. This is because of the greater risk inherent in Internet transactions. (For more information about the security risks of Internet transactions, see Chapter 5, "Online Security Issues and Credit Card Fraud.")

Transaction Fees

In addition to the discount rate, you may also have to pay a fixed transaction fee on every sale you process in your online store. The transaction fee is usually between $0.25 and $0.50 per sale, regardless of the amount of the sale. For example, suppose your transaction fee is $0.30. If you complete a sale for $25.00 on your online store, you owe your bank or merchant account provider $0.30. On a sale worth $40.00, the transaction fee is still $0.30.

Monthly Fees

Some merchant account providers might also charge you one or more monthly fees on top of the discount rate and transaction fee. For example, you may be asked to pay a monthly statement fee (a fee for a monthly summary of the transactions that occurred on your online store), a monthly maintenance or customer service fee, and/or a variety of other monthly charges. Sometimes the monthly fees are lumped together into one lump-sum payment every month and sometimes they are charged separately.

Sometimes there may be a minimum monthly fee that will be instituted in the event your discount rate fees and transaction fees fall below a certain level. For example, suppose your discount rate is 3.25 percent, your transaction fee is $0.30 per transaction, and there is a minimum monthly fee of $25.00. If you processed ten orders and $500.00 in sales in your first month, your transaction fees would total $3.00 (10 × $0.30) and you would also have to pay $16.25 based on a discount rate of 3.25 percent (3.25 percent of $500.00). This brings your total fees to $19.25. However, since your minimum monthly fee is $25.00, you would be required to pay an additional $5.75 ($25.00 − $19.25) to cover the $25.00 monthly minimum.

Equipment Rental Fees

A merchant account might include a fee for the rental of a point-of-sale or swipe terminal. If you do not have a physical retail location and you are planning on processing all of your credit card orders online, you do not need one of these devices. Make sure you don't end up paying for this service if you don't need it.

Fraud-Screening Fees

Some financial institutions or Internet payment service providers may provide a fraud-checking service so you can screen your credit card orders for signs of fraud. There may be an extra charge for this service. For more information about online credit card fraud and the importance of fraud screening, see Chapter 5, "Online Security Issues and Credit Card Fraud."

Chargeback Fees

A chargeback is a request from the cardholder or the card issuer to reverse a purchase made on your online store. Chargebacks occur when a cardholder disputes a charge on his or her credit card statement, perhaps because the person claims to have not received the goods or services ordered, because the goods or services were faulty or damaged, or because the customer's credit card was used fraudulently. When a chargeback occurs, not only do you have to refund the amount of the original purchase, you may also have to pay a penalty, called a chargeback fee, to the organization that issued your merchant account. Chargebacks are an extremely important issue and one of the major risks of operating an online store. You can learn more about chargebacks and how to avoid them later in this chapter, as well as in Chapter 5, "Online Security Issues and Credit Card Fraud."

Holdbacks and Rolling Reserve Funds

To ensure it has the funds to cover any disputed charges, your acquiring financial institution or merchant account provider may withhold or hold back a percentage of your sales (e.g., for thirty days). To avoid being surprised, make sure you understand the holdback policy of your merchant account provider or acquiring financial institution before you apply for a merchant account.

It is also not uncommon for some Internet payment service providers to hold back a percentage of sales in a rolling reserve fund for a specified period, such as six months. This protects the Internet payment service provider in case you receive chargebacks from customers. For example, suppose your total sales in your first month are $1,000.00 and your acquirer holds back 8 percent of your credit card sales in a rolling reserve fund for six months. Eight percent of $1,000.00 is $80.00, so the rolling reserve fund in month

#1 is $80.00. Typically, the $80.00 will be returned to you in month #7. This process continues every month, so in month #8, the money that was held back in month #2 will be returned to you; in month #9, the money that was held back in month #3 will be returned to you, and so on.

Escrow Accounts

Banks and merchant account providers may also require an escrow account to be set up to ensure the merchant can cover any losses.

Other Fees

If you use other services provided by your acquiring financial institution or Internet payment service provider, other fees may apply. For example, some organizations offer an address verification service (see Chapter 5 for a discussion of address verification). If you choose to use this service, a per-transaction fee may apply.

Are There Any Other Fees You Should Be Aware Of?

Yes! Be very careful when examining the fees you will be charged for a merchant account. When comparing merchant account fees, make sure you take all the fees into consideration. An organization with a lower discount rate or transaction fee than another organization may compensate for these lower fees by imposing other charges and/or charging you higher monthly fees.

e-fact

Fifty-five percent of direct marketers who engage in e-commerce transactions are profitable.

Source: Direct Marketing Association (www.the-dma.org)

Access to Funds

When a purchase is made on your Web site with a credit card, the funds owed to you from the purchase will eventually be deposited into your business chequing account. Sometimes the discount rate fee and transaction fee are deducted from the amount of the purchase before the funds are deposited in your account, but in most cases, the fees are deducted separately and appear as one or more charges on your monthly statement.

The length of time it takes for the funds to be deposited into your bank account will depend on the arrangement you have with your acquiring financial institution or Internet payment service provider. In most cases, funds will be deposited into your account within several days. When investigating different Internet payment service providers, make sure you find out how long it typically takes for funds to be transferred to your bank account.

Shop Around!

It's generally a good idea to research your alternatives. The discount rates and various fees associated with merchant accounts will vary from one organization to the next. In some cases, the rates and fees may be negotiable, depending on factors such as the types of products or services you are selling, your credit history, your expected sales volumes, and other criteria. This means that even if two businesses obtain merchant accounts from the same bank or the same merchant account provider, the transaction fees and discount rates each business pays could be completely different. For example, a business with an excellent credit history could have a lower discount rate and transaction fee than a business with a poor credit history.

The bottom line? Don't sign up with the first bank or Internet payment service provider you come across, and don't simply take the merchant account offered by a particular storefront solution without looking at your options. Shop around and compare rates and fees, and don't hesitate to ask a lot of questions. Since each bank and Internet payment service provider may evaluate risk differently, you should get quotes from several organizations before making a final decision. While one bank may regard you as a high risk and therefore quote you a high discount rate, another bank may look at your situation differently and offer you a lower fee structure.

Ask around in your community to see which firms have a good reputation for providing reliable merchant account services. You should also try to talk to people who are already selling online to get their advice on choosing a good bank or Internet payment service provider.

Finally, before signing a merchant account contract with an organization, read the terms and conditions of the contract carefully and make sure you fully understand all the fees you will be responsible for. Don't forget to read the fine print!

Applying for a Merchant Account

In order to apply for a merchant account in Canada, you must have a Canadian business address and a Canadian bank account. Obviously, one of the best starting points when obtaining a merchant account is to inquire through your existing financial institution. You will have an established credit record with them, possibly one or more bank accounts, and in essence, perhaps enough of a history to make the process much smoother. Most financial institutions have information on their Web sites that explains the merchant account application process and some of the particulars related to merchant accounts for that particular financial institution.

As noted earlier, many storefront creation services have partnered with a financial institution or another organization that supplies merchant accounts, and may include a merchant account application right on their Web site. This allows merchants to apply for a merchant account right away if they don't already have one.

If you are using stand-alone shopping cart software or one of the advanced e-commerce software packages, you will usually need to get your merchant account on your own. You can approach any bank or Internet payment service provider, but make sure their system is compatible with the storefront software you are using.

When applying for a merchant account, you could be asked for any of the following types of information:

- General contact information for your business: Address, telephone numbers, legal name of business, Web site address
- Information about the business owners/partners/officers: Names, titles, addresses, phone numbers, etc.
- Information about your business: When it was established, where it is physically based, where you operate the business from (e.g., home office, retail storefront, warehouse, office, etc.), what types of products/services you sell, ownership structure (e.g., sole proprietorship, partnership, corporation, non-profit, limited liability company, etc.), what province the business is incorporated in, etc.
- Sales data about your business: Existing or projected monthly and/or annual sales, sales by source (e.g., in-store, telephone/mail order, Internet)
- Banking references: Information about your business account, including the bank, your contact(s) at the bank, how long your account has been established, total dollar value of the account and average daily balance, and other pertinent information
- Bank routing information for your business chequing account
- Delivery process: How your products/services are delivered to customers, how long it takes before your products are shipped

- Description of your refund/exchange policies
- Marketing and advertising activities: How you promote your business
- Average "ticket" price for your online store: How much you expect the average sale to be
- Names, addresses, and telephone numbers of previous credit card processors (if any) and, if applicable, evidence of sales volumes and/or chargeback experience

In addition to supplying the above information online, you may also be asked to submit the following types of documentation by mail:

- Copies of your federal business tax returns or the personal tax returns of the owners/officers of the company if you haven't filed a business tax return for your company
- Your business plan
- Interim financial statements, balance sheets, and profit and loss statements
- Proof of business registration (if no business tax returns have been filed), such as articles of incorporation (for corporations), a partnership agreement (for partnerships), or other information (for a sole proprietorship)
- Voided cheque from your business chequing account (if your business account does not have chequing privileges, a letter from your bank confirming your business address will usually suffice)

In the absence of a business credit history, banks may look instead at your personal credit history and ask to see your business plan and financial statements for the next couple of years.

If tax returns, financial statements, and other paper documentation aren't required upfront, they may be requested after your application for merchant status has been reviewed. This could be the case, for example, if the financial institution needs more information on your business before granting you merchant status.

If you are applying completely online, the application process is typically very quick and you will be notified within a few days whether your application has been accepted or declined. Usually this notification will come by e-mail.

Why Is the Application Process So Intensive?

The amount of information you have to supply in order to get a merchant account will vary depending on which bank or organization you are applying to. In some cases, the amount of documentation required may seem overwhelming. To understand why so much information is required of you, you have to appreciate the bank or merchant account supplier's position. When a bank or other organization gives you a merchant account, it is essentially giving you an open line of credit. This is explained on the site of a U.S. bank that offers merchant accounts:

> *A merchant credit card processing account is like an open-end line of credit. You send us your credit card transactions for processing, and we credit your business checking account, in most cases, within 24 hours. Those funds are available for you to use as you wish. But on the other end, the transaction is posted to the customer's credit card statement, which states that they have the right to dispute any charges posted. If they dispute a transaction, it can generate a chargeback that may come back to the bank and be debited against your business' account. This may take 120 business days or longer to reach your account. We want to make sure that you can handle any chargebacks. So a merchant account application is like applying for a business line of credit. (Source: Wells Fargo Internet Payment Services FAQ, biz.wellsfargo.com)*

As noted above, chargeback occurs when a customer disputes a transaction that has appeared on his or her credit card statement. A customer may dispute a charge for a variety of reasons, including:

- *Merchandise not as described:* The cardholder states that the merchandise received from you was different from what was described on your Web site.
- *Defective merchandise:* The cardholder states the merchandise received was defective.
- *Credit not received:* The cardholder states that the merchandise ordered from you was returned and he or she hasn't been given a refund or credit yet.

- *Duplicate transaction:* The cardholder states that he or she was billed twice for the same purchase.
- *Non-receipt of merchandise:* The cardholder claims he or she never received the merchandise that was ordered.

Chargebacks also occur when a stolen credit card is used fraudulently to make an online purchase. We discuss online credit card fraud in more detail in the next chapter.

On the Internet, the risk of a chargeback is higher than in a physical retail storefront. When you accept a credit card order in your online store, there is no physical imprint of the customer's credit card, and you don't have the benefit of swiping the credit card into a point-of-sale terminal that has built-in features to identify unacceptable cards. The other problem with an online credit card order is that you don't get a written signature from the customer. As a result, it's much easier for customers to use a bogus credit card number or a credit card number that doesn't belong to them on the Internet than it is in a land-based retail store. It is also easy for customers to claim that they did not use their credit card on your online store even when they did. This is called friendly fraud. In the absence of physical evidence, such as a signature or a physical card imprint, it is hard to prove a customer wrong.

As you'll learn in Chapter 5, merchants are usually responsible for any fraudulent credit card transactions in their online stores. When a stolen credit card number is used on your online store to purchase merchandise, you are responsible for the amount of the purchase. Therefore, if a customer disputes a charge on his or her credit card statement, your bank or Internet payment service provider will usually debit the amount of purchase from your bank account, in effect taking back the money that was put into your account shortly after the purchase was made. When reviewing your application for a merchant account, the bank/Internet payment service provider will look for evidence that you will be able to afford any chargebacks that occur. As noted earlier in the chapter, the risk of chargebacks is why some organizations have a mandatory rolling reserve fund for merchant accounts.

Needless to say, any credits to be processed to a customer's account should be handled promptly. This will reduce the number of chargebacks received and you can avoid unnecessary fees. In addition, a low percentage ratio of chargebacks to overall sales will result in a favourable track record for your online store.

When reviewing your application for a merchant account, banks and Internet payment service providers want to make sure your business is credible, reliable, and reputable. They want to avoid having customers call to complain about defective merchandise or merchandise that was ordered and never delivered. Since there are many things an online business can do to reduce the chance of chargebacks, a bank or Internet payment service provider may want to review your Web site to make sure you've taken the necessary steps to prevent chargebacks from occurring in your online business.

Here are some of the things that a bank/Internet payment service provider may look for on your Web site:

- Your business name and address are clearly listed.
- The product information is clear to the consumer.
- Product images are clear and large enough for the customer to see.
- The price of the product is clear to the consumer.
- A refund/exchange policy is clearly defined.
- A customer service phone number is displayed.

e-fact

Online sales of travel services will reach US $64 billion by 2007—more than double the US $24 billion transacted online in 2001.

Source: Jupiter Media Metrix (www.jmm.com)

Restricted Businesses

You should be aware that many banks and Internet payment service providers will not provide merchant accounts for certain types of businesses (unless there are extraordinary circumstances). Often this is because these businesses are subject to frequent incidents of fraud. For example, Beanstream (www.beanstream.com) states on its Web site that it cannot provide merchant accounts for any of the following types of businesses:

- Lottery tickets
- Collection agency services
- Cheque-cashing services
- Time-share sales
- Gambling or online casinos
- Extended car warranties, except for major car dealerships

- Weight-loss vitamins and pills or powders
- Cult material
- Prepaid phone cards
- Bail
- Credit reporting
- Résumé-preparing services
- Pyramid sales
- Satellite television sales, except if legal in Canada
- Cable television or satellite dish descramblers
- Live animals or illegal animal parts
- Bulk e-mail lists
- Counterfeit items
- Illegal drugs and drug paraphernalia
- Embargoed items (e.g., Cuban cigars sent to the U.S.)
- Adult items (e.g., pornography, escort or call services, massage, videos, etc.)
- Internet game (e.g., Ultima Online, EverQuest, etc.) identities and entitlements
- All firearms, including antique, collectible, sport, and hunting firearms
- All weapons, including military, illegal, or explosive
- Pirated software or descrambling software
- Pirated movies and music, including prereleases or promotionals
- Police badges or any type of false identification
- Travel agencies or airline tickets

Before applying to any bank or Internet payment service provider for a merchant account, make sure your business is one that the bank or Internet payment service provider can work with.

Real-Time Credit Card Processing

Once you have a merchant number for each of the different credit cards you will accept in your online store, you are one step closer to accepting credit card payments from your customers. However, if you want to process credit card transactions in real time, you will need to sign up for real-time credit card processing services.

All online storefront solutions enable you to process credit card transactions in real time, which involves getting authorization for each purchase made in your online store. Authorization ensures that online shoppers with valid credit cards can complete their purchases and shoppers with invalid or stolen cards are prevented from placing orders.

With real-time credit card processing, you encourage customers to place their orders on your Web site using a credit card. A customer selects one or more products from your Web site, inputs the shipping information and credit card data, and then clicks a button to finalize the purchase. Information about the purchase is sent over a secure, proprietary connection (via the Internet) to the cardholder's bank. Within a few seconds, the authorization response is sent back to the merchant and the customer will see a message on the computer screen indicating whether the transaction was approved or declined. A credit card purchase may be declined for a variety of reasons. For example:

- The credit card being used by the customer has been reported stolen.
- The spending limit for the card has been exceeded.
- The credit card has been cancelled.
- The card number is invalid.
- An incorrect expiry date has been provided for the card.

In a traditional retail store, the store clerk would request authorization by swiping a credit card through a physical transaction terminal provided by a bank or merchant account provider. If the transaction was accepted, the store clerk would see an approval message on the transaction terminal. If the transaction was refused for some reason (e.g., the card had been reported stolen), the clerk would see a message on the terminal indicating that the transaction was declined.

However, with real-time credit card processing on the Internet, there is no physical transaction terminal, and the customer is told right away onscreen whether the transaction went through successfully. When you log onto your storefront to review your orders, you'll be able to see whether each transaction was approved or declined. If it's approved, you'll be able to see the authorization code. You may also receive this information by e-mail, depending on how you have the storefront set up to notify you of new orders. Most storefronts and payment processors can provide you with a detailed daily analysis of all the transactions that took place in your online store, which you can access using your Web browser.

Once you've received an authorization for a purchase, you can proceed to ship it as long as you're satisfied that the order isn't fraudulent. As you'll discover in Chapter 5, an authorization from the credit card company does not guarantee that a credit card order is not fraudulent. See Chapter 5 for some of the warning signs of credit card fraud.

The benefit of using real-time credit card processing is threefold. First and foremost is that your customers can place their orders immediately rather than having to print out the order form and either mail, fax, or phone in the order. We know of several online stores that have lost sales because customers had to perform the additional steps of printing and faxing in their orders. Second, the customer is told right away whether the transaction has gone through successfully and a receipt is usually e-mailed to the customer. If the transaction is declined, the customer has a chance to use a different credit card number or fix the problem immediately without abandoning the purchase attempt.

The third advantage of real-time credit card processing is that it's faster and more efficient for you to process orders in this fashion. Although it is possible for you to manually authorize and process credit card orders (such as you would do if you received an order by e-mail, mail, phone, or fax), it's very time consuming. In addition, you would have to chase after customers if the credit card turned out to be invalid or other problems arose with the credit card information. With online processing, you can let the software do the work for you and catch problems before the orders go through! Most merchants on the Internet use real-time credit card processing because of these advantages.

China has the world's second largest at-home Internet population.

Source: Nielsen/NetRatings (www.nielsen-netratings.com)

e-fact

Who Offers Real-Time Credit Card Processing in Canada?

You can obtain real-time credit card processing services from several organizations in Canada. The major credit card processors (sometimes called payment processors) in Canada include Moneris (www.moneris.com), owned by the Royal Bank of Canada and the Bank of Montreal, Global Payments (www.globalpayments.com), which handles merchant services for CIBC, Bank of Nova Scotia (www.scotiabank.ca), TD Canada Trust (www.tdcanadatrust.com), BCE Emergis (www.bceemergis.com), and Desjardins (www.desjardins.com).

If you're a small or medium-sized business, we recommend that you investigate one of the many organizations in Canada that act as Internet payment gateways. An Internet payment gateway offers real-time credit card processing. They are called Internet payment gateways because they have connections or "gateways" into the major credit processors listed previously. Many Internet payment gateways have solutions especially geared for small businesses and they can help you set up real-time credit card processing on your online store quickly and easily. Some of the major Internet payment gateways in Canada are listed below.

Internet Payment Gateways in Canada	
Beanstream	www.beanstream.com
Caledon Card Services	www.caledoncard.com
E-xact Transactions	www.e-xact.com
InternetSecure	www.internetsecure.com
Paradata Systems	www.paradata.com
PSiGate	www.psigate.com

If you decide to build your online store using a browser-based storefront solution or stand-alone shopping cart, you'll find that many of these services have partnerships with a major credit card processor or an Internet payment gateway so you won't need to arrange for real-time credit processing on your own.

You may have noticed that some of the companies listed above are the same companies we identified earlier in the chapter as Internet payment service providers, organizations that help businesses obtain merchant accounts. This is because many Internet payment gateways are also Internet payment service providers. For example, Beanstream, InternetSecure, and PSiGate not only provide real-time credit card processing, they can also help you get merchant accounts without the need for you to go directly to one or more Canadian banks. However, not all Internet payment gateways are Internet payment service providers. For example, E-xact Transactions of Vancouver (www.e-xact.com) only provides real-time credit card processing. They do not offer merchant accounts. Therefore, E-xact Transactions is an Internet payment gateway, but not an Internet payment service provider.

Many Internet payment service providers also offer online storefronts through agreements with one or more online storefront vendors. For example, Beanstream has fully integrated its real-time credit card services with the online storefront services offered by 5Click (www.5click.com).

What all this means is that it's possible to find a single organization to help you obtain your merchant account, set up real-time credit card processing, and find an online storefront provider. Rather than having to go to several different organizations for the different components of your online store, you may be able to find a single organization such as Beanstream, that provides all of the services you need in one place.

Seventy percent of online shoppers have used a site's search engine while shopping online, and 43 percent say it's the most important feature on the site.

Source: PricewaterhouseCoopers (www.pwcglobal.com)

e-fact

Web-Based Point-of-Sale Terminals

Although we recommend that you process your orders online in real time, some customers may still want to fax or phone in their orders because they are concerned about transmitting their credit card number safely online. (You should advise your customers *not* to e-mail their orders to you because e-mail is not secure unless it is encrypted.) Most of the major credit card processors and Internet payment gateways in Canada can provide you with a Web-based point-of-sale terminal (sometimes called a virtual terminal or e-terminal), which will allow you to process purchases received by fax, telephone, e-mail, in-person, or by other means. You can also use your virtual terminal to process returns, adjustments, and refunds.

Choosing a Real-Time Credit Card Processor/Internet Payment Gateway

Before choosing a specific company to deal with for real-time credit card processing (either a major credit card processor or an Internet payment gateway), make sure you think about and ask the following questions:

- What fees do you charge?
- What credit cards do you support?
- What storefront programs or shopping carts do you work with?
- Do you support U.S. dollar merchant accounts? (This is important if you are selling products or services in U.S. dollars.)
- Am I tied to a specific bank or bank platform when I use your services? What happens if I decide to change my bank or merchant number in the future?
- What type of technical support do you offer? (What happens if my credit card processing fails in the middle of the night?)
- Do you offer any type of Canadian address verification service?
- How easy will it be for me to integrate your services with my online store? Will you help me with the integration?
- Will my business name or yours appear on the customer's credit card statement? (You should make sure your business name appears on your customers' credit card statements; otherwise customers will not recognize a charge from your online store and may ask their bank for a chargeback.)
- What type of fraud checking do you do, if any?
- Can I cancel my contract at any time, or am I locked in for a specific period of time?
- What type of sales analysis reports do you offer? (e.g., Do you provide me with daily, weekly, and/or monthly reports that track sales activity in my online store?)
- Is transaction information from my online store available to me twenty-four hours a day, seven days a week?
- Do you offer any storefront hosting services, either yourself or through a third party organization that you are affiliated with?
- Can I get my merchant account from you, or do I have to acquire it separately from another organization?
- How long have you been in business?
- Do you keep off-site backups of all the transactions processed by my online store?
- What type of security features do you offer to protect my customers' credit card data?
- What are the names of some of your clients?
- Do you offer a Web-based point-of-sale terminal?

- Which major credit card processors do you link to through your gateway (in the case of an Internet payment gateway)?
- Are there any other value-added services you offer?
- Are there any other costs I should be aware of?

When evaluating different payment processors, don't hesitate to ask for references. In addition, ask if you can see sample transaction reports as well as a demonstration of their online sales reporting capabilities. This will give you an idea of what your reports will look like when you start processing credit cards in real time.

Real-time credit card processing may sound complex, but it really isn't. It's also much cheaper and more effective than processing credit card transactions manually. It's definitely the way to go if you want to build a serious and successful online store. As Beanstream (www.beanstream.com) notes on their Web site, "It is simply not possible for a clerk to manually process a credit card transaction less expensively than a computer!"

5

Online Security Issues
and Credit Card Fraud

"U.S. merchants reported $1.6 billion in losses from Internet crime in 2000, according to Meridien. Not only do the merchants eat the cost of the lost goods or services—something called a chargeback—but they also get whacked with a penalty fee from Visa or MasterCard. Rack up enough fraudulent transactions over a few months, and credit card companies will sometimes cut a merchant off."

—*"A World of Opportunity for E-Scammers," BusinessWeek Online,*
February 12, 2002

In this chapter, we outline a five-step action plan to help you manage the Internet security risks that might affect your online store.

A Five-Step Action Plan for Securing Your Online Store

1. Learn about Internet security risks.
2. Assess your procedures.
3. Protect the security and integrity of your online transactions.
4. Let customers know your online store is safe.
5. Be vigilant!

First, be prepared to learn about Internet security risks. Regardless of your technical expertise, you must become personally involved in understanding the security risks that can affect your online store from a variety of different perspectives.

Second, assess whether you are satisfied with the security procedures and methods used by the services that build and host your online store. You need to make sure the company that hosts your online store and the people you hire to build it have the technical experience and the know-how to ensure your online store is adequately secured.

Third, secure the transactions that flow through your online store. When customers place credit card orders on your online store, you must ensure the transactions are secure so that credit card numbers cannot be accessed as they are transmitted through the Internet. You should also take steps to prevent bogus or stolen credit cards from being used on your Web site.

Fourth, battle perceptions. Once you are satisfied that you have proper security in place, you must assure your customers that any credit card orders they place on your online store are safe, and that any personal or confidential information they send you is also safe.

Fifth, be vigilant about security. New security weaknesses and vulnerabilities are constantly being discovered on the Internet. You need to stay on top of these issues so you can react to any potential security problems before they get out of hand. You can't afford to have a security slip-up of any type with your online store—it can be the kiss of death.

> By 2003, 50 percent of small and mid-size organizations that manage their own network security and use the Internet for more than e-mail will be attacked over the Internet.
>
> *Source: Gartner (www.gartner.com)*

e-fact

Step #1: Learn About Security Risks

You need to have a good appreciation of Internet security risks. At the most basic level, there are two concerns.

First, the Internet involves many, many computers—literally millions of them. The information stored on each computer is potentially accessible to someone else on the Internet unless specific precautions are undertaken to prevent such access. Over the last several years, there have been many high-profile incidents of hackers breaking into the Web sites used by online retailers. In some cases, credit card numbers have been stolen. In others, credit card numbers have been held ransom.

The second risk is that information transmitted through the Internet from one computer to another is essentially "sent in the clear," meaning that it is not scrambled in any way unless something has specifically been done to ensure it is scrambled.

How Do Security Problems Arise?

With the first issue, in most cases problems arise because necessary precautions to prevent unauthorized access to host computers are not taken, with the result that the Web sites and online stores found on those computers are not properly secured. Many break-ins occur because of negligence or ignorance on the part of those responsible for the system. Hackers are able to gain unauthorized access to a Web site because of errors in the computer code that make up the Web site or because a Web site has been incorrectly configured. In other words, human error is responsible for many of the security breaches that occur on the Internet.

The second problem is the result of programs called "sniffers," which hackers use to see the information transmitted between computers on the Internet. A sniffer program could allow someone to steal credit card numbers as they are passed between customers and merchants on the Internet.

What do you need to do to protect your online store and the credit card numbers you receive from customers? First, make sure your online store software and Web site are configured so as to minimize the risk of a break-in. Second, ensure that when customers send you their credit card information, it is transmitted securely over the Internet so that it can't be accessed by any unauthorized individuals.

Online Security Requires Your Involvement

You should take responsibility for the two issues that we describe above. This might come as a surprise to you; after all, isn't security the responsibility of the organizations that design and host your online store? Not at all. The key to ensuring that your online store is secure is your personal involvement in security issues. Not only should you have a good understanding of the security risks, but you also need to take all appropriate precautions to protect your online store.

If you ignore security and don't become personally involved with these issues, you'll be relying on other people to take care of your online security matters. They may or may not do so. It is more than likely that they'll do a good job, but your lack of involvement increases the likelihood that they will focus less than 100 percent of their attention to important security issues.

We liken the situation to working with an accountant or financial adviser. The more involved you are in understanding what an accountant or financial adviser is doing with your money, the more prepared you'll be to ask questions and the more likely it is that you'll catch mistakes. Dealing with security on the Internet isn't much different. While Internet security can be an incredibly complex topic, a minimal understanding of the issues will make you a much more effective online storekeeper. If you're aware of the issues, you'll know what questions to ask your online store provider, and you'll be more likely to catch mistakes or oversights.

We find it surprising that so many store owners ignore fundamental security issues on the Internet, although they take those issues very seriously when it comes to their land-based stores. Imagine a real store located in a strip mall. Build it without any security or staff to watch what goes on, keep the front door unlocked, and the store will be completely vulnerable. Someone could walk up to the cash register and easily empty the till.

Does that happen in the real world? Not at all. The owners or managers of most retail stores, large and small, implement a wide variety of security measures ranging from security guards to sophisticated alarm systems. Indeed, the retail sector spends quite a bit on store security. Most organizations choose to spend wisely on experts to secure their stores rather than leaving the front door open and the cash register unlocked. Furthermore, the owner or management of the store will take the time to learn about security issues and gain an understanding of some of the fundamental risks and how to minimize those risks.

Security Problems Are Often Due to Negligence, Ignorance, or Human Error

Experience has shown that most online security breaches are due to negligence on the part of those responsible for the technology being used. Only through your prodding and personal involvement can you ensure that the people involved in building your online store will pay sufficient attention and give proper respect to security issues.

As an example of what we mean, consider what happened to Western Union. Hackers were able to break into the company's Web site and access the credit card numbers of over 15,000 customers who had used the Western Union Web site to transfer money. Why did the break-in occur? Western Union admitted that its Web site had been left unprotected while undergoing maintenance and that the incident was entirely due to "human error." As a result, confidential information on the Western Union site was easily accessible to hackers.

If you are using shopping cart software to build your online store (see Chapter 2, "Options for Building an Online Store"), you need to make sure the software you are using has no known security weaknesses that haven't been adequately addressed. Many of these programs have security problems. For example, one survey of eleven popular shopping cart programs conducted by Internet Security Systems (www.iss.net) revealed that they all had security vulnerabilities. Even more shocking was the survey's finding that several of the software vendors did nothing to fix the problems.

What do both of these stories tell us? If the Internet remains insecure, it is often a result of the negligence or technical inexperience of the people who build and maintain Web sites and software for online stores. Some critics point a finger at software vendors who are in such a rush to get merchants online that they don't take the time to address security issues adequately. It is a sad fact, but often very true.

That's why it's important to thoroughly check the reputation, competence, and track record of any company you are considering to host or build your online store. Ask for references and/or look for examples of other online stores that are using the company's software. Contact those organizations and ask about their experiences. Find out if they have encountered any security problems you should know about.

e-fact

Companies conducting e-commerce are twice as likely to have their Web servers attacked by hackers.

Source: Information Security Magazine (www.infosecuritymag.com)

Security Problems Are Usually Due to Break-ins

Many people think the biggest security risk on the Internet occurs at the time of the sale—when a customer's credit card number is sent over the Internet to the merchant's computer. In the early years of the Internet, people were obsessed with the notion that hackers could grab credit card numbers while they were transmitted over the Internet. As a result, merchants focused their security efforts on protecting credit card data so they could travel securely over the Internet without being intercepted—by encrypting it. In reality, most security breaches happen after the sale is completed—when a customer's credit card number is sitting unprotected on the merchant's computer. That's what happened in the Western Union incident described earlier: the credit card numbers were stolen off of Western Union's computers, not as they travelled to the Western Union Web site.

Think about the mindset of someone who wants to steal a few credit card numbers by hacking into your store. There are two ways a hacker might go about it: the hard way and the easy way.

What is the hard way? The hacker might set out to monitor your Internet connection somehow and hope that you aren't using encrypted transmissions to scramble any credit card numbers in transit between your customers and your store. Undertaking such a task probably involves a high level of expertise that isn't beyond the reach of some hackers, but it does require specialized knowledge. All that effort might produce a credit card number or two.

The easy way? The hacker works at breaking into your Web site and store, and then browses around to see if there is a file containing customer information, including credit card numbers. A successful hacker could net a file of several thousand credit card numbers this way.

Obviously, the second method produces "better" results. This means that protecting your Web site is as important—if not more so—than securing the transactions through your site.

Examples of Online Security Risks
There are many different types of security risks that could affect your online store. Here are just some of them.

Snooping Attacks
A snooping attack is what happens when someone "eavesdrops" on your Web site and attempts to capture customer data, such as credit card numbers, as they are transmitted by customers to your online store. You can minimize your vulnerability to a snooping attack by encrypting the information so it's scrambled, making it unintelligible to an eavesdropper. Although the risk of a snooper is slim, this is probably the one security issue that online shoppers are most terrified of.

The easiest and most popular way to scramble a customer's credit card number is to use a method of encryption called SSL (secure sockets layer).

Most online storefront products use SSL to ensure that customers can transmit their credit card data and other personal information to your Web site safely and securely. We discuss SSL in greater detail later in the chapter.

e-fact

Eighty-one percent of online retailers believe that sales would increase if online shoppers were not as concerned about fraud.

Source: CyberSource (www.cybersource.com)

Web Site Break-ins

A break-in occurs when someone forcibly enters an online store or Web site to gain access to sensitive information, such as cardholder data, passwords, or billing records. This type of risk can be reduced by using firewalls and other sophisticated security measures to limit who can gain access to a Web site or a computer network. A discussion of these specific security technologies is beyond the scope of this book, so you should raise this issue with the company that will host your online store.

Security Leaks

A security leak occurs when confidential information is visible on a Web site or online store when it shouldn't be. This usually happens because someone hasn't properly secured the Web site. In addition, security leaks can occur through unauthorized access by an internal party or by someone at an Internet service provider.

Intentional Destruction of Data

Sometimes people break into Web sites with the sole intention of vandalizing the site in some manner. Usually the culprits alter the images or graphics on the Web and add their own in order to make a public statement of some kind. Even the Central Intelligence Agency has been a victim of this type of attack. If your store is not properly secured against unauthorized access, you could find yourself in a very embarrassing and potentially costly situation.

Accidental Loss of Data

You want to protect your online store in the event of a computer crash, power failure, flood, or other disaster at the location of your Internet service provider, storefront service provider, or Web hosting company. You could also lose data or even your entire online store through human error on the part of those responsible for managing your online store. For example, some commands on UNIX operating systems are so powerful that a single accidental command could wipe out everything. Another risk is that the provider of your online store goes bankrupt or out of business, leaving you unable to easily recreate your store. This happened to a number of companies during the dot-com shakeout and many online vendors were left scrambling.

These risks are best avoided by restricting access to the computers on which your online store is located, as well as through regular and ongoing backups of your Web site and online store.

Denial-of-Service Attacks

There have been many high-profile cases of Web sites being shut down or made inaccessible or intolerably slow as the result of what is called a denial-of-service attack. This situation involves someone deliberately blocking access to your online store by bombarding the computer that hosts your online store with a stream of information requests.

The information requests eventually overwhelm the computer, causing it to shut down. Such an attack exploits a problem within the operating system software or other software upon which a Web site or online store is based. The much-publicized attacks in 2000 that temporarily shut down several Web sites, including Yahoo!, Amazon.com, and eBay, were denial-of-service attacks.

Your online store could be subject to a denial-of-service attack by a disgruntled customer, electronic joyrider, or, heaven forbid, a competitor. Denial-of-service attacks can occur because of known bugs in particular software programs, and thus are best avoided by ensuring that the software your online store uses, including the operating system and Web server, is kept up-to-date with the most recent versions.

Unauthorized Modification and Integrity Attacks

If someone can break into your online store, that person probably has the capability to change your prices or product information. This could have an embarrassing or indeed damaging effect on your business, particularly if customers make purchases in your online store based on the incorrect information.

Viruses

Viruses are malicious programs that can damage or delete data on your computer, modify files, steal passwords, and even transfer files from your computer to other computers on the Internet, often without your knowledge. An example is the famous Love Bug virus, which paralyzed hundreds of thousands of computers around the world in 2000. The virus caused an estimated US $15 billion worth of damage and forced thousands of organizations to shut down their e-mail systems. Opening an e-mail or computer file infected with the virus will infect your computer.

Evidence shows that most viruses affect Windows-based systems. The best way to protect yourself if your store is based on a Windows server is to install—and regularly update—virus protection software from companies such as McAfee (www.mcafee.com) and Symantec (www.symantec.com). Both companies provide extensive information on their Web sites to help you learn about viruses and guard against them.

You should also ensure that all the information on your computer is backed up in the event a virus wipes out some or all of the files on your hard drive. Once you begin running your online store, think of all the important data you will have on your computer systems—customer records, order history information, credit card numbers, product data, and more. It would be a disaster if you were to lose all this information due to a virus.

e-fact

"Information security professionals are more concerned about viruses than they are about computer break-ins."

Source: Information Security Magazine (www.infosecuritymag.com)

Domain Name Hijacking

This occurs when someone transfers ownership of your domain name (e.g., nike.com) to another individual without your consent. When this happens, the hijacker is able to take control over your Web address so that when customers type your Web site address into their browser, they are deliberately rerouted to another Web site, such as that of a competitor. This type of attack is more common than you may think. It happens when someone, by forging your identity or through other means, gains unauthorized access to the central registry database that stores the routing information for your domain name.

Unlike the other types of security risks listed here, there is little you can do to prevent this type of event from occurring. Security for Internet domain names rests with the various domain name registries that allocate domain names to individuals and businesses on the Internet. More information about the importance of domain names can be found in Chapter 6, "Marketing Strategies for Your Online Store."

Cyber Extortion

Cyber extortion is what happens if a hacker or criminal breaks into your Web site and promises to destroy data, steal credit card numbers, launch a denial-of-service attack, or commit some other act unless a ransom is paid. This has happened to several firms with Web sites. In one case, an online retailer's Web site was broken into and customer records were accessed. The hacker threatened to publish thousands of customer credit card numbers unless $100,000 was paid. The company refused, and the hacker proceeded to post thousands of customer names, addresses, and credit card numbers on the Internet. This type of blackmail is an unfortunate reality of doing business on the Internet.

A more insidious form involves domain expirations. Many companies do not pay adequate attention to the expiry date of their domain, and fail to re-register it in time. Over the last few years, porn-site operators have developed software that lets them instantly find newly expired domains. They then scoop up the domain name, put up a porn site—and contact the original owner indicating that they'll sell the domain name back for an exorbitant fee. Imagine if you went to the effort to create a sophisticated online store, only to forget to pay the $35 annual renewal fee! Always keep track of the expiry date of any domains that you have and always keep them up-to-date in terms of registration fees.

Step #2: Assess Your Procedures

In Chapter 2, we reviewed a number of different methods for creating an online store. You need to be confident in the security procedures and methods used by the companies you engage to host and/or build your online store. This section presents a checklist of questions to ask to help you undertake this assessment.

Keep in mind that your bank or merchant account provider might require you to demonstrate that you have addressed security to a reasonable degree, so these are not matters to take lightly. You might consider consulting a security expert who can assist you with these issues, both before and after the design of your store. Technology companies such as IBM (www.ibm.com) and consulting firms such as Ernst & Young (www.ey.ca), as well as smaller, independent consultants, offer these types of services.

In addition, you might consider hiring an "ethical hacker," a company or individual who will test your Web site's security by attempting to break into your store. This can help identify potential weaknesses. These services can be obtained from consultants such as IBM and Ernst & Young as well, in addition to organizations such as New Brunswick–based CyberSecure (www.cybersecure.ca). However, hiring a security consultant can be expensive, so it's not usually the type of service that a small business or mom-and-pop online store would use.

Security Checklist for Storefront Hosting Services

1. Is the company security conscious?
2. Do they respond to your questions appropriately?
3. Do they keep up-to-date on security issues?
4. How is staff turnover handled?
5. How is access to the computers restricted?
6. Are unused services on the computers turned off?
7. Are there known risks with the storefront software?
8. Where is cardholder information stored?
9. What backup procedures are in place?
10. How is data transmitted?

Is the Company Security Conscious?

When you select a company to host or build your online store, assess whether the company pays proper attention to security issues. If you have any concerns, make sure they are addressed to your satisfaction.

At a minimum, determine what security procedures and technologies the company has in place to guard against security breaches and the types of problems we described earlier. Don't simply assume that the company has excellent security—ask about it. And don't assume that the company knows what it's doing, as even the experts can get it wrong.

Keep in mind that in the last few years, particularly in the wake of the U.S. terrorist attacks, companies have become extremely security conscious, so you might find that a lot more attention is now given to security. Not only that, but some Web hosting organizations specifically market themselves based upon their security offerings (in addition to other factors such as reliability, redundancy, and uptime. (Uptime is the percentage of time your Web site is fully operational and available to your customers.)) For a good example of such an organization, take a look at Canada's Q9 Networks (www.q9.com), which specializes in providing high-end Web hosting services for major Canadian companies.

Virus attacks are the most common type of computer attack.

Source: Computer Security Institute (www.gocsi.com)

e-fact

Do They Respond to Your Questions Appropriately?
A good e-commerce company will take the time to help you understand the security issues that affect your online store. If the company dismisses your questions or has an arrogant attitude, then you should consider using another company. If an e-commerce company does not respond to your concerns appropriately, it is probably also far too willing to dismiss security issues in general. Don't be embarrassed by your lack of expertise about security. A good e-commerce company will recognize that you are trying to educate yourself and will respond in a professional manner.

Do They Keep Up-to-Date on Security Issues?
New security problems are constantly arising. What is the company doing to keep current on these issues? You want to deal with an organization that takes security seriously by keeping up-to-date.

How Is Staff Turnover Handled?
What security policies are implemented when an employee leaves the organization? What procedures ensure that former employees don't have access to passwords and critical files?

How Is Access to the Computers Restricted?
Find out where the company's computer facilities are located, including the computer(s) used to run and store data from your online store. What steps has the company taken to protect unauthorized physical access? Are the facilities in a secure building? What about online access? Who has

access to the administrative and other special accounts involved with your online store? Are passwords to these accounts changed regularly?

Are Unused Services on the Computers Turned Off?

Security problems often arise because the Web server (the software that runs a Web site) hasn't been set up to screen out certain types of Internet communications. Any methods of gaining access to the Web server that are not required for electronic commerce should be either removed or disabled. This will prevent a hacker or other unauthorized individual from gaining access to your Web site through a back door.

Are There Known Risks with the Storefront Software?

Ask the company if there are any known risks or security problems with the storefront software you have chosen. If there are, find out how those problems are being addressed. Obviously, if there are known security problems with a company's storefront software, they may not be willing to disclose this information to you for fear of losing your business. That is why it is important to ask for references and interview other people who are using the company's software. This will help you uncover any security issues that the company may not have revealed to you.

Where Is Cardholder Information Stored?

Ensure that any customer information your store collects (e.g., credit card information, billing records, telephone numbers, mailing addresses) is securely stored on computers that can't be accessed from the Internet. For maximum protection, it is essential to store customer information and credit card numbers in an encrypted (scrambled) manner behind a firewall. This will make it difficult for a hacker or other unauthorized individual to access the data.

What Backup Procedures Are in Place?

Find out how often backups are performed on your online store. Daily? Weekly? Monthly? As soon as a customer order is placed? Are the backup copies stored in a safe, secure, locked location? Are the backups backed up in case the original copies are accidentally destroyed? If you plan to keep customer credit card information in a database linked to your online store, what is the procedure for destroying old copies of that database? It's crucial that the company has a backup of your online store in case there is a computer crash, natural disaster, or act of vandalism that causes you to lose all or some of the computer files belonging to your on-line store. The more frequent the backups, the better!

How Is Data Transmitted?

Finally, make sure the storefront software you are using will automatically encrypt customers' credit card information and other personal data when an order has been placed. This will prevent unauthorized individuals from intercepting and reading the information as it travels over the Internet to your online store. You should choose an online storefront solution that supports 128-bit encryption using SSL (secure sockets layer) technology. This is the most popular form of encryption in use on the Internet and will adequately protect customer data from being accessed while in transit.

Is All This Really Necessary?

Since it's unlikely that you're an expert on Internet security issues, your natural inclination will be to trust the company you're dealing with. After all, how are you supposed to know whether an e-commerce company has taken all the appropriate security measures? Even if you ask all the questions we've listed above, you have no way to tell whether the company is being perfectly honest with its responses unless you're well versed in technical issues or have access to its facilities. Moreover, it may be difficult for you to contact a person who has enough knowledge to answer all of these questions.

To a great degree, you have to place your faith in the hosting company and software you have chosen. However, any hosting company or store-front hosting firm that takes Internet security seriously should have basic information about its security infrastructure on its Web site and will be happy to answer your questions by e-mail or on the telephone. Many companies are obviously not going to publish sensitive information about their security procedures on their Web sites, so you will probably need to have a conversation with someone in order to get detailed security information. Understandably, however, many companies are reluctant to reveal their security policies—even to a potential customer—in order to protect the integrity of their systems. While a company may not want to reveal publicly how it deals with certain security issues, at the very minimum you should be able to learn how your customers' credit card data will be handled, both in terms of transmission and storage, and what a company's backup policies are.

The bottom line is that you should never take Internet security for granted. Try to get a gut feeling for how various e-commerce companies deal with Internet security.

For example, a company that forwards you a two-page description of the security measures it has taken to protect your online store will likely give you more confidence than one that answers "trust us" to your questions. Finally, check with your bank or merchant account provider as many of these organizations are developing lists of approved hosts, gateways, ISPs, etc., that have met their security qualifications.

e-fact

Global Internet traffic in 2005 will be ninety-three times the volume of traffic in 2000.

Source: International Data Corporation (www.idc.com)

Consequences of Inadequate Data Security

What will happen to online merchants who fail to implement proper Internet security measures? They expose themselves and their customers to tremendous risks by not adequately protecting credit card data and other sensitive customer information such as names, addresses, and telephone numbers. If hackers are able to gain access to a merchant's credit card data, some or all of the merchant's customers could become victims of online fraud.

Think of the resulting public relations damage if word got out that your customer database had been broken into by hackers. Fearing that their credit card numbers wouldn't be safe, customers might stay away from your online store in droves, resulting in a sharp drop in business. The negative media attention that often ensues from a hacker attack could haunt a merchant for years, not to mention the devastating impact on the merchant's reputation.

Consider what happened to Western Union following the hacker attack described earlier in this chapter. The story was immediately picked up by the news media and reported widely. The negative publicity from this event harmed Western Union's reputation and credibility, making many customers think twice about using the company's Web site.

Inadequate security on your Web site could also result in the revocation of your merchant accounts (see Chapter 4 for discussion of merchant accounts). As noted in Chapter 4, every time a fraudulent transaction occurs on your Web site, you'll probably receive a chargeback for the purchase once the real cardholder discovers the fraudulent activity.

If you start to receive a lot of chargebacks due to online fraud, Visa, MasterCard, and American Express reserve the right to revoke your merchant status so you won't be able to accept credit cards anymore. Obviously, this could be devastating to your business. More serious might be the fact that you, the merchant, can't fund the chargeback. That is a more likely risk to legitimate merchants who have a security lapse.

But those aren't the only consequences that merchants may face if they don't pay adequate attention to security. Credit card companies such as Visa are stepping up their enforcement of Internet security and creating mandatory security rules for merchants and their service providers. Visa, for example, has created an "Account Information Security Program," which includes the following fifteen minimum security principles:

1. Establish a hiring policy for staff and contractors.
2. Restrict access to data on a "need-to-know" basis.
3. Assign each person a unique ID to be validated when accessing data.
4. Track access to data, including read access, by each person.
5. Install and maintain a network firewall, if data can be accessed via the Internet.
6. Encrypt data maintained on databases or files accessible from the Internet.
7. Encrypt data sent across networks.
8. Protect systems and data from viruses.
9. Keep security patches for software up-to-date.
10. Don't use vendor-supplied defaults for system passwords and other security parameters.
11. Don't leave paper/diskettes/computers with data unsecured.
12. Securely destroy data when it's no longer needed for business reasons.
13. Regularly test security systems and procedures.
14. Immediately investigate and report to Visa any suspected loss of account or transaction information.
15. Use only service providers that meet these security standards.

These principles *must* be followed by all organizations that store cardholder data, including the merchant, as well as any companies involved with the merchant's online store, such as the e-commerce service provider that hosts a store. In addition, they are recommended for all other merchants, regardless of their size. As you probably noticed, a lot of these rules are simple common sense.

Merchants and their service providers who fail to comply could face disciplinary action. To avoid these penalties, check with your merchant account provider or acquiring financial institution (see Chapter 4 for an explanation of these organizations) to obtain the most current security rules for each of the credit cards you accept on the Internet.

If you are operating your own Internet server(s), you will need to address these issues yourself. On the other hand, if you are paying someone else to host your online store on the Internet, or if you are using one of the storefront creation services such as Yahoo! Store (as we discussed in Chapter 2), you should ensure the company that will be hosting your online store is following these rules.

At a minimum, e-mail or telephone the company you are using or thinking of using for your storefront and ask what security precautions it has taken to safeguard cardholder data. You can compare the response to the list above. If certain items are missing, ask about them. Don't be shy about pressing a company for answers about online security. It's your right to know, and any company that is serious about e-commerce will respect your questions. After all, if something goes wrong and a hacker is somehow able to access your customers' credit card information, you are the one who will bear the brunt of the fallout, not the hosting company you are working with!

Finally, be aware that there might be a verification process by various card companies to determine if you comply with their rules. How Visa or other card companies verify your compliance with their rules will depend on your size and how many transactions you typically store or process. For example, a small mom-and-pop merchant may only be required to complete an online self-assessment checklist. Larger merchants and service providers that process hundreds or thousands of transactions a day may be required to submit to on-site reviews, intrusion-detection testing, and ongoing monitoring of their firewalls.

If you're not sure whether your Web site and computers are adequately protected, hire an Internet security expert to assess your situation for you. It's better to be safe than sorry!

More cyber attacks originate in the United States than in any other country.

Source: Riptech (www.riptech.com)

e-fact

Step #3: Protect the Integrity and Security of Your Online Transactions

In addition to keeping your online store safe from break-ins, natural disasters, vandalism, and breaches of confidentiality, you need to protect the integrity and security of the order process itself. When a customer places an order on your Web site, you need to have security in place so that a customer's order information, including credit card details, can't be stolen or tampered with when it is transmitted over the Internet. This is an encryption issue. You should also take steps to prevent stolen or bogus credit cards from being used on your Web site (i.e., for fraudulent purchases). These two issues are among the most technically complex subjects that you will have to deal with when you set up your online store.

Encryption

To secure the transmission of customer data, most online merchants use SSL (secure sockets layer). SSL is supported by all Web browsers and is in widespread use on the Internet today. SSL encrypts credit card information as it travels from the customer's computer to the merchant's Web site. This minimizes the chance that the credit card information will be stolen while it passes over the Internet. However, despite the widespread use of SSL, consumers remain apprehensive about using their credit cards on the Internet.

This has led some payment card companies to launch single-use credit card numbers that expire immediately after they are used. American Express (www.americanexpress.com), for example, offers users in the United States a service called "Private Payments," which involves the use of disposable credit card numbers. It wasn't available in Canada at the time we were finishing this book, but is a good example of how card companies are responding to the challenges of the online world. American Express cardholders can register for the free service on the American Express Web site. Once a cardholder is registered, he or she can download software that can issue a unique disposable credit card number whenever the cardholder wants to make an online purchase. The disposable number can be used at any online store that accepts American Express cards. Each unique number is valid only for a single purchase on the Internet and expires as soon as the purchase is completed. The merchant gets paid for the sale because each disposable credit card number is linked to the customer's real American Express account.

There are two primary benefits to these single-use credit cards from a security point of view. First, since the disposable number is good only for a single purchase, the number is useless to anyone who intercepts it during an online purchase. Second, even if someone were to break into the merchant's Web site and steal the number, it couldn't be used since the number would have already expired. Thus, even when SSL is used, the use of a disposable credit card number gives the consumer even greater protection.

Single-use credit cards do have a number of drawbacks, however. For example, they can pose a problem for merchants when a customer wants to return an item but can't remember the particular credit card number that was used during the transaction. Moreover, single-use credit card numbers can't be used to purchase a product or service that requires advance billing (e.g., hotel reservations) or recurrent billing (e.g., a subscription to an Internet service provider that is billed to your credit card every week, month, etc.), nor can they be used in situations where the customer is later required to show or use an actual plastic credit card (e.g., airline ticket or movie ticket purchases). Another major disadvantage of disposable credit card numbers is that customers can't store them on merchant Web sites. Many customers like to store their credit card details on their favourite online shopping sites so they won't have to manually enter their billing information each time they shop. This can't be done with disposable credit card numbers because the numbers aren't known in advance.

Fraudulent Purchases

Fraudulent purchases derive from two risks. The first is the risk that someone tries to buy a product with a card that is stolen, invalid, cancelled, or over its spending limit. These are authorization issues. Second, there is the risk that someone tries to use a valid credit card that hasn't been reported stolen but that doesn't belong to him or her. This is an authentication issue. Before we discuss these issues, let's first look at who is responsible for fraudulent transactions once they occur.

In Most Cases, the Merchant Is Responsible for Fraudulent Credit Card Transactions

You may be wondering who is responsible if you unknowingly accept an online order with a stolen credit card and then ship the merchandise to the address provided with the order. The answer is that you are on the hook for any fraudulent transactions on your online store if you are not taking advantage of programs from the card companies that minimize risk (more on this below). This is so important we will repeat it again. You are usually forced to bear the loss for any fraudulent transactions that occur on your online store.

Eighty-three percent of Canadian Internet users who have yet to make a purchase on the Internet say that security concerns are holding them back.

Source: Ipsos-Reid (www.ipsos-reid.com)

e-fact

Here's what would happen if an order was placed on your Web site using a stolen credit card. Let's assume that you process the order and ship the merchandise. Several days or weeks later, the real owner of the credit card receives a credit card statement and notices the transaction that took place on your online store. Since the real credit card owner won't recognize the transaction, the person will probably dispute the purchase. Because credit card statements are usually mailed out to customers only once a month, a customer may not receive a statement and file a complaint until several weeks after the order was made on your online store. By that time, it's quite likely that your bank or merchant account provider will have already deposited the money from this order into your bank account. (As discussed in Chapter 4, money from online orders is usually deposited into your bank account within several days after the order is placed.) Upon being notified of the customer dispute, your bank or merchant account provider will issue a chargeback and, in effect, will take back the money it gave you for the order, leaving you with nothing, even though you have already shipped the merchandise.

Herein lies an important lesson: when online fraud occurs, it is the merchant, not the bank, who is ultimately responsible. It's rather ironic. Throughout this chapter, we've been talking about consumers' fears of using their credit cards on the Internet, but it's the merchants who bear the greater risk. And to make matters worse, online merchants don't usually find out that an order has been disputed until many weeks after the order was placed. By this time, the merchandise is usually long gone, having been shipped weeks earlier by the merchant.

Consider the following advisory that Yahoo! Store (store.yahoo.com/vw/fraud.html) gives its merchants:

> *You often read in the press that consumers are worried about ordering online. In reality, it is not the consumers who have to worry, but the merchants. If you're a consumer, the chance of your credit card number being intercepted as it travels over the Internet is microscopically small. But if you are a merchant, the chance of getting orders with stolen credit card numbers is significant.*

In addition, Moneris (www.moneris.com), which is the merchant card service joint venture of the Royal Bank and Bank of Montreal, has the following warning on its Web site:

- *Mail Order/Telephone Order and Non-Secure E-Commerce Transactions: If you complete mail/telephone order and/or a non-secure electronic commerce transaction you do so at your own risk. Moneris solutions cannot protect you from chargebacks, as we cannot ensure the individual using the card is the owner of the card. An authorization number only confirms the funds are available on the card at the time of the transaction.*
- *If you choose to accept a mail/telephone order and/or non-secure electronic order, please ensure you record the cardholder's name, address, phone number and e-mail address. Once the order has been completed, call back the cardholder to confirm the information given to you.*
- *If possible, have the cardholder fax in the order, with a letter signed by the cardholder, stating they authorize and participate in the transaction.*
- *Obtain an authorization number for the transaction, regardless of the dollar amount.*
- *Clearly state your refund policy in writing before an agreement is reached between yourself and the cardholder. Provide the cardholder with this information.*
- *If you are shipping out your merchandise to the cardholder, please send it by courier or registered mail. Upon receipt of the goods, a signature should be obtained by the cardholder.*

- *If the cardholder is picking up the merchandise, obtain a manual imprint of the credit card and a signature from the cardholder. The merchant should also attach a copy of the previously agreed upon contract and have the cardholder sign it.*

When a cardholder disputes a charge made at an online store, the merchant has no physical proof that the cardholder legitimately made the purchase since the merchant does not see the physical credit card or a customer signature. In essence, with Internet e-commerce, merchants have decided that they will take the risk of accepting credit card orders online, and hence the risk of accepting credit card numbers without any assurance as to the validity of the number. So when cardholders complain that they never made an online purchase that showed up on their credit card statement, the bank often sides with the customers, and the merchant in most cases is forced to bear the loss.

Recognizing that the system usually works in favour of the customer, some consumers buy goods on the Internet with their own credit cards and then deny ever making the purchases once they receive their credit card statements. As mentioned in the last chapter, this is called friendly fraud. Friendly fraud, however, accounts for a very small percentage of online fraud. Many organizations have aggressive programs in place to combat this type of fraud.

New Programs Shift the Burden of Risk

New programs by various card companies, such as Verified by Visa, which we describe later in the chapter, shift the burden of risk from the merchant to the bank. This means that when you implement these programs, in most cases you are no longer responsible for fraudulent transactions that occur in your online store; hence it is in your interest to adopt these new programs as quickly as possible.

In the sections that follow, we'll look at the issues of authorization and authentication, which are related to the issue of how e-commerce risk comes about. Then we'll look at Visa's Verified by Visa program.

Fifty-nine percent of U.S. consumers who do not shop online say they are afraid their credit card information could be stolen while shopping online.

Source: Jupiter Media Metrix (www.jmm.com)

e-fact

Authorization

Online stores can authorize their credit card transactions manually by using a transaction terminal or in real time by using any of the payment gateways we discussed in the explanation of authorization processes in Chapter 4. When you attempt to authorize a credit card purchase, you'll receive an authorization code. If the credit card has been cancelled, reported stolen, or isn't in good standing, you won't receive an authorization code and the purchase will be declined by the financial institution that issued the credit card. This is essentially the same process that occurs in a retail store when a customer makes a purchase.

What Does a Credit Card Authorization Really Mean?

Even if you receive an authorization from the credit card company for an online purchase, it is not a guarantee that the credit card is legitimate or that the person placing the order is the rightful owner of the card. After all, all you know from an authorization is that the credit card provided is a real credit card. You don't know if the owner of the card is the actual person using the card.

And contrary to popular belief, an authorization is also not a guarantee that you'll get paid for the order. In fact, the credit card may be stolen and the owner may not know about it or have reported it yet. If a credit card hasn't been reported stolen, the credit card company has no way of knowing that there is a problem. So when the stolen credit card number is used on the Internet to make a purchase, the credit card company will authorize the transaction as long as the cardholder hasn't exceeded the allowable credit limit.

Authentication

Authorization verifies that a real credit card is being used, but you need some additional assurance that the actual owner of the card is the one doing the transaction. This is a tricky problem with Internet transactions, given their virtual nature.

Hence, one of the biggest challenges confronting merchants and credit card companies is authentication. How do you ensure that the person using a credit card is in fact the owner of that card number? As we explain below, one of the problems merchants face on the Internet is that they can't see the customer's physical credit card, nor can they get a physical signature from the cardholder.

Card-Present Versus Card-Not-Present Transactions

When a customer makes a purchase in a retail store, the store clerk is supposed to compare the signature on the back of the credit card to the signature made by the purchaser. If the signatures don't match, it may be a sign that the purchaser is not the owner of the credit card. A purchase in a retail store is referred to as a "card-present transaction" because a physical credit card is presented to the merchant by the customer. Merchants who follow the guidelines issued by credit card companies for card-present transactions (including authorizing the transaction using the transaction terminal and checking for matching signatures) are not responsible for any fraud that occurs and they are guaranteed payment for the amount of the purchase, less any merchant fees, such as the ones we discussed in Chapter 4.

With an online transaction, the shopper enters a credit card number on the merchant's Web site and confirms the order. Because a physical credit card cannot be presented during an online transaction, online credit card orders are referred to as "card-not-present transactions." And since neither the customer's signature nor any other form of identification has typically been required for online transactions, it has not been possible for the merchant to verify the identity of the cardholder. In card-not-present transactions, as noted previously, merchants are responsible for any fraud that occurs.

It is important to note that card-not-present transaction status is not new. Long before the Internet was around, it applied to mail order and telephone orders (the term "MOTO transaction" is also often used). So don't think that the credit card companies are out to treat you differently because of the Internet. They are simply applying their existing rules to card-not-present transactions.

Since neither a physical credit card nor a cardholder's signature is used in an online transaction, online credit card orders expose the merchant to fraud.

Assessing Your Risk and Comfort Level

In any online store, there is a good chance that someone with a stolen or bogus credit card number will try to place an order. It's important to understand that any online merchant can be affected by fraud, not just those merchants selling high-priced items like jewellery, electronics, or computer equipment. So even if you're selling a low-priced item like hand-painted earrings, you're not immune to online fraud. It can happen to anyone!

However, there are several things you can do to authenticate the identity of a credit card holder. It is your responsibility as a merchant to screen all of your orders before shipping them. In the next sections, we will help you understand many of the manual methods of authentication you might undertake to reduce your risk of loss. We will also talk about some of the computerized methods of authentication, such as Verified by Visa, address verification, and fraud-screening software.

Obviously, many of these procedures will cost you extra time and effort and possibly extra money. Therefore, you have to carefully determine how far you are willing to go in analyzing transactions for potential fraud, as well as how much effort you are willing to make to verify the identity of the individual behind a credit card transaction that might cause you concern. Clearly, if you are selling low-cost items with a very low margin, you might decide to reject any orders that don't pass muster. If you are selling high-priced items with a big margin, you might be willing to undertake additional steps on a suspicious sale to determine if the risk is worth it. The bottom line is what you do depends on what you are selling and the effort that you are willing to apply.

e-fact

Fifty-four percent of online retailers say that online credit card fraud is a very serious problem.

Source: CyberSource (www.cybersource.com)

Manual Methods of Authentication

Here are some manual methods of authentication to help avoid credit card fraud on the Internet.

- Ask for both home and work numbers on your order form and then call to verify the order, particularly if you are dealing with high-value items. Out-of-service telephone numbers are an obvious sign that an order is probably fraudulent. If you don't hear back from the customer, don't ship the order.
- Check both the billing and shipping addresses on your orders to make sure they are legitimate. You might be suspicious if the billing address you have been given differs from the shipping address even

though it is common for billing and shipping addresses to be different. Someone using a stolen credit card number will not want to have the order shipped to the cardholder's billing address, so another address will be given to you for shipping purposes. Be aware, however, that a billing address that differs from a shipping address is not always a sign of credit card fraud. A cardholder may be ordering a product on behalf of another person or shipping the order to a work address, another residence, or to a friend or relative's home.

- Be wary of orders that are placed using free e-mail address services such as Hotmail. This can be an indication that the person placing the order doesn't want to be found, or makes it difficult to verify the legitimacy of the identity used.

- Check to see if the e-mail address used by the purchaser is located near the billing address provided by the cardholder. For example, if you receive an order from an e-mail address in Turkey and the billing address is located in the United States, this is a good indication that the order may be fraudulent. It's not always easy to determine in what part of the world an e-mail address is located, but sometimes you can deduce this information by looking at the domain name of the customer or using a bit of detective work. Some credit card processing services might also provide the IP or Internet address of the purchaser, and you might be able to use this to verify their location. Later in this chapter we will talk about some of the fraud-screening technology that can help you deal with this.

- Be suspicious if the order you receive is unusual, such as an order for several high-ticket items, large quantities of product, or an assortment of products that typically wouldn't be ordered together. Rush delivery on a large-volume or large-value order may be another sign of fraud.

- Be careful when shipping to certain countries, such as Romania, Colombia, Belarus, Russia, and Macedonia. Because a high proportion of fraud originates from these countries (and others), you should treat orders from these countries with caution. Remember that you're not obligated to ship to every country in the world. When you develop a shipping policy for your online store (see Chapter 3, "Tips for Building an Effective Online Store"), carefully consider this issue.

While we are not suggesting that you not ship outside of North America, you should carefully consider requesting payment in advance from some of the high-risk countries.

As a general rule, never ship an order that you're not fully comfortable with. Use all of the avenues available to you to verify the legitimacy of an order if you think it may be suspect, including financial institutions and telephone and address directories.

Don't rely on e-mail as a means of verifying an order. An e-mail message from someone confirming that they've placed an order on your Web site means nothing. How do you know that the e-mail message actually comes from the owner of the credit card used in the purchase? E-mail addresses and e-mail headers can be easily forged or altered to trick the recipient into thinking the message is coming from a particular person.

Remember that there are dozens of free e-mail services on the Internet. Anyone can create an e-mail account to resemble a person's name. That account could then be used with a credit card order so that the order seems legitimate.

Below are the most common signs of credit card fraud, according to Visa. Study this list and be on the lookout for any purchases in your online store that seem suspect.

Twelve Signs of Possible Internet Fraud

Be alert for Internet transactions with several of these characteristics:

- *First time shopper:* Criminals are always looking for new victims.
- *Larger-than-normal orders:* (This requires knowledge of what a normal-size order is.) Because stolen cards or account numbers have a limited lifespan, crooks need to maximize the size of their purchase.
- *Orders consisting of several of the same item:* Having multiples of the same item increases the criminal's profits.
- *Orders made up of big-ticket items:* These items have maximum resale value and therefore maximum profit potential.
- *Orders shipped "rush" or "overnight":* Crooks want these fraudulently obtained items as soon as possible for the quickest possible resale, and aren't concerned about extra delivery charges.
- *Orders from Internet addresses making use of free e-mail services:* For these services, there's no billing relationship and often no

audit trail or verification that a legitimate cardholder has opened the account.

- *Orders shipped to an international address:* A significant number of fraudulent transactions are shipped to fraudulent cardholders outside North America. Develop and maintain a customer database or account history files to track buying patterns and compare and evaluate individual sales for signs of possible fraud.
- *Transactions on similar account numbers:* This is particularly useful if the account numbers being used have been generated using special software available on the Internet (e.g., Credit Master).
- *Orders shipped to a single address but made on multiple cards:* These could also be characteristic of an account number generated using special software available on the Internet, or a batch of stolen cards.
- *Multiple transactions on one card over a short period of time:* This could be an attempt to "run" a card until the account is closed.
- *Multiple transactions on one card or similar cards with a single billing address but multiple shipping addresses:* This could represent organized activity rather than one individual at work.
- *Multiple cards used from a single IP (Internet protocol) address:* More than one or two cards could well indicate a fraud scheme.

Source: Visa

Obviously, if you plan (or hope) to sell a lot of products on the Internet, you may find manual fraud-screening procedures time consuming and perhaps not entirely effective. Hence, you should have a clear understanding of the computerized methods available online to provide you with credit card authentication, the first of which is known as Verified by Visa.

Out of every $100 spent online, between $0.24 and $0.28 is lost to fraud, compared with $0.07 to $0.08 in overall credit card purchases.

Source: Visa International (www.visa.com)

e-fact

Computerized Methods of Authentication

As we noted earlier in the chapter, credit card transactions on the Internet are known as card-not-present transactions because a physical credit card isn't presented to the merchant. This exposes online merchants to fraud because a physical signature can't be obtained from the person making the purchase.

Over the years, a variety of methods emerged to protect merchants against online fraud, such as credit card authorization and address verification services. However, when we describe them below, you will note that some of these methods of authentication have significant weaknesses. For example, authorizations are sometimes given for stolen credit card numbers and unfavourable address verification codes are often reported for perfectly legitimate credit card orders. That's why both Visa and MasterCard are in the process of introducing new buyer-authentication services that will authenticate cardholders when they make purchases on the Internet. MasterCard's solution is called SPA (secure payment application), while Visa's solution is called Verified by Visa.

e-fact

Seventy-one percent of existing online shoppers say that adequate authentication would make them consider shopping online more frequently.

Source: VISA EU (www.visaeu.com)

Verified by Visa

In 2000, Visa announced an online service called Verified by Visa. Verified by Visa is a method of confirming that the person using a credit card during an online transaction is in fact the owner of that card. The major advantage of Verified by Visa is that it's less complicated to implement—and much easier to understand—than AVS (address verification service) and it responds to requests by merchants for better solutions to prevent fraud on the Internet.

For example, Visa cardholders won't require any special software or devices in order to use Verified by Visa. All that is required from cardholders is a simple multistep enrollment process that can be completed on a special Web site hosted by their card-issuing bank. Cardholders will be directed to the appropriate site by the bank that issued their credit card. The registration process takes only a couple of minutes to complete. Once cardholders register, they'll be issued a special password to use whenever they make an online purchase. The password is Visa's way of ensuring that the person using the credit card is actually the owner of the card.

Verified by Visa is coming to Canada, and over time, you will notice a greater number of merchants and cardholders participating in the program. The greatest benefit for online merchants is that in April 2003, when new Visa rules take effect, *merchants who make use of Verified by Visa won't be subject to chargebacks for fraudulent purchases made on the Internet.* Instead, the bank that issued the credit card will be liable for any fraudulent online purchase made using that credit card, as long as the merchant was using Verified by Visa. This means that as of April 2003, any online merchants participating in the Verified by Visa program will have similar rights to merchants operating in brick-and-mortar stores, in the sense that they will not be responsible for fraudulent transactions.

When a merchant uses the Verified by Visa system, the cardholder's bank will provide the merchant with one of three possible answers after the cardholder's password has been checked:

- If the cardholder is authenticated with Verified by Visa, the merchant receives a "Yes" and the merchant can proceed with the transaction.
- If the cardholder is unable to authenticate himself or herself, the merchant receives a "No" answer and should request another card. Under no circumstances is the transaction to proceed if the authentication answer is "No." If a merchant does proceed, then he or she is fully responsible for any chargeback.
- If Verified by Visa service is unable to authenticate a transaction, the merchant will receive a message to that effect. There are specific rules governing liability, which are outlined in the *Verified by Visa Merchant Implementation Guide.*

Merchants can register for Verified by Visa by contacting their acquiring bank. Once enrolled, they will receive a plug-in software program specific to the computing platform and e-commerce server they are using. In some cases, the Verified by Visa software may already be integrated into the e-commerce software the merchant is using in the same way that merchant account applications and payment gateways are prepackaged with many of the e-commerce storefront solutions discussed in Chapter 2.

For more information about Verified by Visa, contact the acquiring financial institution that gave you your merchant number. You should also visit the Verified by Visa Web site for Canadian merchants at www.visa.ca.

How Cardholders Register for Verified by Visa
Here is how the system is designed to work:

1. Visa cardholders register for Verified by Visa by going to a designated "enrollment site" for the bank that issued their credit card, or by using another method specified by their bank.

2. Once at the site, the cardholder will be prompted for account information as well as information known only to the cardholder. This information can vary by bank.

3. At this point, you may ask what happens if a thief steals a customer's credit card and tries to register with Verified by Visa. To prevent someone other than the real cardholder from successfully registering with Verified by Visa, the cardholder will be asked for one or more pieces of "out-of-wallet" information in order to verify that the person is the legitimate owner of the credit card being registered. Out-of-wallet information is data that only the cardholder would likely know, such as the cardholder's maiden name or previous address.

   The cardholder will also be asked to create a "personal message." This phrase will be displayed to the cardholder when he or she is prompted to enter the password during a transaction. It lets the cardholder know that the request to enter the password comes from the card-issuing bank and not an imposter. The personal message can be any phrase the cardholder wishes.

4. Next, the cardholder will be asked to enter a password that will be used to authenticate the cardholder when an online purchase is made. The cardholder will also be prompted for a "hint and response pair." The hint and response are used to confirm the cardholder's identity in case the cardholder forgets the Verified by Visa password. The hint is a question that the cardholder will know the answer to, and the response is the correct response to that question. The cardholder is free to come up with any question as long as it's not a question that someone else would know the answer to. For example, a cardholder might want to use a question like "What street did you grow up on?" or "When is your mother's birthday?"

5. Upon completion of registration, the cardholder is formally enrolled in Verified by Visa and the cardholder's password, hint and

response pair, and personal message are securely stored on the issuing bank's computer network.

Auction fraud accounts for nearly 43 percent of all reported Internet fraud in the United States.

Source: Internet Fraud Complaint Center (www1.ifccfbi.gov)

e-fact

How Verified by Visa Works During an Online Transaction

Verified by Visa is simple to use. In fact, most of the activity takes place behind the scenes and is completely transparent to the cardholder. Here is an overview of the process.

1. A cardholder shops online in the usual way, adding items to a shopping cart, proceeding to the merchant's checkout page, and completing the merchant's checkout forms by providing payment information and the shipping and billing address.
2. When the online shopper presses the "submit" or "complete order" button to complete the purchase, a request is sent over the Internet from the merchant to the cardholder's issuing bank to find out whether the cardholder is participating in Verified by Visa.
3. If the cardholder's issuing bank reports back to the merchant that the cardholder is participating in Verified by Visa, the customer will see a bank-branded pop-up window appear on the screen. The window will attempt to verify the identity of the customer by asking for the password that was supplied during the registration procedure.

    If the cardholder's issuing bank reports back to the merchant that the cardholder is not participating in Verified by Visa, the transaction would proceed as it normally would and a request for authorization will be sent to the cardholder's issuing bank. The merchant would receive an approval or decline message in return, and the customer would be notified onscreen if the order was processed successfully. At this point, the transaction is completed.
4. As noted in Step #3, if the cardholder is participating in Verified by Visa, a window will appear on the cardholder's screen and he or she will be prompted to enter his or her password. Once the cardholder has entered the password, the system checks to see if the password is correct.

5. If the password is verified, the merchant receives a "Yes" response and a receipt containing the card issuer's "digital signature." Think of a digital signature as an electronic method of notarizing a document. The digital signature is important because it lets the merchant know that the authentication response hasn't been generated fraudulently. When the digital signature is returned to the merchant, it's automatically verified to make sure it came from the cardholder's bank. Once this happens, the cardholder is considered "authenticated," meaning that his or her identity has been confirmed, and the transaction continues to the authorization stage.

   If the password is not correct, the customer is given a number of attempts to enter the password correctly. Upon the final invalid entry, the cardholder is provided with his or her hint and asked to provide the correct response. The cardholder is given one chance to correctly enter the response. If the response is incorrect, an "authentication failed" response will be returned to the merchant and the merchant should request another form of payment from the shopper.

6. Once the cardholder has been authenticated, an authorization request is sent from the merchant to the cardholder's issuing bank. Included in the authorization request is certain data provided to the merchant by the card issuer during authentication, along with an "electronic commerce indicator." (We discuss the electronic commerce indicator in the next section.) If the cardholder's account is in good standing, the transaction will be approved, and an authorization message will be delivered back to the merchant from the cardholder's issuing bank.

7. If the credit card transaction is approved, the cardholder will see a message on the screen indicating the transaction has gone through successfully and the merchant will be able to retrieve the order from his or her storefront software.

Remember that this seven-step process takes just a few seconds. Most of all the steps are completely transparent to the customer.

e-fact

It is projected that authentication technologies will lead to a 50 percent reduction in e-commerce-related disputes and fraud.

Source: Visa (www.visa.com)

What to Do in the Event of a Failed Authentication

If the cardholder is unable to authenticate himself or herself, the merchant will receive a "No" answer and you will be required to ask the customer for another credit card. The merchant is not allowed to proceed to authorization if the authentication fails because the transaction is likely fraudulent.

> Only 34 percent of computer security professionals surveyed in the United States say they report computer attacks to the authorities. Seventy-five percent say they do not report intrusions because of the negative publicity that might result.
>
> *Source: Computer Security Institute (www.gocsi.com)*

e-fact

The April 2003 Deadline

Verified by Visa is quickly coming to the Canadian market. All Visa member financial institutions in Canada are required to make this service available to online merchants by April 2003. Even if your customers haven't been able to enroll with their financial institution, you will be protected from fraudulent purchaser disputes when you implement Verified by Visa and attempt to authenticate the cardholder. In addition to this incentive, you would be wise to investigate other means to reduce fraud and improve order efficiency at your doorstep before trying to pass responsibility back to the cardholder's bank. For example, you should ensure that you don't waste time shipping orders to incorrect addresses or fraudulent customers.

Electronic Commerce Indicator

Prior to the late 1990s, credit card transactions were classified as coming from either a brick-and-mortar retail store or from a mail or telephone order business (MOTO). Under this classification system, merchants selling products or services on the Internet were classified as MOTO merchants.

However, since the late 1990s, both Visa and MasterCard have required merchants to identify transactions that originate on the Internet by using a special code, called an electronic commerce indicator (ECI). Visa began requiring electronic commerce indicators in October 1997. MasterCard also introduced electronic commerce indicators in October 1997 and made them mandatory in October 2001. The purpose of the ECI is to differentiate Internet merchants from other types of merchants and identify the type of security used. The specific value for the electronic commerce indicator ranges from 5 to 9 and indicates the level of authentication used for each transaction.

Under the new rule, whenever a merchant requests authorization for an online purchase, the merchant must send the electronic commerce indicator electronically to the bank along with the authorization request. Many merchants are not aware of this requirement. However, it is mandatory and an essential part of using Verified by Visa properly. The company that hosts your Verified by Visa software (which can be an Internet payment service provider, an acquiring bank, or a major credit card processor) is responsible for setting you up so you are compliant with the electronic commerce indicator rules.

Computerized Methods of Authentication—Address Verification

You may have heard about a fraud-prevention service called address verification. It originated in the U.S. and is used widely by stores based in that country. However, it is not generally available in Canada, at least in the manner by which it operates in the U.S. Instead, an AVS-like service is available from some Canadian payment processors, such as the Card Holder Verified service available from Caledon Card Processing.

As you explore your options for processing payments, you will find that a great number of credit card processors will refer to AVS. It is important to understand how it works, even though it might not be available to you. What you can do is look for some unique Canadian alternatives based on AVS concepts that have emerged.

How does U.S.-Based AVS work?

In the United States, an address verification service checks to see whether the billing address and zip code provided at the time of the transaction match the cardholder's actual address and zip code on file with the issuing bank. When you accept orders on the Internet, you will be required to ask shoppers for both a billing address and a shipping address. If someone has stolen a credit card or the owner of the credit card has unknowingly lost the card, the person in possession of the card may attempt to use it fraudulently to purchase something in an online store. Experience has shown that most perpetrators of fraud do not know the billing address of the cardholder whose account they are using. As a result, they will usually make up a fictitious address, use a real address that belongs to someone else, or make the billing address the same as the shipping address.

This is where address verification comes in. When an online order is placed, the address verification service takes the zip code and the numerical part of the street address (excluding suite or apartment numbers) from the billing address and compares it to the information on file with the cardholder's issuing bank.

The result of the comparison is usually delivered to the merchant in the form of an alphabetic response code. The code will tell you whether there was an exact match, a partial match, no match on the information, or if the card issuer is in a foreign country.

The primary benefit of an address verification service is that it can help you undertake an extra review of the information provided with an order to determine if you feel comfortable fulfilling the order. When you review the orders in your online store, you'll be able to see the address verification code that each order received. What a merchant might do at this point will depend on how much risk he or she is willing to accept, keeping in mind that an Internet merchant is financially responsible for any fraudulent transactions that occur in an online store. Internet merchants are responsible for coming up with their own guidelines for handling address verification service codes.

You'll read quite a bit about AVS as you explore your payment options online. Although it is not generally available in Canada, you may find variations of AVS offered to you by your bank or merchant account provider. However, AVS isn't the best way to prevent fraud in your online store because criminals can easily work around it. Criminals are adept at using reverse look-up information on the Internet and elsewhere and can easily guess a cardholder's billing address. Because of this inherent weakness, Verified by Visa is a much more effective tool for fraud prevention. AVS does have a role to play in ensuring that cardholders have not unintentionally provided incorrect addresses, but, unfortunately, criminals can easily outsmart the system.

Fortune 500 companies only spend an average of 0.0025 percent of revenue on security.

Source: Forrester Research (www.forrester.com)

e-fact

Suggestions for Verifying the Legitimacy of Online Credit Card Orders

If you use some derivative of AVS, how do you handle orders that might seem suspicious, based on an inadequate address match?

If an online order you receive seems suspicious, or if you get an unfavourable address verification code, you can resort to directory assistance or online telephone directories such as Canada411 (canada411. sympatico.ca), Switchboard (www.switchboard.com), or InfoSpace (www.infospace.com) to verify the street addresses (both billing and shipping) and telephone numbers of individuals. You could also use one of the many reverse look-up services on the Internet (for Canada, check Infospace at http://www.infospace.com/info/reverse_ca.htm, and for the U.S., AT&T's AnyWho service at www.anywho.com), which will give you a name and telephone number for a given street address. You might even use an online mapping site such as MapQuest (www.mapquest.com) to verify that the addresses provided are legitimate.

However, keep in mind that only customers with listed phone numbers will appear in online or offline telephone directories. Also, if the customer has moved, the telephone directory may still list the customer's old address information, so you shouldn't assume that an order is fraudulent just because you couldn't verify the order information using a directory.

If the information you've been given matches the information in the phone directory, at least you'll know that the phone number belongs to, for example, John Smith, when you call the number to verify the order. If you call up John Smith and he denies placing the order, you'll know right away that the order is fraudulent. On the other hand, if John Smith confirms placing the order on your Web site, you still have no way of knowing that John Smith is actually the owner of the credit card that was used on your Web site. Although it is very unlikely that a thief would use his own address and phone number on a Web site when committing credit card fraud, anything is possible. To verify his identity, ask John Smith to give you the address that the bank has on file so you can run the address verification check again. If he is indeed the owner of the credit card, he should have no problem giving you another address that will match the one the bank has on file. This should result in a favourable address verification code.

While an address verification service or a Canadian derivative of such a service can help you cut back on fraudulent credit card orders, it isn't perfect. Also, it is obviously time consuming for a merchant to manually check or follow up on orders that seem suspicious. This is why it's important to implement Verified by Visa once it becomes available.

Authorization Versus Address Verification
It is important not to confuse authorization with address verification. They are completely different procedures. The authorization process checks the card number to see if it's valid, checks the customer's credit limit, and verifies that the credit card hasn't been reported stolen.

As explained earlier, authorization doesn't guarantee that the credit card isn't stolen. In contrast, an address verification service only confirms that the billing address provided on the merchant's Web site matches the cardholder data on file at the issuing bank. It is fully possible, therefore, for a credit card purchase to be authorized and receive an unfavourable address verification code at the same time. When a person places a credit card order on a Web site, an authorization request and address verification request are usually sent together over the Internet to the cardholder's issuing bank. The merchant will receive a response containing both the service's code and an authorization number.

If the address verification code is unfavourable (i.e., a mismatch or only a partial match), it will not result in the transaction being declined. The address verification code does not influence the authorization process in any way.

Seventy percent of merchants surveyed by the Worldwide E-Commerce Fraud Prevention Network say that fraud prevention tools can keep online fraud to a minimum.

Source: Worldwide E-Commerce Fraud Prevention Network
(www.merchantfraudsquad.com)

e-fact

Computerized Methods of Authentication—Fraud-Detection Software
Some payment processors have implemented fraud-screening services aimed at helping online merchants reduce the number of fraudulent transactions they process. Many of the services use neural network technology, which can analyze patterns in data and distinguish between a legitimate online order and one that is potentially fraudulent. Fraud-detection software takes many different factors into account when determining whether

an order may be fraudulent. For example, among other things, it will usually look at the IP address (a unique number assigned to every computer network connected to the Internet) of the purchaser and determine whether that address is located near the billing address provided by the customer. If the IP address is in Cairo and the billing address is listed as Rhode Island, the transaction will likely be flagged as potentially fraudulent.

Merchants will receive a "score" for each online order they receive, which will indicate the likelihood that the order is fraudulent. Based on this information, a merchant can decide whether or not to accept the online order. The cost of fraud-screening technology varies depending on the supplier, but it is usually priced on a fee-per-transaction or a flat fee-per-month basis. Examples of fraud-screening services include HNC Software (www.hnc.com) and Internet Fraud Screen from CyberSource (www.cybersource.com).

The benefits of using fraud-screening programs are numerous. Most importantly, by flagging potentially fraudulent transactions for you, these programs can help reduce the costly losses from online fraud. In addition, by using fraud-screening technology in your online store, you are providing a valuable service to your customers and consumers everywhere. Why? You are helping to stop credit card thieves in their tracks. This will help you develop goodwill with both your current and future customers.

In addition to considering the use of fraud-screening services in your online store, ask the company that is processing your credit card transactions what measures it has taken to minimize the occurrence of fraud. Some credit card processors maintain a "negative database" of credit card numbers and/or e-mail addresses that have been used to commit fraud in the past so they can automatically identify those purchases as fraudulent.

How to Implement Fraud-Detection Software in Your Online Store

If you plan to use one of the entry-level storefront creation services described in Chapter 2, fraud-screening software may already be built into the service or it may be available from the credit card processors or payment gateway you are using. Check with the storefront service or payment processor you are thinking of using to see if any type of fraud-screening service is available. If you are planning on using shopping cart software, you should investigate the different payment gateways supported by the software to see if any of them offer fraud protection. You may want to make fraud protection one of the features you look for when comparing different storefront solutions.

If you are building your own online store using more advanced e-commerce software, you can approach companies such as HNC Software and CyberSource directly and integrate their fraud-screening software directly into your Web site. However, keep in mind that these are expensive solutions.

More than 18 percent of U.S. online consumers say they are combating online fraud by using safeguards offered by Visa or MasterCard.

Source: GartnerG2 (www.gartnerg2.com)

e-fact

How Big Is Online Fraud?

One of the most hotly debated issues regarding online fraud is the extent of the problem. Some reports have suggested that fraud can be as high as 40 percent of online sales. Other studies have indicated that online fraud is a much smaller problem than most people think. So which is it? First, part of the reason for the discrepancy is that merchants experience different fraud rates depending on the products they are selling. For example, merchants selling adult entertainment services or digital goods, such as downloadable music, generally experience higher fraud rates than merchants in other product categories. Second, the amount of fraud a merchant experiences will depend on the precautions that merchant is taking. Merchants who carefully scrutinize every order looking for the warning signs of fraud, as listed above, will unquestionably experience lower rates of fraud than merchants who don't take similar measures. Third, many online merchants don't report fraud for fear of scaring away their customers or ruining their reputations. As a result, it is hard to know the exact amount of credit card fraud that occurs on the Internet.

Where Do Stolen Credit Card Numbers Come From?

Thieves can get valid credit card numbers from a variety of places, most of which don't require the thief to have access to a physical credit card. They may break into a merchant's Web site on the Internet to get numbers, as happened to Western Union. Alternatively, the thief may have "inside" access to credit card records at a store or business where you've previously made a purchase. Fraud is sometimes committed by people who work inside an organization and have authorized access to customer credit card files. It is also possible that your credit card number came into the hands of a thief via one of the credit card number generators on the Internet. These are programs or Web sites that randomly generate credit card numbers that seem to be valid but that might not have been issued. And, of course, a thief could get your credit card the old-fashioned way— by stealing it from your home, wallet, or some other location where it may have been left unprotected.

e-fact

Internet transaction fraud is twelve times higher than in-store fraud.

Source: GartnerG2 (www.gartnerg2.com)

Track Occurrences of Fraud

One of the most effective means of combating fraud is to keep good records. Keep an accurate list of all your chargebacks and the reasons for them. If you don't keep good records, fraud may be significantly cutting into your profits without your realizing it! By carefully documenting all of your chargebacks, you'll always know how much of a problem fraud is in your online store and you'll be able to identify weaknesses in your fraud-prevention techniques before they escalate. As we explained in Chapter 4, a chargeback can occur for a variety of reasons, such as defective merchandise, not just in cases of fraud.

Knowing why chargebacks are occurring in your online store can help you pinpoint problems and take corrective action. You need to determine whether the chargebacks are due to fraud or some other problem. For example, if your recordkeeping reveals that fraud is responsible for 80 percent of your chargebacks and 10 percent of your sales, you know that you have a problem with fraud. Further investigation may reveal that 75 percent of your fraud occurs with international orders. With this information in hand, you may decide to revise your policies for accepting foreign orders.

On the other hand, your investigations may reveal that most of your chargebacks are due not to fraud but to some other reason. For example, you may find that 80 percent of your chargebacks are due to unhappy customers who complained that the merchandise they received from you was not as described or pictured on your Web site. If this were the case, you would need to check the product descriptions and/or pictures on your Web site to ensure that they accurately describe the merchandise you are selling.

Obviously, you can't make the right decisions if you don't know why chargebacks are occurring and to what extent fraud is affecting your sales, which is why meticulous recordkeeping is so important. At a minimum, you should always know how big fraud is as a percentage of your gross sales.

As part of your recordkeeping, make sure you keep details of each fraudulent transaction that occurs in your online store, including the name that was used, shipping address, billing address, e-mail address, telephone numbers, and credit card number. This is called a fraud avoidance file. Keeping a fraud avoidance file will allow you to identify patterns in the data so you can protect yourself from future occurrences of fraud. For example, you may notice that several of your fraudulent transactions have the same shipping address. You could then flag that address and be on the lookout for any other orders that come through with the same shipping address. Depending on what payment gateway software you are using, you may be able to set up your online store to automatically reject any orders with that shipping address. Some of the payment gateway software in use on the Web today allows merchants to screen out orders that match specific card numbers, names, e-mail addresses, or billing/shipping addresses.

In addition, monitor the transactions in your online store for any suspicious activity that may indicate fraud. For example, purchases from overseas for high-ticket items should set off a red flag. Also be on the lookout for multiple purchases on the same credit card for valuable items that can easily be resold (e.g., electronics). You should also get in the habit of maintaining what's called a "negative card list." This is a list of problem credit card numbers that you should constantly screen your orders against. According to a security report from GartnerG2 (www.gartnerg2.com), it's not uncommon for merchants to be victimized multiple times by the same person!

Step #4: Let Customers Know Your Online Store Is Safe

Once you've addressed the issues we've discussed in Steps 1 to 3, you need to reassure your customers that your online store is secure.

It's difficult. The inherent insecurity of the Internet has led to problems with online stores and the concept of online shopping since the earliest days of the World Wide Web. After all, when the Web was born—around 1994 or 1995—many early pioneers set up what would now be considered primitive online stores. These stores usually consisted of Web pages that detailed products for sale, all of which pointed to a simple form that people could fill out to make a purchase. When the form was completed, it would be e-mailed to the owner of the store or would be printed automatically. At this point, the credit card number used in the transaction would be authorized using traditional telephone or terminal authorization methods.

e-fact

One in six online consumers has been the victim of credit card fraud; one in twelve has been hit with identity theft.

Source: GartnerG2 (www.gartnerg2.com)

Such methods of conducting a credit card transaction were insecure because the information was sent "in the clear" through the Internet. This meant that the credit card information, whether transmitted via the Web or e-mail, was never encrypted to make it inaccessible. In those early days, media reports soon began to emerge that it was not safe to use credit cards on the Internet. This was true, given the basic design of the Internet.

From the earliest days of the Internet, many people realized that the Internet was fraught with risk. The result was a great deal of consumer misapprehension and distrust. These concerns linger to this day. Despite the development of technologies like SSL, which are virtually impenetrable, many online shoppers are still reluctant to use their credit cards on the Internet.

Battling the Internet Security Myth

When you are selling products on the Internet, it is important to do two things:

1. Remind customers that their online transactions are secure.
2. Show them what you have done to protect their credit card information.

Remind Customers That Their Online Transactions Are Secure

First, assure customers that credit card transactions on the Internet in general, and more specifically on your online store, are secure. Let's put it this way: it's estimated that it would take someone a trillion years to break the strongest encryption forms (SSL uses 128-bit encryption) in use on many online stores today. That's how hard the technology is to penetrate. But even if an online store doesn't use SSL, the chance that someone could obtain credit card numbers transmitted over the Internet is very remote. Every day, tens of thousands of credit card transactions take place on the Internet. In the last several years, there have been few, if any, reports of credit card information being stolen as it passed from one computer to another. Consumers are at more risk giving their credit card numbers to a waiter in a restaurant than they are giving their credit card numbers to an online merchant. Therefore, the perception that credit card transactions on the Internet are inherently dangerous has little merit. Nevertheless, to be absolutely sure that no one steals the credit card numbers customers give you over the Internet, and to make your customers feel comfortable, use SSL encryption or some other form of encryption transmission.

Show Customers What You've Done to Protect Their Credit Card Information

Next, demonstrate to your customers that you've gone to great lengths to ensure that credit card transactions on your Web site are secure. To gain their confidence, we recommend you follow the advice about building online credibility that we provided in Chapter 3, "Tips for Building an Effective Online Store."

To recap, first describe how an online transaction works on your Web site. Walk customers through the process so they can see the security measures you've taken. In addition, tell them what technology you're using to protect them. For example, are you using SSL? Are firewalls in place to protect confidential data? Do you encrypt credit card numbers on your computers? Consider implementing a security guarantee or safe shopping guarantee on your Web site. As discussed in Chapter 3, security or a safe shopping guarantee is a promise by your organization that credit card transactions on your Web site will be safe.

Keep in mind that Visa, MasterCard, and American Express all have a zero liability policy for their credit card holders for purchases made online. This means that customers are never responsible for unauthorized transactions on their credit cards. It's a good idea to promote these policies on your Web site so customers will know they have nothing to fear when shopping online.

Step #5: Be Vigilant!

Finally, good online store security means constant vigilance. Find out what your Internet service provider or Web hosting company does to monitor newly emerging Internet security issues or, in the case of your own systems, what your information technology staff does. If you are using a storefront software package or shopping cart software, visit the vendor's Web site frequently and subscribe to any mailing lists offered to keep abreast of product enhancements and security issues. You should also visit the Web sites of anti-virus software vendors regularly to learn about new viruses before they strike. Most importantly, be alert for new Internet security threats that might affect your online store. As a step in this direction, you may want to consider obtaining a free membership in the Worldwide E-Commerce Fraud Prevention Network (www. merchantfraudsquad.com). Established by American Express, Amazon.com, and a variety of other e-commerce companies, the organization's goal is to help online merchants of all sizes fight e-commerce fraud.

Merchants who join the Network receive a number of benefits, including free advice to help combat online fraud and a directory of companies that specialize in anti-fraud technology. A membership registration form is available on the Network's Web site.

Finally, you need to recognize that online security is an issue that will never go away. Online storefront services, Internet service providers, credit card companies, financial institutions, security software companies, and online store owners are constantly introducing new technologies into the marketplace to help merchants protect the security and integrity of their online transactions. Because the online security technology marketplace changes so rapidly, it is important to keep an eye out for new products or services to help you protect both yourself and your customers from security threats and credit card fraud. In particular, monitor your competitors to see what products they are implementing.

---

e-fact

The risk of online fraud is greater for merchants who have high-volume transactions and/or a high percentage of cross-border sales. Fraud risk is also higher for merchants who sell digital content, electronically delivered software, or high-cost physical goods that are easily resold.

Source: GartnerG2 (www.gartnerg2.com)

Reviewing Your Five-Step Action Plan

We've covered a lot of ground in this chapter. Here, in summary, are the five key steps for securing your online store:

1. Develop a basic understanding of Internet security issues so that you can be a more effective advocate of good security on your online store. You don't need to become an Internet security expert—just educate yourself so you can protect your business and look out for the best interests of your customers. Also, make sure you comply with the requirements of your bank or merchant account provider.

2. Assess whether the company that builds your online store (if you've hired one) as well as the company that hosts it are taking appropriate security precautions. This will also give you a gut feeling for how serious they are about online security issues. As part of this interview process, find out what security measures, both physical and computer-related, they have implemented to protect your Web site from being accessed by hackers, vandals, and other unauthorized individuals.

3. Remember that there are two fundamental credit card transaction issues you need to address. First, make sure you encrypt credit card transactions on your online store. Currently the best technology for doing this is SSL. Second, protect yourself against fraudulent purchases. Because an authorization from the credit card company doesn't guarantee that a credit card isn't stolen, use the fraud checklist we provided earlier in the chapter to monitor your credit card orders for signs of fraud. Never ship an order that you think may be suspect.

    We highly recommend that you take advantage of new authentication methods such as Verified by Visa as they are introduced. Not only will these services make your customers feel safer, they will shift the liability for fraudulent online purchases to your bank and reduce your exposure to costly chargebacks originating from credit card fraud. For additional protection against fraud, keep good records and follow the suggestions we offered earlier in the chapter.

4. Include a section on your Web site to let customers know that you don't take security issues lightly. Describe what steps you've taken

to protect their credit card data and other personal information. As we suggested earlier, a security guarantee would be a good idea.

5. Finally, be alert for any new security holes or problems that might affect your online store. In addition, keep abreast of new technologies that can help you better protect your online store from vandals. Don't ever let your guard down.

6

Marketing Strategies for Your Online Store

"Four out of five Internet users arrive at a new Website via a search engine, so it's not surprising that search sites are increasingly viewed as the most important aspect of any online marketing campaign."

— *"The Great Search Engine Debate," Marketing Week,* November 29, 2001

Below are fourteen ways to promote your online store:
1. Know your audience
2. Your brand name
3. Offline marketing
4. Your retail store
5 Gift certificates
6. Product referral services
7. Affiliate programs
8. Permission marketing
9. Search engines and Web directories
10. Search engine optimization
11. Online shopping directories
12. Online advertising and sponsorships
13. Keyword-based advertising
14. Links from other Web sites

As the number of shoppers on the Internet has grown, so too has the number of Web sites and land-based businesses clamouring for a piece of the multitrillion-dollar e-commerce pie. As many Internet companies have discovered, even with a multimillion-dollar marketing campaign, it's difficult to get the attention of Internet users, even for just a split second. After all, Internet users are bombarded with so many advertisements every day and see so many Web sites that it's hard for any one firm to stand out.

One of the most difficult jobs you'll have as an e-commerce merchant is deciding on what combination of offline and online marketing techniques to use to promote your Web site. If you're a small business, that challenge is even greater on a tight budget. The right marketing mix depends on many factors, including the types of products you are selling, the types of people you are trying to target, and, of course, your budget.

In this chapter, we'll review a variety of different techniques for raising the profile of your online store and attracting shoppers to your Web site. Marketing your Web site is not an easy task, nor is it a short one. You'll need to work hard continuously to make sure your online store doesn't get lost among the estimated 2 to 3 billion pages of information on the Web.

Know Your Audience!

The key to successful marketing is very simple: know your audience. Before you spend any time or money on marketing, you need to know who your target market is. What types of customers are most likely to buy the types of products you are selling? For example, males or females? What age bracket? What income bracket? Are you trying to reach people with certain interests or skills? Once you know the profile of your typical customer, you need to find ways of reaching customers with that demographic profile. This may involve online advertising, offline advertising, or a combination of the two. But don't even begin to think about spending money on marketing until you've spent time thinking about who you are trying to reach. You may even need to do some market research to find out this information. We can't emphasize this step enough. Your marketing efforts won't be successful unless you are spending your marketing dollars in the right places.

Your Brand Name

One of the most important marketing assets you have is the name of your online store. Give it careful consideration. You should pick a name that's easy to remember yet distinct from other similar names on the Internet. Closely related to the issue of picking a name is choosing a suitable domain name. The domain name is the part of your Web site address that appears after "www." For example, the domain name for RadioShack Canada is radioshack.ca and the domain name for Hudson's Bay is hbc.com. Therefore, RadioShack's Web site is at www.radioshack.ca and Hudson's Bay's Web site can be found at www.hbc.com.

To avoid confusing your customers, you will want to have a domain name that is as close as possible to your organization's name. This will also make it easier for customers to find your Web site. For example, customers looking for Future Shop's Web site would probably start by typing "www. futureshop.ca" or "www.futureshop.com" into their Web browsers.

> Sixty-three percent of online shoppers in the United States rely on brand awareness as the leading factor in purchasing online.
>
> *Source: Goldman Sachs (www.goldmansachs.com), Harris Interactive (www.harrisinteractive.com), and NetRatings (www.netratings.com)*
>
> **e-fact**

.ca Versus .com

You have two basic choices when registering a domain name. You can register a domain name that ends in either .ca or .com. Some organizations choose to get both. For example, Future Shop owns both the futureshop.ca domain as well as futureshop.com (typing either "www.futureshop.ca" or "www.futureshop.com" into your Web browser will take you to the same Web site). .com stands for "commercial," while .ca stands for "Canada."

> The world's most valuable brands own an average of just over 1,000 domain names each.
>
> *Source: NetNames (www.netnames.com)*
>
> **e-fact**

What's the difference between a .com and a .ca address? If you have a Web site address that ends in .ca, you'll be immediately identified as a Canadian merchant. By their nature, .ca addresses promote your online store as being Canadian. This may discourage some American and international shoppers from clicking on your Web site address if they see it on a search engine or another Web site. On the other hand, .com addresses are more generic and simply identify you as being a for-profit organization. While .ca addresses can be used only by Canadian companies, .com addresses can be obtained by anyone in the world. In fact, there are thousands of Canadian companies with .com addresses.

Whether you use .com or .ca is up to you. Many online stores in Canada have chosen to promote a .com address rather than a .ca address. For example, even though Hudson's Bay Company has registered both hbc.com and hbc.ca, it promotes its online store as hbc.com. Future Shop does exactly the opposite. Although it owns both futureshop.ca and futureshop.com, it promotes its online store as FutureShop.ca. If you are part of a multinational retail organization with stores in the United States, you may need to use a .ca address if the .com address is already in use by your U.S. counterpart. For example, RadioShack's online store in the United States can be found at www.radioshack.com. RadioShack's Canadian online store is at www.radioshack.ca. However, even though your preferred .com address may be taken by another organization, it doesn't preclude you from registering a different .com address. For example, RadioShack Canada also registered radioshackcanada.com, so customers can use either www.radioshackcanada.com or www.radioshack.ca.

Because it's hard to predict what customers may type into their Web browsers when looking for you online, it's usually a good idea to register a couple of different domain names for your online store. For example, Hudson's Bay not only registered hbc.com and hbc.ca, they also registered hudsonsbay.com. Not only is this a good strategy to help customers find your online store, it will prevent cybersquatters from registering your domain name and then trying to sell it back to you. Whatever domain names you decide to use, it is important that they be short, easy for your customers to remember, and intuitive.

Finally, keep in mind that you don't have to have "www." in your Web address. Some organizations have chosen to drop it entirely, e.g., RadioShack Canada promotes itself simply as RadioShack.ca. If you do this, make sure your Web site is set up so people can get to it if they leave off the "www" portion of your address.

---

e-fact

Only 12 percent of North American companies' Web sites have multilingual versions.

Source: Convey Software (www.conveysoftware.com) and IDC (www.idc.com)

Domain Name Suffixes

Although most online stores in Canada have a domain name that ends in either .com or .ca, they are not the only domain name suffixes you can use for your online store.

Not-for-profit organizations usually have a domain name that ends in .org, which stands for "organization." If you are a not-for-profit organization, it is recommended that you use either a .ca address or a .org address, but not a .com address.

Another domain name extension you will come across is .net, which is used by many online stores on the Internet. Although .net addresses were originally intended for organizations that provided network-related (i.e., technical) services on the Internet, .net addresses have been used by organizations of all types in recent years.

Although .com, .net, .org, and .ca are the suffixes most commonly found on Web sites in Canada, a number of new suffixes have been introduced to accommodate the growth in the number of businesses and individuals using the Internet. They include suffixes such as .aero (for air transport companies), .biz (for businesses), .name (for individuals), .info (for use by anyone) and .museum (for use by museums). However, since these suffixes are so new, it will be a while before Internet users are accustomed to seeing and using them. Of all the new domain name extensions, the most appropriate one for for-profit businesses and online stores is .biz.

If you are setting up your company for the first time, you may want to find a suitable domain name first, and then decide on the name for your company and online store based on the domain name you have selected. Why? Domain names are a scarce commodity. Suppose you decide you want to set up an online store to sell scooters. You decide to call your business "The Scooter Shop" and you decide to incorporate your business. After the business is incorporated, you attempt to register the domain name scootershop.com, only to find out that's it already owned by someone else. Next, you try to register scootershop.ca and you find that it's also taken.

This is a hypothetical situation, but this is exactly the type of problem that many businesses encounter. They have registered or incorporated a business name only to find out later that they can't get the domain name they want because someone else has already registered it. That's why it's usually a good idea to secure a domain name before you choose your business name. By doing this, you avoid having a domain name that doesn't match your business name.

If you find yourself in a situation similar to the one we've described above with scootershop.com, you have a couple of options. The simplest option may be to find an available domain name and change the name of your business to match the domain name you've found. Alternatively, you could continue searching for a domain name that is similar to your company name, but that won't cause too much confusion with your customers. For example, you could see if a domain name like thescootershop.com or thescootershop.ca is available. However, even if thescootershop.com were available, you might not want to choose this domain name. Why not? It's too similar to scootershop.com, which, as noted earlier, is already owned someone else. In fact, if you go to www.scootershop.com, you'll see that the owner has already set up a Web site at this address.

This is problematic because your customers may inadvertently leave the "the" off when typing your address in their Web browsers, and they would end up at the above-mentioned site instead of yours. In essence, you'd be giving business to a competitor!

As this example illustrates, it's important that both your brand name and your Web site address be as distinctive as possible to avoid confusion with other similar companies selling on the Internet. There are tens of thousands of merchants on the Internet, all vying for attention, making it difficult for online merchants with similar names to get noticed. Even if the domain name you want is available, you should find out if similar names currently used by online stores might compete with yours. Many online merchants have found it necessary to change their names because their names were being confused with other similar names on the Internet.

Issues to Consider When Choosing a Name for Your Online Store
- Can you get a Web site address (i.e., domain name) for that name?
- Is the name too long?
- Is the name easy to pronounce?
- Are there other Web sites or online stores with similar-sounding or similar-looking brand names or domain names?
- Is your name unique or distinctive enough?
- Is your name memorable and does it make an impression?
- Is the name consistent with the image you want to project?

If you really want to have a domain name that someone else has already registered, such as scootershop.com, you could approach the owner and see if he or she is interested in selling the domain name to you. Many companies register domain names but never activate them. Even a company that is using a domain name may consider selling it to you for the right price.

Finally, if you believe that someone else has registered a domain name that infringes on a trademark you own, you can pursue legal action against the owner of the domain name in question.

How to Get a Domain Name

A good Canadian site you can use to see if a domain name is available is Webnames.ca (www.webnames.ca). To avoid paying for domain names in U.S. dollars, we recommend that you use a Canadian-based domain name registrar. Webnames.ca is just one of many organizations in Canada accredited to allocate domain names to organizations and individuals on the Internet.

The allocation of domain names in Canada is overseen by an organization called the Canadian Internet Registration Authority, or CIRA (www.cira.ca). The CIRA Web site provides a good overview of how to register a domain name in Canada. CIRA's site also provides a list of CIRA-certified registrars in Canada that you can choose from.

The cost to register a .ca domain name varies depending on the registrar you choose to work with. You don't need to have a Web site in order to register a domain name and most registrars will hold your domain name for you until you are ready to activate it on your online store. Many of the browser-based storefront solutions we discussed in Chapter 2 allow you to set up a domain name for your online store when you set up your account. This eliminates the need for you to go directly to a domain name registrar.

Once you have registered a domain name, you should make sure that no one is registering similar names or taking out a trademark similar to your name. To automatically track your name, consider using a service such as NameGuard, offered by NameProtect (www.nameprotect.com). NameGuard is free and it will constantly monitor new U.S. trademark applications and domain name registrations for you and flag any applications/registrations that are identical or very similar to your domain name. It's a great way to keep informed of any potential threats to your brand name. This service will also help you identify companies that may be trying to register your domain name as a trademark. This is a potentially serious situation as you could lose your domain name if a trademark similar to your brand name is granted to someone else.

Offline Marketing

Perhaps the most important piece of advice we can give you in this chapter is this: don't restrict your advertising and promotional efforts to the Web. Online stores often rely too heavily on online advertising at the expense of more traditional advertising vehicles that may actually produce better results.

Throughout this chapter, we'll review a number of different ways for you to promote your online store on the Web, but it's important not to get too dependent on online marketing for your success. Think about the types of customers you are trying to attract and what the best methods would be to reach those customers. Rather than spending your money advertising on the Web, you may find that a more effective strategy would be to place advertisements in a couple of well-targeted magazines. For example, Noggintops (www.noggintops.com), an online hat retailer, has spent very little on Internet advertising. Instead, the company did some market research and identified a number of magazines that appealed to the company's target market—outdoorsmen. Ads featuring the company's Web site address were then placed in those magazines. In fact, the bulk of Noggintops's marketing budget has been spent on offline ads. Our point is that you shouldn't ignore traditional advertising vehicles. Think about how you can use both print (e.g., newspapers, magazines, journals) and broadcast media (radio and television stations) to reach your target audience. Be realistic with your expectations.

It is important to use your imagination when looking for ways to raise awareness of your Web site. Don't limit yourself to radio, television, and print media. Why not advertise your Web address in buses or subways? How about on newspaper polybags, the plastic bags that newspapers are wrapped in when they are delivered to your front door? Or in movie theatres? Some organizations have even gone so far as to include their Internet addresses on bananas! The possibilities are endless.

In many respects, marketing a Web site is no different from marketing any product or service. The challenge is to find innovative ways to get the word out.

Online consumers can be divided into eight different categories: Shopping Lovers, Adventurous Explorers, Suspicious Learners, Business Users, Fearful Browsers, Shopping Avoiders, Technology Muddlers, and Fun Seekers.

Source: Brigham Young University (www.byu.edu)

e-fact

Your Retail Store

If your business has a brick-and-mortar retail presence, use it to promote your online store aggressively. Include your Web address on your receipts, invoices, and shopping bags, and print it on your catalogues and sales literature. Make sure your Web address is advertised prominently both within your store and outside if you can. Many retailers, unfortunately, don't leverage their retail presence in this way.

Gift Certificates

Brick-and-mortar stores give out gift certificates, so why not online stores too? Consider offering an online gift certificate that your customers can purchase online and then e-mail to a family member or a friend. Gift certificates purchased online make great last-minute gifts because they can be sent by e-mail to arrive almost instantly. The recipient can then visit the store's Web site and apply the gift certificate toward the purchase of any products offered by the store.

Electronic gift certificates not only make great gifts, they're a great way to attract new customers into your online store! Keep in mind that you could increase the attractiveness of gift certificates significantly if you allow customers to specify that they be e-mailed on a particular day, thus becoming the perfect gift for a birthday, anniversary, etc.

Product Referral Services

Many people find out about Web sites through word of mouth. So make it easy for your customers to tell other shoppers about your online store.

For example, as customers browse through your Web site, they may come across products that their friends, co-workers, or family members may be interested in. Or a customer may want to tell a friend or family member about a product that he or she would like to receive as a gift. That is why you should make it easy for customers to refer friends and relatives directly to specific product pages on your site. For an excellent example of how this can be done, visit Hudson's Bay's online store (www.hbc.com). On every product page is a link that says, "e-mail a friend." Customers who click on the link will see a window pop-up on their screen, and they'll be asked to provide the name and e-mail address of a friend. Once the customer fills out the required information, the friend will receive a notice by e-mail with a link to product information on HBC's online store. A referral mechanism like this is an effective way to bring more people into your Web site!

Affiliate Programs

Many online merchants have built successful affiliate programs for their online stores. An affiliate program involves paying owners of other Web sites a commission for referring customers to your online store. In other words, you reward other Web sites for sending new customers to you. The idea is to find Web sites with visitors who are likely to be interested in your products. To this end, Web site owners usually try to find merchants who sell products or services related to their own Web sites. A Web site with movie reviews may try to affiliate with a merchant who sells movies, and a Web site devoted to golf may align itself with a Web site that sells sporting goods or athletic apparel.

It's in a Web site owner's best interests to identify merchants with compatible products because it will increase the likelihood of making lots of sales. For example, suppose you sell travel guidebooks. You could sign up travel agencies to your affiliate program and invite them to create links from their Web sites to yours. You would then pay the travel agencies a commission on any book sales and/or leads you get from their customers.

Online retailers with affiliate programs compensate affiliates in different ways. Some merchants pay affiliates strictly for sales (pay-for-sale), while other merchants compensate affiliates if the referred customers turn into potential leads (pay-per-lead). Other programs may compensate affiliates if a person clicks on an ad on the affiliate's site, regardless of whether that person turns into a lead or ends up purchasing a product. This is called a pay-per-click program. There are also pay-for-performance programs, where an online store pays an affiliate if a referred visitor performs a specific action, like filling out a form, completing a survey, or viewing a specific page of information.

Affiliate programs can be extremely powerful because they allow you to increase your revenues by having your brand name displayed on dozens (if not hundreds) of complementary Web sites. There are literally thousands of affiliate programs on the Web. Staples (www.staples.com), the office supply chain, is one of many online stores that have been successful with their affiliate programs. Staples.com reports that over 30,000 Web sites have signed up since the program was created.

The commission that you offer your affiliates is up to you. Some firms, like Staples, offer a percentage of sales; other firms offer flat fees. Commission structures can range from less than 1 percent to as high as 50 percent. Flat-fee commissions, on the other hand, can range anywhere from $0.05 to $50.00 or more.

Affiliate programs are popular because they're an inexpensive way of attracting customers to your Web site. In essence, you are getting other Web sites to market your online store for you. Moreover, it doesn't cost a lot to get such a program underway. Best of all, you can pay affiliates only if they generate sales or leads for you.

Nine out of ten Canadian Internet users receive an average of twenty-two e-mails every day.

Source: Ipsos-Reid (www.ipsos-reid.com)

e-fact

Affiliate programs do have a number of drawbacks, however. It can be a burden to keep track of all your affiliates and process all the commission cheques. Keep in mind that the number of affiliates you have really has no direct bearing on how successful your program will be. For example, even though Staples.com has over 30,000 affiliates, what really counts is the number of affiliates that are sending significant amounts of business to Staples.com. A lot of online stores have found that many of the Web sites that sign up for their affiliate programs bring in very little business. That is why when you are setting up an affiliate program, your focus should not be on signing up as many Web sites as possible, but on finding those Web sites that can generate the most sales for you. Obviously, it's hard to screen Web sites in advance, but eventually you will discover which affiliates are valuable and which are irrelevant to your business.

As you might imagine, setting up an affiliate program can take a lot of time and effort, especially once you begin to sign up hundreds of affiliates. You need to screen applicants, track sales from each affiliate, prepare commission cheques, and spend time on other administrative functions that take you away from running your online store. For this reason, many online retailers hire organizations called affiliate program providers, which specialize in running affiliate programs on behalf of online stores. Three of the biggest affiliate program providers are Be Free (www.befree.com), Commission Junction (www.cj.com), and LinkShare (www.linkshare.com).

The cost of using an affiliate program provider varies. For example, Be Free (which prefers to deal with large organizations with annual revenues in the millions) charges a one-time fee of $5,000 plus a monthly commission of $3,000. Commission Junction, on the other hand, is more suitable for small businesses. Commission Junction charges a one-time set-up fee of US $1,295 and receives 30 percent of payout rates of US $1 or greater and US $0.30 per transaction of payout rates less than US $1, with a monthly minimum of US $250. For example, if you decide to pay your affiliates US $10 every time a referred customer buys a product from your online store, you would pay Commission Junction 30 percent of US $10, or US $3, for a total of US $13 per transaction (US $10 goes to the affiliate and US $3 goes to Commission Junction).

Which affiliate program provider is best? It all depends on how big you are and what you are looking for. Services and program features vary from one affiliate program provider to the next, so make sure you carefully consider all your options before making a final decision.

One of the major benefits of using an affiliate program provider is that these organizations will help you find Web sites that can begin linking to your online store immediately. If you're a small business with very little brand name recognition, how is anybody going to find your Web site to learn about your affiliate program? Affiliate program providers maintain a directory of participating online stores so that interested Web sites can quickly find merchants they want to work with.

e-fact

By 2005, online advertising will be an US $18.8 billion market in the United States.

Source: GartnerG2 (www.gartnerg2.com)

Affiliate program providers enable merchants to screen applications and reject those Web sites they don't want to work with. Typically, once an application is submitted by a Web site owner, it is forwarded to the merchant, who reviews it and decides whether to accept the site into its affiliate program. Merchants aren't obligated to accept every application. The merchant must consider factors such as how much traffic the Web site receives and the type of content it contains.

Understandably, merchants are very selective about which Web sites they choose for their affiliate networks because they want to protect their image and not associate themselves with any sites that may not reflect the company's tastes or standards. Merchants usually choose to work with those Web sites that have content and objectives similar or complementary to their own.

Seventy-five percent of online consumers think banner ads are annoying.

Source: Valentine Radford (www.valentineradford.com)

e-fact

If you're interested in setting up an affiliate program for your online store, start by contacting the various affiliate program providers we listed earlier. When comparing affiliate program providers, think about the following questions:

- How much does the affiliate program provider charge you to set up an affiliate program? As explained earlier, affiliate program providers have different pricing schemes, so make sure you understand how you will be charged. Also find out if there is a minimum escrow amount you must pay the affiliate program provider (this money is used to pay commissions to your affiliates).
- What types of affiliate programs are offered?
- What type of performance tracking is provided? How sophisticated is the performance tracking? What information do the performance reports contain? How frequently are the reports updated? Are the reports delivered by e-mail in addition to being available on the Web?
- How user-friendly is the affiliate management software? What account management features does the software offer? How easy is it for you to update or replace the ads being served by your affiliates?
- What tools exist for communicating with your affiliates, both through the affiliate program provider's Web site and by e-mail? Can you target certain affiliates with special offers?

- Who issues the commission payments to your affiliates? Do you have to, or will the affiliate program provider do that for you?
- How does the affiliate program provider guard against fraud? For example, what happens if the same person clicks on a link to your Web site fifty times? Do you have to pay for that?
- Is there any flexibility regarding payout rates? Can you customize payout rates for different affiliates, or do you have to give the same commission structure to everyone?
- Does the affiliate program provider offer any client services to assist you with the implementation of your affiliate program, or are you expected to do it on your own? What technical support is available for both affiliates and merchants? Are any consulting services offered?
- How easy is it for Web site owners to join an affiliate program and create links from their Web sites to yours? To get the answer to this question, we recommend you visit some of the leading affiliate program providers on the Web and try signing up with some of their merchants. By doing this, you'll get a first-hand look at how the process works from an affiliate's point of view.
- What types of link options are available for your affiliates?
- Does the affiliate program provide support for e-mail-based affiliate programs? For example, how easy is it for an affiliate to include links to your Web site in their e-mail messages to customers?
- How many affiliates are part of the company's network? What is the company doing to recruit new affiliates into their network?

If you decide to work with an affiliate program provider, don't rely solely on its Web site to promote your program. You should also promote it on your own Web site and get other Web sites excited about the possibility of joining your affiliate program. For a good example of how this can be done, visit the Web site of Victoria, B.C.-based Abebooks.com (www.abebooks.com), an online bookseller. They have implemented a successful affiliate program in partnership with Commission Junction, and they promote the program on their Web site.

One final note about affiliate programs: many merchants, in addition to running their own affiliate programs, have become affiliates of other Web sites in order to generate some extra cash. If you are thinking about becoming an affiliate of another Web site, we recommend that you proceed carefully. Having an advertisement for another company on your Web site can compromise your image and credibility. Sometimes the mere presence of an advertisement on your site can make you look unprofessional to potential and existing clients, especially if it promotes products or services unrelated to your current line of business. Accepting advertising for another company is an implied endorsement of that organization and its product or services. Make sure you are prepared to make that type of public statement. Keep all these factors in mind when considering whether to accept advertisements for other merchants on your Web site.

This advice may seem contradictory since the whole purpose of an affiliate program is to get other Web sites to display advertisements for your company. Won't they look unprofessional by displaying advertisements for you? Maybe. When you create an affiliate program, you have to keep in mind that you're inviting other companies to display your brand name on their Web sites and it's never a good idea to let another company take control of your brand name. Sometimes it's hard to control how your affiliates display your advertisements and in what context. When launching an affiliate program, make sure you carefully screen your affiliates. In addition, you may want to build some rules into your affiliate program so you will have some recourse in case an advertisement for your company is presented in a way you find objectionable.

Permission Marketing

You may have heard the term "permission marketing" before. It refers to a method of online marketing where the merchant asks permission from online shoppers to market to them directly by e-mail. Permission marketing is also known as opt-in e-mail.

Permission marketing follows two main principles. First, you market only to those customers who have specifically told you that they are interested in receiving e-mail messages from you. Second, you must give away something in order to get a customer's e-mail address. In other words, shoppers are more likely to give you their e-mail address if you give them an incentive or reward for doing so. This incentive could be a discount on a future purchase, entry in a sweepstakes or contest, or just the promise of relevant advice by e-mail.

The easiest way to undertake permission marketing is by establishing a mailing list that customers can join. You can then use the mailing list to

e-fact

Seventy-nine percent of Canadian Internet users say they have received junk e-mail.

Source: Ipsos-Reid (www.ipsos-reid.com)

send out a newsletter or promotional messages to your customers. Your challenge is to find ways to get customers to join your mailing list. In the box below, we've listed some of the more common techniques to hook customers into giving out their e-mail addresses.

Six Ways to Get Customers to Join Your Online Mailing List

1. Place a sign-up box on your home page or on every page of your online store.
2. Have a pop-up window appear on the customers' screens when they visit your Web site, inviting them to join your mailing list.
3. Run a contest or sweepstakes. Customers get a chance to win by joining your mailing list.
4. Invite customers to join your mailing list when they are making a purchase from your online store.
5. Ask customers if they want to join your mailing list whenever they contact your organization by telephone or e-mail. If you operate a retail store, have your salespeople ask your customers for their e-mail addresses when they are making a purchase.
6. Invite your customers to suggest the names and e-mail addresses of people they know who may be interested in being added to your mailing list. Then contact those individuals and invite them to join!

Electronic mailing lists are an excellent marketing tool and one we'll talk more about in the next chapter on customer loyalty.

Another Way to Conduct Permission Marketing: E-Mail Brokers

In addition to setting up your own mailing list, you may want to consider using the services of a permission marketing firm or e-mail broker to help you develop and implement an e-mail marketing campaign. E-mail messages typically have higher response rates than banner advertisements, so this type of marketing is gaining more popularity. In Canada, one of the leading e-mail brokers is 24/7 Canada (www.247canada.com), a subsidiary of 24/7 Media, a large Internet-based advertising network. 24/7 Canada has several million Canadian e-mail addresses in its permission-based e-mail database that you can use to reach your desired target audience.

> More than half of U.S. companies do nothing to customize their Web sites for global visitors.
>
> *Source: International Data Corporation (www.idc.com)*

e-fact

Other e-mail brokers include NetCreations (www.netcreations.com) and PostMasterDirect (www.postmasterdirect.com). PostMasterDirect, for example, has accumulated e-mail addresses from thousands of Internet users who have signed up to receive advertising messages targeted to their personal interests. Incredibly, PostMasterDirect's database now exceeds 50 million e-mail addresses! You can "rent" these e-mail addresses and use them to advertise your online store.

> Adding the phrase "click here" or "click now!" to a banner ad increases the response rate between 10 percent and 40 percent.
>
> *Source: Beyond Interactive (www.gobeyond.com)*

e-fact

Another firm active in the permission marketing industry is Yesmail.com (www.yesmail.com), which has a database of over 31 million e-mail addresses (yes, 31 million!).

Many businesses feel awkward about sending marketing messages by e-mail because junk e-mail is disliked by almost everyone on the Internet, but as we noted earlier in the chapter, the very essence of permission marketing is getting an Internet user's permission to market to them by e-mail. Although it seems hard to believe, every person in the Yesmail database has consented to having his or her e-mail address added to the database, so you shouldn't worry about offending anyone.

> The weather influences online shopping! Residents of colder states were the most likely of all U.S. consumers to shop online during the 2001 holiday season.
>
> *Source: BizRate.com (www.bizrate.com)*

e-fact

Definitely explore the use of e-mail brokers and permission marketing firms, but make sure any service you hire has obtained permission to use the e-mail addresses in its database, otherwise you risk annoying hundreds, if not thousands, of Internet users with your advertising.

Search Engines and Web Directories

Many online shoppers use a search engine or a Web directory to find something on the Internet. A search engine is a Web site that indexes the contents of millions of Web pages. A Web directory, on the other hand, organizes Web sites by category so Internet users can easily browse them.

The search engine and directory businesses have undergone massive changes in the last few years. During the early Internet years and leading up to the explosion of dot-com businesses in 1998, 1999, and 2000, there were lots of popular search engines. Everyone seemed to use different search engines, so making sure visitors could find your Web site meant submitting your Web site to each of the major search engines. Today, the number of popular search engines and directories has shrunk and most people seem to use either Google (www.google.ca) or Yahoo! (www.yahoo.ca). Nevertheless, this doesn't mean you should completely ignore some of the remaining search engines and directories. While sites like Lycos and AltaVista don't have the following they used to have, they still attract significant numbers of Internet users.

In the box on the facing page, we've listed the names and addresses of the most popular search engines and Web directories. Take the time to ensure that your Web site is registered with all of these sites. By registering with all the major search engines and Web directories, you have the best chance of being found by online shoppers regardless of which search engine or Web directory they use.

In years past, getting your Web site added to a search engine or directory was a trivial affair. You simply went to the search engine or directory's Web site and typed your Web site address into a form. Within a few days or weeks, your Web site was added to the search engine or directory's database. There was no cost to do this and most search engines wouldn't have dreamed of charging companies who wanted to get listed in their databases. It was also frowned upon for a search engine or directory to give preferential treatment to advertisers.

Popular Search Engines

AltaVista	www.altavista.com
AOL.COM Search	search.aol.com
Ask Jeeves	www.askjeeves.com
Excite	www.excite.com
FAST	www.alltheweb.com
Google	www.google.ca
Overture	www.overture.com
Hotbot	www.hotbot.com
Lycos	www.lycos.com
MSN Search	search.msn.ca or search.msn.com
Teoma	www.teoma.com

Popular Web Directories

LookSmart	www.looksmart.com
Open Directory Project	www.dmoz.org
Yahoo!	www.yahoo.ca or www.yahoo.com

Today, virtually all of the search engines and directories charge for listings and give you a way to increase the prominence of your Web site on their search results pages. In the next section, we'll show you how to get your Web site listed in a search engine or directory.

Search Engine and Directory Databases

Before you submit your site to any search engine or Web directory, you need to understand how their databases are developed. A search engine database is significantly different from a directory database. Automated computer programs called spiders develop search engine databases. These programs scour the Internet and index the full contents (i.e., all of the words on a page) of the millions of Web pages they find. These databases help you find instances of words or phrases on Web sites, similar to a book index.

Web directory databases, on the other hand, list Web sites that have been selected by people and organized into distinct categories. These databases are similar to the Yellow Pages, which organize businesses by topic, and are more useful when you are interested in a specific topic.

The confusion comes from the fact that all the major search engine Web sites now have not only a search engine database, but also a directory database. Often when you do a search on such a Web site, the results that are returned include information from both databases. This is also true of Web directory sites, most of which have a search engine database in addition to the directory database.

As an Internet merchant, the ideal situation is to have your Web site included in both databases of any search engine or directory Web site.

e-fact

Only 1 percent of Internet users have tried to block online ads using ad-blocking software.

Source: Forrester Research (www.forrester.com)

Submitting Your Web Site to a Search Engine Database

When you launch a Web site, make sure it is included in the search engine databases of both search engine Web sites and directory Web sites. There is a good possibility that the spider programs these Web sites use will find your Web site, index it, and add it to their search engine database. However, it could take months for these spiders to discover your site, if they ever do. For these reasons, it's generally a good idea to visit each search engine and directory Web site and manually submit your Web site for inclusion in their search engine databases.

Getting Added to a Search Engine's Database

To add your Web site to a search engine, go to the particular search engine site and look for a link or button somewhere on the main page that says "Add Your Web Site," "Add a Page," or "Add URL." (URL stands for uniform resource locator. It means the same thing as "Web address.") Click on the button or link, and you'll usually be directed to a Web page where you can fill out a form and submit your Web site.

Getting Added to a Web Directory's Search Engine Database

Web directory sites may have their own search engine spiders that develop their search engine database, but quite often the Web directory partners with an existing search engine. For example, the Yahoo! directory has partnered with the Google search engine. When you do a search in Yahoo!, it looks for matches within category names and Web site titles and comments as they appear in the Yahoo! directory, and then looks for matches in the content from individual Web pages found by the Google search engine. If you are listed in Google, this means you will also appear on the search engine portion of Yahoo! (i.e., it's a two-for-one deal). These alliances are very common, so it is worth the time to find out who is partnered with whom and submit your Web site to all the relevant search engines. This will maximize the number of search engine databases you appear in.

> Forty-five percent of online shoppers choose e-commerce Web sites based on word-of-mouth recommendations.
>
> *Source: Jupiter Media Metrix (www.jmm.com)*

e-fact

Submitting Your Web Site to a Directory Database

First and foremost, make sure you register your Web site with the major directories we listed earlier in the chapter, as well as with any other Web directories that pertain to your industry. Look for information on their home pages explaining how you can submit your Web site to their database. You generally have to decide which category and subcategory would best represent your site. In some cases you do not have a choice. For example, if you are an online store wanting to be listed in Yahoo! you must list your site in the "Business and Economy" section. Look through each Web directory's help section to make sure you understand what is required and how to go about properly registering your site.

Second, visit the Web site of each of the major search engines and determine who provides their Web directory listings. (When you submit a Web site to a search engine, your Web site is added to the search engine's full text database, but it does not necessarily get your Web site included in the directory portion of the search engine.) Then visit each of those Web directories and submit your Web site if you haven't already done so.

Is There a Charge to Submit Your Web Site to a Search Engine or Web Directory?

In most cases, the answer is yes. Submitting your site to a search engine or directory used to be free, but in an effort to become profitable and give businesses more control over how their pages are included in search engine directory listings, most search engines and directories now charge for submissions. In some cases, you may be given an option to submit your site for free, but there is usually no guarantee that your Web site will ever get into the search engine or directory this way, plus it could take weeks or even months for your site to appear.

In some cases, paying a search engine or directory to get your Web site included in their database only guarantees that your Web site will be *considered* for inclusion. Check each search engine and Web directory's help files for specific information.

---

e-fact

By 2005, U.S. revenues from e-mail advertising will total US $1.5 billion.

Source: GartnerG2 (www.gartner.com)

Should You Pay to Have Your Web Site Included?

You may be wondering whether it's a good idea to pay to have your Web site included in a search engine and/or Web directory. If a paid submission service is available, we recommend that you use it. In some cases, it's the only way to get your Web site added to a search engine or Web directory. In other cases, paying a fee may expedite the inclusion of your Web site in a search engine or directory.

On those Web sites where both free and paid submission services are offered, we still recommend that you opt for the paid submission. Why? As noted earlier, with free submission, there is no guarantee that your Web site will ever make it into the search engine or Web directory. By paying, you guarantee that your Web site will at least be considered for the search engine or Web directory in a timely manner. If you use the free submission option, you could wait forever!

One search engine service you should definitely consider paying for is Inktomi (www.inktomi.com). Inktomi doesn't provide a search engine on its own Web site, but it provides the technology that powers popular search engines like AOL Search (search.aol.com) and MSN Search (search.msn.com). Inktomi allows you to pay to have a Web page, series of Web pages, or even your entire site added to the Inktomi database. Once your Web site is included in Inktomi's database, your site will automatically be included in all the search engine sites that use Inktomi's search engine, including Microsoft and America Online. We suggest you visit Inktomi's Web site for the latest available pricing information.

Using Automated Submission Programs

It doesn't take a lot of time to register your Web site yourself with each of the major search engines and Web directories. However, some online store owners prefer to use a commercial service such as Submit It! (www.submitit.com) or Position Pro (www.positionpro.com), which automatically registers your Web site with selected search engines and directories. If you want to use a commercial search engine submission service, stick to services such as Submit It! or Position Pro, which are run by well-known, reputable companies. We strongly recommend that you steer clear of companies that send you unsolicited advertisements by e-mail, promising to list your business in hundreds of search engines for only a couple of hundred dollars. There are countless search engine submission scams out there, and most of them will get you nowhere.

However, a few words of caution. Before using any automated submission service, find out which search engines and Web directories it will submit your site to. Don't expect these services to submit your Web site to all the major search engines/directories and remember that even though there are dozens of search engines and directories out there, only a handful are used by a significant number of people. Be skeptical of any search engine submission program that promises to submit your Web site to "hundreds" of search engines because there are only a handful that really matter. In addition, you should recognize that some of these services may not be able to submit your site to the search engines and Web directories that require payment for listings. Therefore, before you sign up with any of these services, make sure you fully understand what you are getting.

Increasing Your Likelihood of Success

Throughout this section, we have talked about the process of submitting your site to search engines and Web directories, and we indicated that you might or might not manage to get listed. If you are paying a search engine or Web directory to be considered for inclusion in their site, you might want to know if there are ways to design your site so it is more acceptable for inclusion. Look through the help files of search engines and Web directories to see if they provide any hints, tips, and other guidance for your site. Some, such as LookSmart (www.looksmart.com), have submission criteria you should follow.

There are no hard and fast rules—it can be a very subjective process. You can be judged on content, appearance, relevance of your site, and other factors. All we can suggest is that you make your site and/or online store as comprehensive and professional as possible, which will undoubtedly increase the likelihood of being listed.

Are Search Engines and Web Directories Effective Marketing Tools?

Working with search engines and Web directories can easily consume a lot of time, and many Web site owners wonder whether the effort is really justified. As noted in the opening quote of this chapter, Internet users rely heavily on search engines and Web directories when they are looking for information on the Web, so it's definitely worth your time to ensure that your Web site is included in all the major search engines and Web directory sites. At the same time, we caution you against going overboard and relying too much on search engines and Web directories to attract traffic to your Web site. Search engines and Web directories are just one part of the marketing mix. Your marketing activities should include using offline media such as radio, television, and print, as well as the other techniques we discuss in this chapter.

Later in the chapter, we discuss the use of Web site analysis tools such as WebTrends, which can help you analyze which search engines and Web directories your customers are using to find you. These types of tools can help you understand how much traffic on your Web site originates from search engines and Web directories. Furthermore, by using these tools, you'll be able to quantify the importance of being listed on various search engines and Web directory sites.

---

e-fact

Shoppers between the ages of forty-five and fifty-four are more likely than younger shoppers to be extremely satisfied with their online shopping experiences.

Source: Retail Forward (www.retailforward.com)

Search Engine Optimization

As we noted at the beginning of this chapter, there are billions of Web pages on the Internet and thousands upon thousands of online stores, all clamouring for attention. When you submit your Web site to a search engine, you typically don't have any control over where your Web site will show up in the site's results list when someone searches for your company name or a keyword related to your business. For example, suppose you open an online store selling pasta products. If someone goes to a search engine and types in "pasta," you're not going to be very happy if your Web site shows up on the seventh page of results. Most people won't bother looking past the second or third page of results when they are doing a search on the Internet. In fact, many won't even bother looking beyond the first page of results. This means that if your Web site doesn't show up in the top ten or so results for a specific search such as "pasta," the chances of your Web site being seen by Internet users diminish considerably.

Hence, an important part of online marketing involves a process known as search engine optimization—ensuring that your Web site receives prominent placement on all the major search engines. Ideally, you want your Web site to show up on the first page of results when a potential customer searches for a keyword related to your business. Since Web directories are typically compiled and organized by people rather than machines, you really can't optimize your position on a Web directory (unless you pay for positioning). That's why the practice of optimization is typically limited to search engines, which use complex algorithms to rank Web pages according to a user's search criteria.

Before we go any further, you need to understand three things. First, there is no simple method or magical formula for achieving good rankings on search engines. Second, every search engine uses different ranking criteria. This is why the same search performed on different search engines will yield different results. It is also why your Web site may be ranked number one on one search engine but appear in the twentieth position on another. Third, search engines are constantly changing the algorithms they use to index Web sites, so your site's ranking on any given search engine may be in a continual state of flux. Many search engines provide some information on their Web sites to help you understand how they rank Web pages. Visit each search engine, read the help files, and try to accommodate as many of the suggestions as possible. Reading help files like this will help you understand what you need to do to get a good ranking for your Web site.

Eighty-eight percent of online consumers have made a purchase as a result of receiving permission-based e-mail.

Source: DoubleClick (www.doubleclick.com)

e-fact

There are some general tips we can offer to help you improve your Web site's ranking on various search engines:

1. Don't use graphics at the expense of text. When you create the front page of your Web site, make sure you include lots of text that accurately describes your business. When search engines index your Web site, they can't read images. If your home page consists of a bunch of graphics and very little text, it's difficult for the search engine to properly index your Web site. This means it will be hard for Internet users to find it when they are using a search engine to find products and services. We're not suggesting that you eliminate graphics on your home page. However, if you use graphics, make sure they are accompanied by lots of text.

2. Integrate important keywords into your text. Choose important keywords related to your business and make sure those keywords are strategically positioned on your Web site. For example, this is the advice that Lycos provides to Web site owners: "Decide two or three terms or phrases on which to focus your efforts—the 'hot' keywords that our seven million users are most likely to search for. Give those words priority in your HTML. Important words should appear more frequently in larger headings and closer to the top of the screen if not actually in the page title. An introductory paragraph with descriptive text that mentions your 'hot' keywords will help our software create a better abstract of your site."

   This doesn't mean you should blatantly repeat the same words over and over again on your Web site. Rather, when building your Web site, think carefully about the words you choose to use on your home page. Make sure you integrate words and phrases into your Web site that you think Internet users will use to search.

3. Use meta tags. Meta tags are pieces of HTML code that you in- clude in your Web site to influence the description that search engines give your Web site (this is called a description meta tag) and to influence the words that search engines associate with your site (this is called a keywords meta tag).

   If a Web site is using meta tags, you can see them by looking at the site's HTML code (the hypertext markup language is the computer code used to build pages on the World Wide Web). If you are using the Netscape Web browser, you can look at a Web site's HTML code by choosing "View" from the list of options at the top of your browser, then selecting "Page Source" or "Document Source." If you are using Microsoft's Internet Explorer browser, select "View" from the menu bar, then "Source." As noted earlier, there are two types of meta tags you should consider using on your Web site—a description meta tag and a keyword meta tag.

To show you what a description meta tag looks like, we've reproduced below the one from HMV's (www.hmv.com) Web site:

<meta name="description" content="HMV offers you the largest selection of CDs, Cassettes, Videos and DVDs to buy online at great prices.">

The information in a description meta tag is used by the search engine to create a summary description of your Web site. When an Internet user is browsing through a list of search results on a search engine, the summary description from the meta tag is sometimes used to create the abstract that appears under the title of each Web page. In the case of HMV, the abstract that would show up on a search engine is "HMV offers you the largest selection of CDs, Cassettes, Videos and DVDs to buy online at great prices." Since many Internet users rely on these abstracts to help them decide which Web sites to visit, it is important to create a site summary for your Web site that accurately and concisely reflects its purpose.

Your keywords meta tag should contain a list of keywords related to the products or services you sell. Usually, businesses include keywords that their customers would most likely search for on the Internet. For example, a company selling music products, like HMV, would include keywords related to different types of music as well as keywords related to the types of music products they sell. HMV's keywords meta tag is reproduced below:

<META NAME="keywords" CONTENT="HMV music DVD CD video canada online store records DVD store HMV Music CDs DVDs new music new releases movies classical music hmv.com gifts super audio rock music country music jazz music blues music techno music soul

music alternative music piano music swing music folk music reggae music funk music HMV Canada hmv canadian music compact disc compact discs pop R&B urban classical videos cassettes speciality music pop music soundtracks r&b urban music heavy metal electronica hard rock adult contemporary classic rock rock and roll rock & roll new music indie indie music modern rock movie soundtracks rap music rap acid jazz dance music singles CD singles hip hop DJ rhythm & blues opera baroque contemporary classical composer orchestral music instrumental music operetta vocal performance choirs choral choral music classical video classical DVD zydeco music cajun music big band instrumental jazz jazz solo gospel music bluegrass new country karaoke francophone new age music world music sound effects spoken word instrumental cds on sale videos on sale DVD on sale online shopping ecommerce buy online top ten new releases box sets boxsets service selection">

As you can see, HMV's keywords meta tag includes dozens of keywords related to its business. A keywords meta tag increases the likelihood that your Web site will appear higher on a search engine's results list whenever someone does a search using any of the words or phrases that appear in your tag. When creating your keywords meta tag, we recommend that you don't repeat the same keyword multiple times in order to increase your Web site's ranking. Some search engines have been known to lower a Web site's ranking in their index or remove the site altogether if they discover this type of abuse.

e-fact

Opt-in e-mail advertising is the most effective online advertising tool for converting Internet users into actual buyers.

Source: Survey of 2,000 companies by Harris Interactive (www.harrisinteractive.com) and Jupiter Media Metrix (www.jmm.com)

We mention meta tags in this book because so many Web sites use them and because they are often cited as an important online marketing technique. However, the main problem with meta tags is that only some of the large search engines recognize them—many ignore them altogether. Furthermore, on search engines that do pay attention to meta tags, the tags are only one of several factors used to rank your Web site for users' searches. Therefore, meta tags are not a guarantee for getting your site to the top of search engine results list. They are just one of many ways to improve your site's chances of being found on the Web. If you want to find out whether a particular search engine recognizes meta tags, visit its Web site and read the online help files.

Depending on what type of storefront software you used to build your online store, you may or may not be allowed to modify the HTML code that makes up your Web site. In order to create and modify your meta tags, you will need to access the HTML code behind your Web site. Check with the company that hosts your online store to see if this is possible. If you are not technically inclined or if you're not familiar with HTML code, you may want to hire someone to create your meta tags for you.

4. Give your Web site a descriptive title. Make sure the title of your Web page describes your business rather than simply mentioning the name of your business. The title of your Web site is what appears at the very top of the Web browser's window—it is not what appears on the front page of your Web site. For example, Foot Locker has been using the following title on its Web site: "Foot Locker | Jordan basketball shoes, running shoes and football shoes by Nike, Reebok, and Adidas."

Many search engines pay special attention to the words in your Web site's title when they index your Web site. In other words, you may increase the likelihood of appearing higher up on a search engine's results list if the words in your title closely match what an Internet user is looking for. By using the terms such as "Jordan basketball shoes" and "football shoes" in its title, Foot Locker may improve its ranking in a search engine when someone is searching for those terms. What you shouldn't do is create a title like "Welcome to my Web site" or "Welcome to Foot Locker's Home Page." Titles like this are much too generic. You should try to create a title for your site that is as descriptive as possible.

Your Web site title is also important for another reason: it often appears in a search engine's list of results. Creating a good descriptive title for your Web site is one way to make it stand out from the rest. Internet users are most likely to click on Web sites that have clear, descriptive titles. The title of your Web site is controlled by a line of HTML code in your Web site called the title tag. For example, if you look at the HTML code used by Foot Locker's Web site, its title tag looks like this: <TITLE> Foot Locker | Jordan basketball shoes, running shoes and football shoes by Nike, Reebok, and Adidas</TITLE>

You may need to have access to your online store's HTML code in order to change or modify your Web site's title.

5. Get other Web sites to link to you. Contrary to popular belief, many search engines look at factors other than what's on your Web site in order to determine where to rank your site. For example, if many other Web sites link to you, this can help you get a good ranking on some search engines. For example, Google (www.google.ca) takes the number of Web sites that link to you into consideration when deciding where to rank your site when someone does a search on its site. Generally speaking, the more Web pages that link to your Web site, the more "popular" your Web site is, and the higher your Web site will rank on Google. We'll discuss the issue of Web site linking in more detail later in the chapter.

e-fact

Thirty-five percent of companies say they would not pay for complete performance monitoring of their Web presence from a third party.

Source: Zona Research (www.zonaresearch.com)

Using a Search Engine Optimization Company

Many Web site owners, sometimes in sheer desperation or frustration, have enlisted professional help to improve their rankings on search engines. The reason that search engine optimization (SEO) firms are in such demand is explained well by Aaxis (www.aaxis.com), one of many companies that specialize in search optimization: "Over the years the search engines and directories have gotten smarter and keep changing to the point where we have to work very hard to keep up to date on what techniques work best (or at all). Search engine optimization has become a very complex, sophisticated practice that requires constant research, practice, and reevaluation to be effective." In other words, understanding how search engines work is a complicated business and most Web site owners don't have the time, inclination, or skill to manage their own Web site rankings.

Search engine optimization has become a popular business in recent years. Players in this industry include such firms as Aaxis (www.aaxis.com), iProspect.com (www.iprospect.com), Outrider (www.outrider.com), and Web-Ignite Corporation (www.web-ignite.com). There are also many small organizations that offer search engine optimization services. Many Web design and online advertising firms have also entered this market.

Search engine optimization firms use a variety of practices to improve Web site rankings for their clients, practices that are beyond the scope of this book. If you're thinking of hiring a SEO firm, evaluate your options carefully. While many search engine optimization companies do honest, legitimate work, there are just as many companies that use unethical or useless techniques and are looking for a way to earn a fast buck. We know of one company, for example, that was duped out of over $2,000 after hiring a company that promised to get it listed in the top ten rankings of all the major search engines. The rankings never materialized, and the company never saw its money again. If the company you hire uses unacceptable techniques to boost your search engine ratings, you could wind up having your Web site banned from a search engine forever.

Search engine optimization is such a complicated business that it's hard to know what techniques a company is using. Even if they're explained to you, you might not understand, and this of course makes it difficult for you to figure out whether a certain practice is ethical or unethical. Before choosing a SEO company to work with, check references and ask to see the company's client list. This will help ensure that you are dealing only with legitimate companies that use industry-accepted practices.

Where to Learn More About Search Engines and Search Engine Optimization

The search engine industry is in constant flux, so it's important to stay on top of changes in the industry. The resources listed in the box on the next page will help you keep up-to-date on the latest news and opportunities in this fast-moving field.

Search Engine Watch (www.searchenginewatch.com), perhaps the best online resource for the latest search engine news, has two free newsletters that you can subscribe to—"Search Day" (a daily newsletter) and "The Search Engine Report" (a monthly newsletter). If you purchase a Search Engine Watch membership (approximately US $89 per year), you'll receive a subscription to "The Search Engine Update," a twice-monthly newsletter on search engine promotion and optimization issues. For more information any of these three newsletters, visit searchenginewatch.com/about/newsletters.html.

In addition to the three newsletters mentioned above, we highly recommend the I-Search mailing list, a free electronic discussion group devoted to understanding search engine technology. You can access the archives and subscribe by visiting www.adventive.com.

Online Resources About Search Engines and Search Engine Optimization

About.com Guide to Web Search	websearch.about.com
Search Engine Watch	www.searchenginewatch.com
Search Engine Forums	www.searchengineforums.com
Search Engine Showdown	www.searchengineshowdown.com

Online Shopping Directories

Many of the major search engines and Web directories have shopping areas on their Web sites that showcase selected merchants and list merchants by product category. In Canada, sites like Yahoo! Canada (www.yahoo.ca) and Canada.com (www.canada.com) have entire sections to devoted to online stores. There are also sites like RetailCanada.com (www.retailcanada.com), which provides a directory of hundreds of Canadian merchants that sell online.

Many Internet users use shopping directories when looking for online merchants, so it's a good way to get exposure for your online store. However, to get your online store included in one of these shopping directories, or to become one of its "featured stores" or "premier merchants," you may need to pay for a listing or be an advertising partner. America Online, for example, has advertising agreements with a number of large retailers that give these retailers prominent positioning on AOL's shopping directory.

Online Advertising and Sponsorships

A common online marketing strategy is to advertise on or sponsor other Web sites that attract the types of people who may be interested in buying your products and services. For example, if you sell luggage products, you could advertise your online store on Web sites that attract travellers. You could also approach a travel Web site, such as one of the popular travel-booking services like Travelocity.com (www.travelocity.com), about sponsoring a section of their site. In addition, many of the popular travel magazines, such as *Condé Nast Traveler* (condenet.com/mags/trav/), have their own Web sites and accept advertising.

Plain text is the most popular form of e-mail marketing.

Source: Direct Marketing Association (www.the-dma.org)

e-fact

Most Web sites that accept advertising have a section somewhere on the site that provides contact information for advertising inquiries as well as a general overview of advertising and sponsorship opportunities. Before choosing to advertise on or sponsor any Web site, make sure the site is reputable. You don't want to advertise on any Web site with a doubtful reputation or credibility. You should also obtain audited statistics that tell you how many visitors the site receives on a daily, weekly, and monthly basis. Also try to obtain as much demographic information as you can— data on what types of people the site attracts, including average age, income, and spending habits. You want to ensure that the Web site is attracting the same types of people who buy your products; otherwise your advertising dollars will be wasted. You should also find out what types of advertising or sponsorship packages are available and how much they cost. Will the Web site let you track how well your ad is performing? How frequently can you access usage statistics?

In the sections that follow, we'll look at some of the most important and best-known forms of online advertising.

Banner Advertisements

Online advertisements come in all different sizes and shapes, just like newspaper ads. However, online advertising often appears in the form of a banner ad. A banner ad is a small rectangular graphic that can be either animated or static. You can design it yourself, or have someone design it on your behalf. People can click on a banner ad to be immediately connected to the advertiser's Web site.

Banner advertisements are usually sold on the basis of page views (every time a person accesses the Web page that contains the banner ad that a page view occurs), and page views are usually purchased on a cost-per-thousand (CPM) basis. For example, if you are told by a Web site that the cost of banner advertising is $10 per CPM, this means that you pay $10 for every thousand page views. This might represent 1,000 people looking at that page, or it might mean 500 people each looking twice at that page. There are hundreds of thousands of Web sites on the Internet that accept banner advertising, including all the major search engines and Web directories. The key is to find Web sites that attract the types of customers you are interested in reaching. There is no sense in buying banner advertising on a Web site if its visitors aren't in your target market.

As we will discuss shortly, advertisers have had limited success with banner ads. That fact, combined with a slump in the technology sector, has meant that the cost of banner ads has fallen dramatically in recent years. The cost of a banner ad may also be influenced by the length of the contract you sign and where on the Web site the banner ad will appear. For example, a banner ad placed in the health section of a Web site may cost more than an advertisement in the gardening section if the health section attracts more visitors. As you might expect, banner advertising on high-traffic sites like Yahoo! is typically more expensive than banner advertising on less popular sites.

The cost of purchasing banner advertising (or any type of online advertising for that matter) is also affected by the way a site charges for advertisements. The cost may be based upon the number of "impressions" or page views (i.e., the number of times your ad is actually viewed on a Web page), or instead it might be based upon the number of "click-throughs" (i.e., the number of times people actually click on the ad).

When purchasing banner advertising, you may come across terms like "run of category," "run of site," "run of network," and "fixed category," especially if you are inquiring about advertising on a search engine or Web directory. Run of category means your banner advertisement will be rotated throughout a specific category area on the site (e.g., gardening, travel, etc.), run of site means your banner ad will be rotated throughout the entire Web site, and run of network means your banner ad will be rotated throughout a network of other Web sites that are somehow related to the site you are advertising on. Fixed category advertising allows you to display your banner ad on the same page within a category all the time.

If you need help putting together a banner advertising campaign for your online store, there are a couple of options. One is to use a company like 24/7 Canada (www.247canada.com) or DoubleClick (www.doubleclick.com), which have expertise in online ad campaigns. You could also contact an advertising agency to get their assistance in putting together a banner ad campaign for your online store. An advertising agency can help you plan the campaign and identify Web sites that reach the types of demographics you are interested in. Another alternative is to contact one of the big media conglomerates in Canada, organizations such as CanWest Global and Bell Globemedia. These organizations own dozens of Web sites for the newspapers and broadcasters they manage, and they may be able to help you run a banner campaign across their respective Web sites. Some major Web sites handle their own advertising sales, while others have appointed an online marketing firm such as 24/7 Canada to sell advertising opportunities on their behalf.

Finally, you may want to hire an online advertising consultant to help you with an online advertising campaign. The Internet Advertising Bureau of Canada (www.iabcanada.com) may be able to refer you to someone if this option is of interest to you.

Of the 8,000 Web sites selling advertising in the United States, the top twenty sites receive 80 percent of the revenue.

Source: GartnerG2 (www.gartnerg2.com)

e-fact

How Effective Are Banner Ads?

We won't kid you—companies have had mixed success with banner ads. Many online shoppers say they ignore them. Indeed, only 3.2 percent of online advertisers surveyed by Forrester Research said that banner ads were effective in attracting traffic to their Web sites.

The problem is that most Web users who see banner advertisements don't click on them. In fact, the average click-through rate for banner ads is less than 1 percent. In other words, no more than 1 percent of all the Web users who see banner ads on the Internet actually click on them. That's an even lower response rate than direct mail! But such a dismal click-through rate doesn't mean that banner ads are ineffective. Some companies run banner advertising campaigns with the goal of increasing brand awareness. If this is the goal of your online advertising campaign, the number of click-throughs isn't as important as the number of people who see your banner ad. However, if you are trying to attract traffic to your Web site, you may find that banner advertising is not a good investment.

Given the disappointing performance of banner ads for many businesses, if you're thinking of purchasing banner ads to attract visitors to your online store, make sure you keep your expectations in check.

Pop-Up and Pop-Under Ads

While banner ads remain one of the most visible types of online advertising on the Web, they're not necessarily the most effective means of online advertising. In fact, as we noted previously, the click-through rates for banner ads are very low. In recent years, companies have begun experimenting with other types of online advertisements, the most popular new format being pop-under ads. A pop-under ad (sometimes called a pop-behind ad) is an online advertisement that suddenly appears underneath your Web browser while you are looking at a Web site.

> **e-fact**
>
> Nearly half (49 percent) of active Internet users agree strongly that pop-up ads get noticed, compared to 33 percent for banner ads.
>
> *Source: Knowledge Networks/Statistical Research (www.statisticalresearch.com)*

It's hard not to notice pop-under ads if you use the Web because they are constantly popping up on your screen. Ironically, what makes these ads so annoying is what makes them so effective—you can't ignore them and you have to click the ads to make them disappear from your screen. In fact, some companies report that pop-under ads are ten to twenty times more effective than traditional banner ads.

A pioneer in the use of pop-under ad technology is a U.S. company called X10 Wireless, which manufactures miniature surveillance cameras. X10's pop-under advertisements have been seen by so many millions of Internet users that one particular month, it was reported that 33 percent of the entire online population had visited their Web site. Needless to say, that's an incredible success rate.

In addition to pop-under ads, there are also pop-up ads, which are ads that appear or pop up on top of the Web site you are viewing.

Despite their apparent effectiveness at attracting traffic to your Web site, both pop-under and pop-up ads tend to be intrusive and therefore may annoy consumers. If you end up using this form of online advertising, be aware that you might end up receiving complaints from some of your current and prospective customers. However, despite the risks of using these types of radical advertising techniques, many companies feel that the benefits far outweigh the disadvantages.

> Sixty-two percent of Web users say that pop-up ads interfere with their use of Web sites.
>
> Source: Knowledge Networks/Statistical Research (www.statisticalresearch.com)

e-fact

Other Advertising Formats

The limited success that companies have had with banner ads has led to a search for other effective forms of online advertising. Besides static banner ads, other online advertising formats include skyscraper ads (a fixed-position vertical banner ad), floating ads (ads that always stay in view, even when you scroll up or down a Web page), multimedia ads (ads that have sound or moving images), and interstitials/transition ads (large-screen ads that are displayed on a user's screen before a desired Web page appears).

If you want to learn more about the different types of online advertising formats, excellent sources of information include the Interactive Advertising Bureau (www.iab.net) and the Internet Advertising Bureau of Canada (www.iabcanada.com). Yahoo!'s Marketing Solutions Web site (solutions.yahoo.com) also contains a wealth of information on the different ad formats that Yahoo! supports, along with pictures and rates.

> Seventy-two percent of Internet users close pop-behind ads (ads that pop open underneath your Web browser window) without looking at them.
>
> Source: E-Poll (www.e-poll.com)

e-fact

Keyword-Based Advertising

Many Web sites, including all of the major search engines and directories, offer keyword-based advertising. Here's how it works: You purchase one or more words and/or phrases related to your business. When a customer searches for any of those words, an advertisement for your Web site will appear. The advertisement may be a banner ad or another type of online advertisement that you create. For example, suppose you own a business that sells pools and spas. You could purchase the word "pools" on Yahoo! so that whenever someone searches for this word, a banner ad for your company will appear on the search results screen.

Keyword-based advertising doesn't necessarily involve banner ads. For example, Google (www.google.com), one of the Internet's most popular search engines, allows you to create text ads for your company that will be displayed whenever an Internet user searches for a keyword you've selected. Google's program, called AdWords (adwords.google.com), is affordable for small businesses because no minimum deposit or spending minimum is required. The cost of an AdWords campaign on Google depends on how many times your ad is displayed (the number of "impressions" it receives) and the position of your ad (ads are rotated through different positions on the page based on their performance).

Keyword Research

Part of the challenge in using keyword-based marketing on the Internet is to pick the keywords your customers are most likely to use when they are searching for the types of products or services you sell. This will likely require a bit of brainstorming for you and your staff. Once you've come up with one or more keywords you want to use, services like Google's AdWords will show you how popular they are. This will give you an estimate of how many times your ad is likely to be displayed and how much your ad campaign will cost. What Google doesn't do, however, is help you come up with the right keywords. That's your job.

Some search engines publish what Internet users are searching for, and the results can be quite fun to look at. For example, Lycos has a service called "The Lycos 50 Daily Report" (50.lycos.com), which shows some of the most popular search terms on its site. Google publishes a similar list of popular search terms called Google Zeitgeist (www.google.com/press/zeitgeist.html). You may also want to check out MetaSpy (www.metaspy.com), a service operated by MetaCrawler, one of the popular search engines on the Internet. MetaSpy will show you what Internet users are searching for right now. You'll certainly find these services entertaining, if not inspirational as well!

Bidding on Keywords

Some search engines (and directories) make it possible for merchants to bid on keywords so that their Web sites will show up near the top of the results list whenever someone searches for those words. These are called pay-for-performance or pay-per-click search engines. The price you pay depends on how much you are willing to spend every time someone sees your listing and subsequently connects to your Web site. For example, if you bid $0.25 per click-through, you would pay $0.25 for every visitor the search engine sends you. The company that bids the highest for a certain keyword will be listed first whenever someone searches for that keyword; the company that bids the second-highest will be listed second, and so on. Merchants can bid against one another, which means your ranking on the site is never guaranteed as long as there is another merchant willing to bid more than you.

Under this type of a bidding system, you don't pay each time your ad is displayed—you pay only for the visitors who come to your Web site. However, this introduces a problem—the more customers that come to your Web site, the more you have to pay. This type of spending could get out of hand if your campaign is very successful. For this reason, most sites that offer keyword bidding will allow a cap on the amount of money you spend.

The two most popular sites for keyword bidding are Overture (www.overture.com) and Google (www.google.com). Google's service is called AdWords Select. Overture was one of the first search engines to offer this type of advertising opportunity to Web site owners and was the only major search engine offering such a service until Google introduced their own competing service in 2002. The nice thing about these services is that you can sign up immediately with your credit card. With Google's AdWords Select, your ads appear instantly!

> Pay-per-placement search engines produce the highest return on investment of any Internet advertising technique.
>
> *Source: Survey of 2,000 companies by Harris Interactive (www.harrisinteractive.com) and Jupiter Media Metrix (www.jmm.com)*

e-fact

When bidding on keywords, pick words or phrases that potential customers would use to find Web sites like yours. The more keywords you bid on, the more traffic your Web site can potentially receive. Don't restrict yourself to only one keyword. For example, if you sell pasta sauces, don't just bid on the word "pasta"—bid on terms like "pasta sauce" or "gourmet pasta" as well.

One word of caution—when bidding on keywords on a search engine or directory, there is no guarantee that your Web site will receive lots of traffic. It all depends on how many people are searching for the keywords you select. In some cases, you may find that your investment results in a minimal amount of traffic to your site.

To learn more about pay-per-click search engines, a useful resource is PayPerClickSearchEngines.com (www.payperclicksearchengines.com).

Links from Other Web Sites

One of the least expensive online marketing techniques, but perhaps one of the most effective, is getting links from other Web sites. Contact suppliers and manufacturers you work with to see if they will link from their Web sites to yours. Why is this important? Customers often visit the Web sites of manufacturers or suppliers when they are researching a purchase. If the manufacturer provides a link from its Web site to yours, the customer may end up making the purchase online from you. This manufacturer benefits from the sale as well, given that you are selling more of its product, so it's in the manufacturer's best interest to link to you. You should also contact any industry associations you belong to and ask if they will link to you. The idea is to get as many Web sites to link to you as possible. As noted earlier, this can even help you with your placement on search engines, since many search engines take a site's links into account when they decide where to rank it.

If you want to see how many other Web sites are linking to your site, a really useful resource is a Web site called LinkPopularity.com (www.linkpopularity.com). Just enter your Web site address into the box on the LinkPopularity.com Web site. The site will generate a free report listing all of the Web sites linked to yours. You can also use the LinkPopularity.com site to monitor how many Web sites are linking to your competitors' Web sites. If appropriate, you can contact these Web sites directly and ask them to link to your online store, too!

Monitor Activity on Your Web Site

Once you invest in an online store, you owe it to yourself to monitor how well your investment is paying off. The number of sales you receive is only part of the picture. You also want to track the number of people who visit your online store, where they come from, and which search engines and directories they use to find you. This information is vital to your business because it will help you assess whether your marketing activities—both online and offline—are succeeding or failing.

If you don't already receive daily traffic statistics from your Internet service provider, Web hosting service, or online store service, or if the reports you receive don't provide enough detail, consider signing up for one of the many third-party Web site analysis services. In the box below, we've listed some of the more popular programs for monitoring how your customers are using your Web site.

Popular Web Site Analysis Programs

Vendor	Web Site
HitBox	www.hitbox.com
SuperStats	www.mycomputer.com
WebTrends	www.webtrends.com
Stats4You	www.stats4you.com

These programs will prepare reports that show you how many visitors your site receives every day. Depending on the program, you may also be able to receive valuable marketing reports that will show you which Web sites your customers are coming from, how much time customers are spending on your Web site, and which Web pages on your site are the most popular. There may also be a variety of technical reports that show you everything from which operating systems your customers have to which browsers they are using.

In Chapter 3, we pointed out that two-thirds of all online shoppers abandon their shopping carts before making a purchase. Some Web site analysis programs can help you with this problem by analyzing what path customers are taking through your site and what the most popular "exit pages" are so you can minimize customer abandonment. (The exit page is the last page visited by the customer before the customer leaves your site.)

One of the most powerful Web site tracking programs is WebTrends (www.webtrends.com). WebTrends has a number of different versions of its program, ranging from a free "Personal Edition" to an "eCommerce Edition," which will allow you to track sales activity on your Web site. WebTrends is capable of generating very detailed sales reports for your Web site.

Most Web site analysis programs work over the Web so you won't need to install or configure any software. You simply cut and paste some code into your Web site and the service will start to track your Web site immediately. You'll be given a password and user name, and you can log onto the vendor's Web site at any time to access your reports. In some cases, you may have the option of purchasing Web site analysis software and installing it on your computer. Users of WebTrends, for example, can choose between browser-based versions that provide real-time statistics over the Web and software versions that can be installed on your computer and integrated with internal databases. Several versions of WebTrends software are available depending on your reporting needs and the complexity of your Web site. If you decide to go with a software solution, you will need to have access to the Web servers of the company that hosts your online store. Check with the company hosting your online store to find out if you can use WebTrends. Free fourteen-day trial versions of several of the WebTrends software programs can be downloaded at www.webtrends.com.

e-fact

Unsolicited e-mail messages account for 10 percent of the total e-mail volume in the United States.

Source: eMarketer (www.emarketer.com)

When evaluating a Web site analysis program, don't buy strictly on the basis of price. Examine the types of reports you are getting (many services will give you a free trial period or access to sample reports on their Web site) from two perspectives. First, how easy are the reports to read and understand? Second, what type of reports are available and how much detail is provided? In particular, find out if the program will allow you to do any type of advanced e-commerce tracking, such as tracking sales or the performance of your advertising campaigns. While WebTrends, for example, has an e-commerce edition that can track sales information from an online store, most of the entry-level Web site analysis programs do not provide this type of e-commerce tracking. If you are interested in tracking orders on your Web site and monitoring sales activity for all the products in your online store, you should be prepared to spend significantly more for a product with these capabilities. However, you may not need these types of tracking options if the storefront solution you are using already provides them.

A final note—some Web site analysis services provide free versions of their programs that you can install on your Web site and use immediately. In addition, from time to time, you may come across companies offering free Web site counters that provide very basic visitor tracking on your Web site. Although these services are free, we suggest you think carefully before using them. Why? Many of these free services require you to place an advertisement on your Web site. For example, the free version of the WebTrends service requires you to place a small advertising button on the Web pages you are tracking. Although your Web site visitors can't see your reports, the button is essentially an advertisement on your Web site, and you have to decide whether this is acceptable to you. Some of the free services require you to place a counter on your Web site that displays the number of visits your Web site has received. Do you really want to disclose this information publicly? For example, a customer may visit your Web site and decide not to place an order with you because your counter shows that your Web site has received only twenty visitors in the last six months!

Where Can I Get More Tips on Online Marketing?

The world of online marketing is constantly changing, and there are some great Internet resources that you should read regularly to stay on top of the latest trends and opportunities in this area. We've listed some great marketing-related Web sites in the box below. If you're new to Internet marketing, we recommend that you look into the University of British Columbia's Internet Marketing Certificate Program. You can take the course completely online, so you can enrol from virtually anywhere in Canada. For more information, visit www.tech.ubc.ca/netmark.

Internet Resources for Online Marketing	
ClickZ	www.clickz.com
Iconocast	www.iconocast.com
Internet Advertising Bureau of Canada	www.iabcanada.com
Internet.com	www.internet.com
MarketingSherpa.com	www.marketingsherpa.com

Another great source of information on Internet marketing in Canada is AIMS, the Association for Internet Marketing and Sales (www. aimscanada.com). Membership is free and is open to senior decision makers in the Canadian Internet and new media industry who are interested in sharing their knowledge and experience with their peers across Canada. AIMS has an active mailing list for its members, which provides an open forum for the exchange of information about best practices and experiences with Internet marketing and sales. There are more than 2,800 subscribers on the list, so it's an extremely valuable source of information for anyone interested in Internet marketing and sales issues, especially as they pertain to Canada.

7

Building Customer Loyalty
in Your Online Store

"Acquiring customers may be Job One for many e-tail marketers. But only those e-tailers that convert new customers into loyal ones will thrive over the long term."

— "The Kings of Repeat E-Business," *E-Commerce Times,*
February 21, 2002

One of the best indications of success in online retailing is how many repeat customers you have. This is a much more important measurement than how many customers you have because repeat customers tend to be more loyal and spend more than first-time customers. In addition, it costs more to acquire a new customer than it does to keep the customers you already have. Hence, when creating your online strategy, you should focus not only on acquiring new customers but on keeping them so they will return to your online store again and again.

In this chapter, we review a variety of different techniques to help you keep customers coming back to your store and spending more. They are:

- Customer service
- Site registration/personal accounts
- Contests and promotions
- Limited time offers and Internet-only specials
- Gift reminder services

- Reorder reminder services
- Online communities
- Interactive events
- Compelling content
- Loyalty programs
- Opt-in e-mail
- Personalization

By no means are we suggesting that you implement all of the different ideas we recommend in this chapter. The types of loyalty strategies you use will depend on the type of business you're in, the types of customers you cater to, and, of course, your budget.

Customer Service

Perhaps it goes without saying, but we would be remiss if we didn't mention it here. The most important thing you can do to build customer loyalty on your online store is to provide excellent customer service and a satisfactory shopping experience for your customers. That, more than anything else we suggest in this chapter, will bring customers back to your store again and again.

What does a satisfactory shopping experience entail? Many things, including selling high-quality, reliable products, delivering your products on time, answering e-mail messages promptly, giving customers a broad range of delivery options, making the checkout process as fast as possible, providing a user-friendly and easy-to-use Web site, and following all the advice we offered in Chapter 3, "Tips for Building an Effective Online Store." We'll repeat what we said at the beginning of Chapter 3: selling on the Internet is all about exceeding customer expectations.

e-fact

Sixty-three percent of U.S. companies say that e-mail marketing was their most effective customer-retention tool.

Source: Direct Marketing Association (www.the-dma.org)

Site Registration/Personal Accounts

In an effort to increase customer loyalty and make online shopping more convenient, many online retailers allow customers to register for their own personal shopping accounts.

When customers register for a personal account on an online store, they usually receive special benefits such as faster checkout times, advance notification of promotions, online wish lists, and other features that aren't available to shoppers who don't register on the site. Gap (www.gap.com) is one of many online retailers that offer site registration on their online stores.

Giving customers personal accounts is really no different from getting customers to store their billing information and address books on your Web site for faster checkout, strategies that we discussed in Chapter 3. One of the benefits of getting customers to register with you is that you can collect their e-mail addresses and, with their permission, send them information about special offers and promotions by e-mail.

> Seventy-five percent of online consumers who participate in loyalty pro-
> grams say they are not what motivates them to make an online purchase.
>
> *Source: Jupiter Media Metrix (www.jmm.com)*

e-fact

By offering personal accounts to your customers, you ultimately benefit from increased customer loyalty. After all, wouldn't you be more inclined to use an online retailer that sends you special offers by e-mail and that stores your preferences on their Web site so you can make your purchases faster? The key is to make online shoppers feel like they are getting something special when they set up an account with you.

How you package services on your Web site can make a big difference in how they are perceived by your customers. For example, Avon (www.avon.com) has a program called the A-List in which customers receive "VIP advantages" in exchange for registering on its Web site. Customers who join Avon's A-List receive e-mail notification of new products and special sales at the Avon online store. In addition, they can store their shipping and billing information on the site so they won't have to enter it each time they order. Joining is free and only requires customers to fill out a registration form. In essence, by bundling site registration into its A-List VIP program, Avon is promoting its site registration in a way that's more appealing to customers. Avon calls its registered customers "members" and plays up the special benefits that customers get by registering on the site.

Preferred customer programs like the one Avon has implemented are a great way for online merchants to build long-term relationships with their customers. The more special features and benefits you can offer your customers, the more convenient and appealing it will be for them to shop with you. Naturally, if you make it easy for customers to do business with you, they'll return again and again.

If you decide to implement a preferred customer program, make sure you display your privacy policy and respect your customers' privacy when collecting information for your program.

Contests and Promotions

Promotions can be a great way to grab the attention of a customer who has entered your online store and to build interest in your products. You could give away one of the products you sell, a service related to your business, or even a gift certificate for your online store. Consider asking one of your suppliers to give you a couple of products that you can give away as part of a contest on your Web site. In return, the supplier gets exposure for its products on your Web site.

Contests are also a good way to get customers to register on your Web site. People are busy, so it can be difficult to get customers to take a few minutes out of their hectic schedules to register with you, but a contest can be a great hook. For example, when RadioShack (www.radioshack.com) wanted to entice customers to register on its Web site, it created a sweepstakes (with prizes including personal computers and digital cameras) and promised that customers would be entered in the contest for free if they took two minutes to register on the Web site. Of course, contests don't need to be linked to site registration. Many online retailers regularly have contests on their Web sites to keep customers coming back.

Whenever you run a contest on your Web site, keep in mind the privacy issues we discussed in Chapter 3. When asking shoppers for any personal information, remember to state that any information collected will be used in accordance with your privacy policy.

Limited Time Offers and Internet-Only Specials

From time to time, consider offering your customers special deals and promotions that are available only for a limited amount of time. Not only can this strategy keep your customers coming back to your online store again and again to check for the latest special offers, these types of deals can often be hard for customers to resist.

If you have a retail store, you may also want to consider offering customers Internet-only specials available only to those customers who shop online. Home Depot (www.homedepot.com), for example, has featured Internet-only promotions on its Web site. This will give customers an extra incentive to shop online.

While limited time offers can be an effective sales strategy, it's important not to go overboard with promotions that will dramatically reduce your profit margins or cause you to lose money on every sale. Be smart about the promotions you offer, and make sure they aren't harming you financially. If you decide to make a limited time offer available to your customers, make sure you display the offer prominently on your home page.

Gift Reminder Services

Several online stores have implemented gift reminder services that allow customers to store personalized lists of important dates such as birthdays and anniversaries. Customers who register with a gift reminder service will be notified by e-mail when an important date approaches. The reminder notice is usually accompanied by an advertisement or a subtle promotional message from the company operating the service. Since reminder services are usually provided free to customers, they don't generate any direct revenue. However, they are an excellent opportunity for online retailers to promote their brands, attract traffic to their Web sites, and provide a valuable service to their customers at the same time.

To see an example of this strategy, visit the online store for Hallmark (www.hallmark.com). Registered members of Hallmark's Web site can store dates for important birthdays, anniversaries, and other special occasions on the site. In advance of the date, customers will receive a reminder e-mail from Hallmark's Web site, accompanied by a subtle message reminding them to return soon to "send free e-cards or shop our selection of gifts and fresh-cut flowers." A reminder service like this one can be an incredibly useful service for your customers that can promote your online store at the same time!

Reorder Reminder Services

If you sell the types of products that customers need to reorder regularly, why not offer customers an online reminder service?

For example, customers of Walgreens (www.walgreens.com), a large drugstore chain in the United States, can schedule e-mail reminders so they know when it's time to refill a prescription or reorder a product. Similarly, Home Depot (www.homedepot.com) has a lawn and garden e-mail reminder service that will periodically e-mail customers to let them know when it's time to buy new lawn and garden care products.

These reminders are optional, of course, but they're a good way to keep those customers who opt to receive them returning to your online store on a regular basis.

Online Communities

Some online merchants have found that a great way to build customer loyalty is to provide discussion groups on their Web sites where online shoppers can gather, make new friends, and chat about topics that interest them.

Of course, one of the keys to using this strategy effectively is building a community that is relevant to the products you are selling. In other words, don't set up a discussion area and let your customers chat about anything. Provide discussion groups that will draw targeted customers to your site and bring them back again and again. An excellent example of this strategy can be found on REI's online store (www.rei.com). REI, a retailer of specialty outdoor gear, has created an online community for outdoor enthusiasts in which participants share ideas, opinions, and experiences with one another. There are discussion groups for a variety of outdoor activities, including hiking, cycling, fishing, snow sports, and climbing.

While online communities such as such as the one offered by REI.com can be an excellent loyalty-building tool, there are several risks you should be aware of.

e-fact

For every dollar spent online, another five dollars are spent offline as the result of online research.

Source: Jupiter Media Metrix (www.jmm.com)

First, you need to set some ground rules for your customers and make sure they observe them. Otherwise, you will end up with customers who use vulgar language in your discussion forums, or who use them solely as a vehicle to advertise penny stocks and other products and services. Forum participants could also end up getting into heated discussions and launching personal attacks on one another.

To avoid these types of problems, REI has established some rules for its discussion groups that customers must follow or be banned from participating. If you decide to create an online community for your online store, you'll want to create and post some rules of your own.

Of course, not everyone will obey the rules, so you've got to monitor your discussion groups closely to make sure no problems arise. This can be very time-consuming, and will distract you from your main job as an online merchant—selling products. The other risk is that some of your customers will use the message boards as a way to vent their frustrations with your company and its products. Needless to say, this can be a potentially embarrassing situation and you'll quickly find yourself in damage control mode.

Before creating discussion groups on your Web site, think carefully about the benefits and drawbacks of offering this type of interaction to your customers.

Interactive Events

Many online stores hold interactive events on their Web sites to attract customers and build long-term loyal relationships with online shoppers. Hallmark (www.hallmark.com) provides a good example of this strategy. Using a service called TalkCity (www.talkcity.com), Hallmark hosted a series of live chats with ornament artists on its Web site. It's a great way to turn your static Web site into a two-way conversational and interactive medium that your customers can truly benefit from!

Compelling Content

Customers will visit your online store more—and stick around longer— if you offer valuable information or reference tools on your Web site that relate to the product area you specialize in. This lets your customers know you're interested in more than just a quick sale. It also gives shoppers a reason to come back to your store again and again.

You probably have much of this information readily available at your disposal. All you have to do is convert it into a format that can be displayed on the Web. If the information isn't your own, make sure you obtain any necessary copyright and trademark clearances. Alternatively, you can hire a local expert to contribute articles, commentary, or tips to your Web site, or you can contract with an industry publication to feature its articles on your Web site. You might find that industry experts and industry publications are willing to contribute free content to your online store in exchange for the publicity your Web site would generate for them.

Consider what PETsMART (www.petsmart.com) has done on its online store. The site's main purpose, of course, is to sell pet food and supplies. But the site also includes valuable information for pet owners, including product advice, pet weight guides, an online pet library featuring full-length books that can be read online, a dog food calculator, nutrition tips, and much more. For example, customers with cats can consult an online article called "Choosing the Correct Food for Your Cat" so they can make a more informed buying decision.

Starbucks provides another excellent example of how to supplement your online store with valuable educational content. Starbucks' Web site (www.starbucks.com), besides selling coffee to consumers, offers articles devoted to coffee education, including information on the history of coffee, tasting tips, and advice on how to brew a great cup of coffee.

Think about how you might add similar content to your Web site. Remember to keep the content fresh by regularly adding new features and information. If your content becomes stale, customers may lose interest in regularly visiting your Web site.

Loyalty Programs

Loyalty programs work well in traditional marketing, so it's not surprising that many online stores have implemented loyalty programs in their online stores. For example, Canadian Tire has implemented a program called "Canadian Tire 'Money' Online" in which online shoppers are awarded money whenever they make an online purchase over a certain amount. While the money can't be redeemed for actual cash, it can be applied toward future in-store or online purchases. Customers can check the balance or status of their reward dollars online at any time.

e-fact

The United States accounts for 40 percent of all money spent online.

Source: International Data Corporation (www.idc.com)

e-fact

Forty-six percent of retailers use sales as the primary metric for judging the success of their Web sites.

Source: Jupiter Media Metrix (www.jmm.com)

Keep in mind that your loyalty program doesn't have to give away discounts on future purchases in order to be perceived as valuable by your customers. When it comes to purchasing online, consumers may be much more interested in issues such as product selection, customer service, and easy returns than they are in a small discount on a future purchase. In fact, a study by Jupiter Communications found that these issues encourage loyalty much more than online loyalty programs do. Customers couldn't care less about earning reward points from your online store if the customer service is terrible and it's a hassle to return unwanted items. If you want your customers to give you repeat business, make sure you address critical issues such as customer service before you launch an online loyalty program.

With this in mind, a preferred customer loyalty program that offers benefits such as faster checkout times may be a better way to improve customer loyalty than a program that gives discounts on future purchases in exchange for repeat business. For example, the Avon preferred customer program that we described earlier in the chapter offers immediate benefits, including faster checkout times and online storage of your shipping details. Hudson's Bay Company has a similar membership program on its Web site (www.hbc.com). Customers can sign up for free to become HBC.com members, and can enjoy a wide range of benefits including express checkout, online order history, personalized wish lists, and more.

Opt-in E-Mail

In the last chapter, we introduced you to the concept of permission marketing. Permission marketing, also known as opt-in e-mail, means getting permission from customers before you market to them by e-mail.

Many online stores have discovered that permission marketing also works as an excellent loyalty-building technique and therefore have built permission marketing strategies into their own Web sites. The idea is to encourage customers to give you their e-mail addresses so you can send them news and information by e-mail. Regular e-mail communication not only keeps your name in front of your customers, it can strengthen customer relationships and increase repeat visits to your online store.

There are two types of general e-mail communications you may want to have with your customers: (1) e-mail alerts or updates that keep your customers informed about special promotions in your online store, new products, and new content on your Web site; and (2) an online newsletter that provides articles, product tips, or other value-added information of interest to your customers.

An online newsletter is a bigger commitment since it requires more content and should be sent out on a regular basis. In contrast, e-mail alerts can be sent out as required, should be brief, and don't need to adhere to any type of release schedule. It's up to you whether you want to offer one or both of these types of e-mail to your customers. Some customers, for example, don't want to receive sales information from your online store, but would gladly sign up for an online newsletter if it offered valuable information.

There is a fine line between an e-mail update and a newsletter, and many online merchants have rolled both into a single e-mail list with both functions. Not only is it less confusing to customers when they have only one e-mail list to sign up for, you don't have to worry about maintaining two separate e-mail lists. For example, PETsMART (www.petsmart.com) has a weekly electronic newsletter called PawsPectives. The newsletter includes helpful information about pet care, Web site news, and information on product specials.

> **e-fact**
>
> Seventy-nine percent of Internet users in Canada have opted to receive e-mail information from Web sites.
>
> *Source: Ipsos-Reid (www.ipsos-reid.com)*

When implemented correctly, opt-in e-mail is a powerful way to keep in touch with shoppers and keep them coming back to your online store on a regular basis. Here are ten tips to help you start your opt-in e-mail strategy on the right track:

1. *Provide value:* Customers will be turned off by an online newsletter if it is nothing more than a sales pitch. Focus on providing relevant, useful information to your customers.
2. *Let customers know what they are getting:* When customers sign up for your e-mail list, tell them what they're signing up for. What will they receive? Information on changes to your Web site? The latest store specials? Feature articles? Don't mislead your customers and then surprise them with information they're not expecting.
3. *Communicate the benefits:* One of the problems with e-mail is that we receive too much of it. Many customers will hesitate to sign up

for a service that will potentially generate even more clutter in their e-mail box. For this reason, make sure you tell your customers what's in it for them. What are the benefits of signing up for your e-mail list?

4. *Get permission first:* Remember that permission marketing is based on the customer's agreement to receive information from you by e-mail. Send your newsletter only to customers who choose to subscribe. Don't send it to customers who haven't asked for it, and don't assume that because a customer has bought a product from you, it's permissible to add that customer's e-mail address to your distribution list.

5. *Make it easy for shoppers to subscribe to your e-mail list:* Shoppers may be less inclined to subscribe if it takes more than a couple of seconds to join. If you make customers answer a long list of questions, they may decide that it isn't worth the hassle. As a result, many online stores allow shoppers to add themselves to their electronic mailing lists with little more than an e-mail address. A good example can be found on the online store for GUESS Jeans. Customers who want to receive e-mail updates from GUESS only need to enter their e-mail address. No other personal information is required.

Three out of four Canadian Internet users who opted to receive e-mail marketing messages from a specific company later opted out either because they found the marketing uninteresting or too frequent.

Source: Ipsos-Reid (www.ipsos-reid.com)

e-fact

6. *Catch customers as they register or check out of your online store:* In addition to promoting your newsletter or mailing list on the front page of your Web site as many merchants do, you can also promote it during the registration process (if you have one) and when customers are checking out of your online store. Always give the customer the option of saying "yes" or "no" to your newsletter.

7. *Make it easy for customers to unsubscribe:* Customers may want to remove themselves from your e-mail list for various reasons. For

example, they may not like it, they may be going away for an extended period of time, or they may be changing their e-mail address. Regardless of the reason, ensure that customers are provided with clear, easy-to-follow instructions on how to unsubscribe from your e-mail list. Many online stores send subscribers an initial welcome message with instructions on unsubscribing. However, our experience has been that most customers end up deleting this information or misplacing it, so a better strategy is to include removal instructions at the end of every message you send out. Your customers will appreciate this and you will too. It will save you from having to respond to dozens of angry e-mail messages from customers who want to get off your e-mail list but don't know how.

8. *Don't overdo it:* Online shoppers hate spam, the Internet term for junk mail. Don't subject your customers to too much information. For example, sending out an e-mail message several times a week is overkill.

9. *Don't sell your e-mail addresses:* In Chapter 3, "Tips for Building an Effective Online Store," we discussed the importance of having a privacy policy on your Web site. Make sure your privacy policy (or a link to it) is clearly displayed when customers sign up for your e-mail list. Let them know that you're not going to sell their e-mail addresses or any other personal information they give to you. If you abuse the information customers give you, you'll lose their trust—and their business. When customers of Patagonia's online store (www.patagonia.com) sign up to the company's e-mail list, they are told: "We respect your privacy. Email addresses are not released to third parties."

10. *Use a mailing list program or permission marketing firm:* Some businesses attempt to maintain their e-mail lists manually without the aid of any special software, but this can become extremely time consuming, especially as the number of subscribers to your e-mail list grows. You'll have to deal with e-mail addresses that stop working as well as with people who want to be added or removed from your list. In addition, if you want to target your e-mail messages based on customer tastes and preferences, demographic information, or purchase history, and then track customer response to your

e-mail campaigns, you'll need e-mail management software that can handle these tasks.

Eighty-eight percent of online consumers have made a purchase as a result of receiving permission-based e-mail.

Source: DoubleClick (www.doubleclick.com)

e-fact

If you want to set up a mailing list for your online store, there are a variety of options available to you. First, check with the storefront solution you are using to see if it includes any sort of mailing list capability.

Alternatively, you may want to use a third-party e-mail management service such as List Builder, which is part of a group of small business services offered by Microsoft's bCentral service (www.bcentral.ca). List Builder allows you to set up a mailing list on your Web site in just a few minutes without the need for any technical knowledge.

List Builder's annual plan costs US $299 per year, which includes 10,000 monthly e-mails, although additional upgrade packages are available if you need to send more messages. There is also a less expensive annual plan if you expect your e-mail volumes to be minimal. List Builder is a powerful service, allowing you to collect demographic information from your customers, import and export subscriber lists, and send targeted messages to your customers based on their profile information.

Permission Marketing Firms

If you're a large retailer, more advanced solutions for setting up an e-mail list on your Web site are provided by permission marketing specialists such as ClickAction (www.clickaction.com) and Responsys.com (www.responsys.com). Lands' End (www.landsend.com), for example, uses software from Responsys to manage its e-mail marketing campaigns. As part of the sign-up process, customers are asked what type of information they want to receive from Lands' End and how frequently they want to be contacted. Using a Responsys software package called Interact, Lands' End can create targeted e-mail messages based on the profile information supplied by customers. The Responsys software also enables Lands' End to build profiles of its customers and send personalized e-mail messages to customers based on their buying patterns, Web site behaviour, and response to previous e-mail campaigns. The software is easy to use, and online store owners can schedule their own e-mail campaigns through their Web browsers.

Similarly, ClickAction's (www.clickaction.com) e-mail marketing technology is used by a wide range of online retailers, including Talbots (www.talbots.com), Hershey's (www.hersheygifts.com), Dean & DeLuca (www.deandeluca.com), and Columbia House (www.columbiahouse.com). ClickAction's software enables online retailers to collect e-mail addresses and profile information from customers.

The benefit of using permission marketing solutions provided by companies such as Responsys and ClickAction is that they enable you to develop highly targeted e-mail campaigns so you can build better relationships with your customers and increase sales as a result.

The cost of some of these services, however, can be prohibitive for a small business. If you're a small business, you may be better off using an e-mail list service such as Microsoft's List Builder.

Personalization

Many merchants believe some form of personalization is an effective way to increase sales and customer retention. There are many ways to personalize the content and services that customers receive in your online store, including:

- Site registration
- Personalized mailings
- Data analysis tools

Site Registration

First and foremost, as noted earlier in the chapter, if you can get customers to register on your Web site and set up a personal account, you can offer express checkout services, online wish lists, access to previous orders, gift reminders, address books, and other personalized services that make customers feel special. You can also greet customers by name as they sign into your online store.

Earlier in the chapter, we pointed out how retailers like Gap and Avon have implemented site registration as a way of increasing customer loyalty and personalizing the services for online shoppers. For another example of how site registration can be used to personalize a customer's online shopping experience, visit Canadian Tire's online store (www. canadiantire.ca). Canadian Tire has an online service called "My Canadian Tire," which gives shoppers numerous personalized benefits including online tracking and express checkout services once they register.

Personalized Mailings

We discussed electronic mailing lists earlier in the chapter and pointed out that they can be an effective marketing tool because they can draw customers to your online store. But most online newsletters send out the same information to everyone.

One alternative to a generic mailing list (where the same newsletter goes out to all your online shoppers) is to have your customers select what types of information they want to receive from you by e-mail. Although it can be more expensive to implement technology that sends out personalized e-mail messages, you're able to target customers in a way that's not possible with a regular mailing list.

As an example of what's possible, visit Hershey's online gift store (www.hersheygifts.com). Customers who want to sign up to receive e-mail from Hershey's can choose what types of special offers they are interested in, and they will receive e-mail updates tailored to their personal interests.

A more extensive example of personalized e-mail can be found on Amazon.com's Web site. Amazon.com has a feature called Amazon.com "Alerts," which will notify customers by e-mail whenever new products are released featuring their favourite authors, artists, actors, or directors. Customers specify who they want to track (e.g., Britney Spears), and Amazon.com will send out an e-mail alert whenever a new product is released that matches a customer's interests.

Don't Overpersonalize!

We would be remiss if we didn't point out the danger of getting too personalized. For example, if you start inviting customers to select specific topics they want to receive information about, such as Britney Spears, customers will expect to receive information about Britney Spears and nothing else. Thus, if you want to send out an e-mail message about a special contest you're having in your online store, you really shouldn't be sending it out to the customers who have said they only want to receive information about Britney Spears—even though many of those customers would probably be interested in that contest. That's why it's generally a good idea to have a generic e-mail list that customers can join in addition to inviting customers to receive special mailings on topics of interest to them.

Data Analysis Tools

Many online retailers use data analysis tools (sometimes referred to as data mining tools, marketing analytics software, or customer intelligence tools) to monitor customer behaviour in their online stores. Some retailers use custom-developed software programs while others use analytic programs from such companies as Net Perceptions (www.netperceptions.com), NetGenesis (www.netgenesis.com), Personify (www.personify.com), Coremetrics (www.coremetrics.com), Siebel (www.siebel.com), and Accrue (www.accrue.com), which specialize in helping online businesses to analyze how customers are using their Web sites. These programs collect information about which Web pages customers are clicking on, which paths customers take through your site, which online advertisements customers have seen, which products they are buying, how customers found out about your site, which online promotions are working or failing, and more. This data is then analyzed and can be used to calculate retention rates, customer acquisition costs, and other useful statistics. The data can also be used to create promotions for shoppers as well as to personalize the content or messages that an online shopper sees. For example, data analysis software could help you identify all the customers who purchased from you at least three times in the past but who haven't made a purchase in the last six months.

Using all of this data, online retailers can set up rules-based personalization strategies that target messages to clients based on their behaviour on the site. For example, suppose you are selling designer jeans on your Web site. You could set up a rule that says any customer who has returned more than twice to your designer jeans page should be shown a coupon for $15 off a designer belt. This type of personalization is attractive because it allows retailers to offer real-time promotions to their customers without knowing the identity of the customer. The customer remains anonymous because the personalization is based on the user's clicking behaviour and activity on the Web site.

---

e-fact

By 2004, marketers in the U.S. will send more than 200 billion e-mail messages annually.

Source: Forrester Research (www.forrester.com)

Higher levels of personalization are possible when retailers combine their rules or click-through data with information that customers voluntarily provide on the site. For example, many retailers encourage customers to register on their site and provide information about their interests, geographic location, and lifestyle. This customer-provided information can be combined with data about how the customer is using the Web site so that promotions and special product offers can be generated on the fly.

Collaborative Filtering

In addition to the basic rules-based personalization techniques mentioned previously, many online retailers are implementing advanced personalization strategies they hope will increase both customer loyalty and customer spending in their online stores.

Jeff Bezos, the CEO of online bookseller Amazon.com, once said, "If we have 4.5 million customers, we shouldn't have one store, we should have 4.5 million stores." The idea is that customers are more likely to return to your online store and buy products from you again and again if you personalize your online services and tailor them to each customer's needs and interests. As an example of this approach to online selling, Amazon.com (www.amazon.com) has built a service called "Your Recommendations" on its Web site, which customizes product recommendations for its customers.

Customers use an online "recommendations wizard" to tell Amazon what types of products (e.g., books, music, etc.) they are interested in. Amazon then uses this information, as well as information gleaned from other shoppers with similar interests, to recommend other products to the customers. For example, Amazon.com may notice that you are interested in buying Anne Rice and Stephen King novels. It will find other people in its database who are also fans of Anne Rice and Stephen King to see what other books they are purchasing, assuming that these books may also be of interest to you. The more products you tell Amazon.com about, the more accurate its recommendations become.

The analytical process that Amazon.com uses to make product recommendations to its customers is called collaborative filtering. Collaborative filtering can determine what a given customer may be interested in based on what other customers with similar tastes and interests have purchased, and it's surprisingly accurate. The upside for online retailers is that they can potentially increase their online sales if they do a better job at identifying products customers may be interested in.

Collaborative filtering and other data mining techniques are expensive solutions to implement, but for those online retailers who can afford to experiment, they have a great deal of potential.

Other Approaches to Personalization

There are many other ways to personalize the online shopping experience for your customers. Your imagination is the limit!

In the apparel industry, one very successful approach to personalization was developed by a Montreal-based company called My Virtual Model Inc. (www.myvirtualmodel.com). My Virtual Model has two core technologies that are now being used by some of the largest apparel retailers on the Internet. The first, My Virtual Model Dressing Room, allows shoppers to try on clothes on the Internet. The other, My Virtual Model Fit, matches a customer's body measurements to the manufacturers' sizing specifications so customers can determine the correct size and fit of an item of clothing before they make a purchase.

To see the My Virtual Model Dressing Room technology in action, visit Lands' End's online store (www.landsend.com). Lands' End was one of the first online retailers to introduce the My Virtual Model service on its Web site, and it's been a hit with customers.

All customers need to do is provide Lands' End with information about their hair colour and hairstyle, eyes, face shape, skin tone, and body measurements. Using this information, a virtual model resembling the customer is displayed on the customer's computer screen. Customers can then try on outfits to see how they look.

The type of personalization technology has two important benefits. First, it helps online retailers increase revenues because consumers are more confident in the products they are buying. Second, this type of personalization reduces returns by helping customers pick the types of clothes that are most likely to fit.

In addition to Lands' End, other online retailers using My Virtual Model Dressing Room include American Eagle Outfitters (www.ae.com) and GUESS Jeans (www.guess.com). My Virtual Model Fit technology can be seen at Kenneth Cole's online store (www.kennethcole.com).

Drawbacks of Personalization

Many organizations have found they have to strike a delicate balance between collecting information from users and relying on data gleaned from online behaviour. Depending on your business, you may find that customers don't want to offer a lot of information about themselves because of privacy concerns, forcing you to personalize offers based more on their online behaviour. On the other hand, online behaviour analysis isn't always appropriate either.

For example, if you are selling to businesses, you can't personalize offers based on how the purchasing manager is using your Web site! The offers you make to a business need to be based on the needs of the whole company and not on the needs of individual employees who are browsing through your online store. In these situations, you need to focus on customizing content for the entire organization.

> Forty percent of Internet users credit e-mail communications as a primary reason for loyalty to online merchants.
>
> Source: DoubleClick (www.doubleclick.com)
>
> **e-fact**

Another drawback with personalization is that it isn't always accurate or even appreciated. For example, many customers find it annoying when a Web site is continually trying to cross-sell products. It's like being in a retail store with a salesperson who won't leave you alone! In addition, the technology behind personalization software is still rudimentary in many cases, causing shoppers to receive inappropriate product recommendations. It's also easy for a Web site to give recommendations to the wrong person. For example, in families where several people use a single computer, a family member visiting a Web site such as Amazon.com may receive personalized information that is actually intended for another person in the household who was previously on the site.

Finally, as noted earlier, you also have to be careful about overpersonalizing your Web site. If you give your customers too much personalized content, you limit your sales opportunities because you are offering customers a narrow rather than broad selection of products.

What Does It Cost?

Personalization schemes can be inexpensive or they can be costly (as much as millions of dollars), depending on what you are trying to accomplish. Many of the collaborative filtering technologies we discussed earlier can cost you well into six figures.

In the box below, we've listed some of the leading vendors of personalization software. You should also investigate the companies we listed earlier in the chapter in our discussion of data analysis software as many of these companies also sell personalization solutions. As noted above, the cost of personalization software can be prohibitive for a small business. If you can't afford the services offered by these companies (and most small businesses can't), speak with the company that is developing your online store to see if there are features you can implement to personalize the online shopping experience for your customers. At the very least, consider implementing one or more mailing lists or online newsletters so customers can sign up to receive information from you by e-mail.

Examples of Companies Selling Personalization Software

Blaze Software	www.blazesoft.com
KANA	www.kana.com
BroadVision	www.broadvision.com
E.piphany	www.epiphany.com
Likeminds by Macromedia	www.macromedia.com
Net Perceptions	www.netperceptions.com
Personify	www.personify.com

8

131 Tips from
Online Merchants in Canada
and the United States

"Find a business in an area you enjoy and in which you have a flare, but at the end of the day be governed by your head rather than your heart."

—Anna Burton, Founder and Owner, Stylocracy Elegant Gifts,
Prince Albert, Saskatchewan

Although electronic commerce represents only a tiny percentage of total consumer and business sales in the Canada, it's growing fast. In spite of the continuing growth in e-commerce revenues, the last couple of years have been anything but a smooth ride for companies selling online. Many online retailers have failed, pushed into bankruptcy by unrealistic expectations and poor business models. Other companies have been experimenting with different approaches to selling online in an effort to find the right formula for success. To help you benefit from the experiences of other online retailers in both Canada and the United States, we convened a panel of twenty-three companies that are selling online and asked them what they've learned so far and what advice they would have for other organizations that are thinking of opening their own online stores. Our merchants range from small mom-and-pop businesses like One of a Kind Kid.com, a business operated by a mother out of her home, to larger retail operations like RadioShack Canada and Payless ShoeSource.

Our Panel

Anna Burton
Founder, Stylocracy
Location: Prince Albert, Saskatchewan
Industry: Giftware
Web Site: www.stylocracy.com

Tane Chan
Owner, The Wok Shop
Location: San Francisco, California
Industry: Woks and cooking products/accessories
Web Site: www.wokshop.com

Bonnie Clewans
Owner, The Bead Gallery
Location: Buffalo, New York
Industry: Beads
Web Site: www.beadgallery.com

Michelle Donahue-Arpas
Owner, Genius Babies!
Location: Charlotte, North Carolina
Industry: Baby gifts and toys
Web Site: www.geniusbabies.com

Richard Flynn
President, Red Trumpet, Ltd.
Location: York, Pennsylvania
Industry: Collectible CDs, LPs, DVDs, and preowned vinyl records
Web Site: www.redtrumpet.com

Jason Friedman
Director of Internet Commerce, J&R Music and Computer World
Location: New York, New York
Industry: Home entertainment and computers
Web Site: www.jandr.com

Kevin Gorman
Owner, WebCyclery, LLC
Location: Bend, Oregon
Industry: Cycling products
Web Site: www.webcyclery.com

Chris Harrower
Chief Information Officer/Director of Sales & Marketing,
   Choo Choo Barn
Location: Strasburg, Pennsylvania
Industry: Train-related merchandise
Web Site: www.choochoobarn.com

Bodega Bob Homme
Chief Engineering Officer, The Submarine Store
Location: Gaithersburg, Maryland
Industry: Submarine-related merchandise
Web Site: www.submarinestore.com

Dave Mack
Director, Dealer Sales and Alternate Channels, RadioShack Canada
Location: Barrie, Ontario
Industry: Electronics
Web Site: www.radioshack.ca

Kim Michaux
Owner, One of a Kind Kid.com
Location: Roanoke, Virginia
Industry: Baby and children's clothing and gifts
Web Site: www.oneofakindkid.com

Ron Mis
President, Galeton Gloves
Location: Raynham, Massachusetts
Industry: Work gloves
Web Site: www.galeton.com

Lynn Moller
General Manager, Lynn's Collectibles
Location: Edmonton, Alberta
Industry: Collectibles
Web Site: www.lynnsclub.com

Diane Morgan
Sole Proprietor, Morgan Mailboxes & More
Location: Tewksbury, Massachusetts
Industry: Hand-painted mailboxes
Web Site: www.dianemorgan.com

Christopher M. Mott
President, Mott's Miniatures Inc.
Location: Buena Park, California
Industry: Miniatures and dollhouses
Web Site: www.mottsminis.com

Sherry Peterson
Vice-President, Main St. Toys
Location: Lindsborg, Kansas
Industry: Toys
Web Site: www.mainsttoys.com

Ray Ritchey
Founder, Childbook.com
Location: Rowland Heights, California
Industry: Chinese children's books/videos/music/software
Web Site: www.childbook.com

Sue Schwartz
Owner, YarnXpress.com
Location: West Milford, New Jersey
Industry: Yarns
Web Site: www.yarnxpress.com

Rob Snell
President, ystore.com
Location: Starkville, Massachusetts
Industry: Web site development for Yahoo! Stores
Web Site: www.ystore.com

Richard Snow
President, Pull Up Our Sox
Location: Toronto, Ontario
Industry: Apparel/Socks
Web Site: www.sox.org

Deb Steinberg
President, Nickers & Neighs, Inc.
Location: Whitesboro, Texas
Industry: Horse-related merchandise
Web Site: www.nickers.com

Rhonda Wells
Director of E-commerce, Payless ShoeSource
Location: Topeka, Kansas
Industry: Shoes
Web Site: www.payless.com

Doug Young
President and Founder, Noggintops.com, Ltd.
Location: Congerville, Illinois
Industry: Outdoor hats
Web Site: www.noggintops.com

We asked each panel member to address the following six questions:

1. What are the keys to success when operating an online store?
2. What was the most difficult obstacle or challenge that you faced when you created your online store?
3. What lessons have you learned as a result of setting up your Internet business?
4. What key piece(s) of advice would you offer someone who is thinking of setting up an online store?

5. What is the best feature you've built into your online store?

6. Has your venture into online retailing met your expectations?

In the pages that follow, we present a selection of their responses, organized in a way that highlights important themes and lessons learned. Whether you're already selling online or just beginning the process of setting up an online storefront, the over 100 tips and pearls of wisdom presented in this chapter will help you build a more successful online business.

Question #1:
What Are the Keys to Success When Operating an Online Store?

Over-Deliver on Customer Service
Dave Mack, RadioShack Canada
When it comes to the fulfillment of product, I can't stress enough the importance of under-promising and over-delivering. If your company can typically ship anywhere in Canada in two days, then commit to under three-day delivery and exceed the majority of your customers' expectations.

Treat Your Home Page like Your Front Yard
Diane Morgan, Morgan Mailboxes & More
The most important element of an online store is the Web site itself. This is the first impression that a customer gets when they come to your store. I think of my home page as my front yard. I want it to appear welcoming to the people riding by ... I don't want flashing banners, jumping frogs, advertising, music, etc., to clutter up my front yard. The home page should be quick to load, neat, clean, and easy to navigate so the person will open your door and come in to visit.

e-fact

Online buying through TV and wireless devices will account for one in ten consumer e-commerce sales in the United States by 2005.

Source: GartnerG2 (www.gartnerg2.com)

Hire an Expert
Sherry Peterson, Main St. Toys
Unless you are very knowledgeable about computers and the technical aspects of Web sites and their design, hire someone who is. We feel that

it is a necessity to work with someone who is excited about our store and the merchandise we sell, and who is easy to work with. Our technical consultant designed our Web site for us and did all the technical aspects of getting our site up and running. We also receive a lot of e-mails from companies wanting us to subscribe to various services that they provide for a fee. We forward all of those to our consultant and he tells us which ones we should consider, based on his knowledge and expertise. When we were first getting our Web site set up, there were things that we thought we would like to do but we had no idea how to do. That's where a good technical person is a must. He is gradually teaching us how to do changes and additions to our catalogue ourselves so that we will eventually become more proficient, but we could never had made it happen in the first place without him.

Give Your Customers as Much Information as Possible
Christopher Mott, Mott's Miniatures
The more information you can put on your site, the better off you will be. This includes product information, as well as information about your policies and shipping information. If it takes you two weeks to ship out an order after you get the order, put that on the Web site. Get it out in the open right up front.

Recognize That the Old Rules of Business Still Apply
Doug Young, Noggintops.com
From the beginning, I had a strong belief that e-commerce isn't really a new way of doing business, it is simply a new medium for conducting business. In other words, all the old rules for building a successful business still apply. The hype and the technological glitter of the Internet make it tempting to disbelieve that, to instead believe the size and power of the Internet will carry you … but it's a fatal mistake. The Internet is powerful, but it is not magic.

Be U.S. Friendly
Anna Burton, Stylocracy
You need to offer Americans prices in their own money. Our market has turned out to be 95 percent U.S. and we have no option but to cater to this market. Americans will be scared off by the unknowns of foreign Canadian dollars and possible duty fees, so you want everything in U.S. funds and assure them you'll cover any duty charges should they arise.

Be Flexible with Your Web Design
Chris Harrower, Choo Choo Barn

Be flexible ... if one design doesn't work, try another (and another ... we are on our third version of the Web site right now, and I'm working on some changes once again). Ask questions of your customers. What do they like (or, more importantly, what didn't they like about your site)? What would they like to see? What would make their shopping experience better (easier, quicker)? And ask questions of other business associates, both locally and across the Net. There is even a mailing list called I-Help/Webreview that allows others to comment on your design and offer their insights into prospective improvements ... join it and use it! [You can join the mailing list by visiting www.audettemedia.com/subscribe.html and selecting I-HelpDesk.]

Have a "Professional" Web Site Design
Bodega Bob Homme, The Submarine Store

If a business is going to be a serious player on the Web, the site must be professionally done. The days of cutesy, schlocky, or homespun Web sites are long gone, at least in the business arena. We invested about $16,000 in the initial site development and, believe me, it was worth every nickel! A professionally done site engenders trust and security among its visitors. We've added about $3,000 or $4,000 of improvements and additional development since its launch. Hey, the Web site is our workhorse! We have never, and will never, sacrifice quality for cost in its development nor will we complain about the money we put into it.

The visitors to an online store cannot touch the products, can't speak directly with a retail representative, and in many cases can only verify a business's credibility or validate its performance after a purchase has been made. Our investment in a site design that not only stimulates purchase (note that it's an all-American red, white, and blue—our market tends to be very patriotic as you might guess)—but incorporates elements that engender trust in our visitors—posted privacy statement, security and data handling information, satisfaction/return policy, detailed contact information, testimonials from customers—all elements that help a site visitor get a better feel for the company behind the Web site. The result is a greater sense, on the part of the visitor, that we are a company that they would be secure doing business with, would want to do business with, and that we would meet their expectations of performance.

Eighty percent of Internet users agree that their purchasing decisions are strongly influenced by the ability to buy from known, trusted retailers and to buy known, trusted brand names.

Source: PricewaterhouseCoopers (www.pwc.global.com)

e-fact

Deb Steinberg, Nickers & Neighs
Build a clear, easy-to-navigate Web site design that lets visitors know up front what your business is all about. Include links to inform them about the ownership of your business, your privacy policy, and shipping rates, but don't clutter up your front page with that ... not everyone cares about the details.

Stay Committed to a Vision
Lynn Moller, Lynn's Collectibles
When I started Lynn's Web site, I was lucky to have great support from family and friends. Even with this support, my belief in the idea was constantly tested. To be successful you, really need to be committed to a vision. Imagine what the end result will be and never compromise the important parts of the vision.

A desire to help people, an important part of my vision, will guide you to make the best decisions. Customers will happen naturally if you are providing value. Take the time to understand your customers, why they use the web, and what value they are looking for. I was surprised by how many customers had become dissatisfied with the customer service in their local brick-and-mortar stores. Product knowledge, store hours, and advice were important to my customers.

Find Good Employees
Jason Friedman, J&R Music and Computer World
Hire the appropriate staff to support your technical, creative, and marketing visions. The applicant who demands the highest salary isn't necessarily the right fit for your type of business.

Remember That Customers Come First
Rhonda Wells, Payless ShoeSource
The real key to success is to always keep your customers' satisfaction as the first and last question of every decision. This is the only test to setting

strategies that will be successful. Internet technology is changing so fast that it is easy to get caught up in the excitement of what is new and to spend lots of money and resources putting together a strategy that your customer might not expect or value.

Doug Young, Noggintops.com
"It's the customer, stupid." The long-term survival of your business is directly tied to your ability to completely satisfy your customers. No amount of marketing genius, financial savvy, or technical wizardry will save you from the growing Dot-Com Hall of Flame if you can't keep customers coming back … and bringing their friends.

Think about it, people who are shopping on the Web are some of the most communication-savvy, interconnected people in history. They fire off dozens of e-mails daily to coworkers and friends. They may receive twice as many. They visit chat rooms. They put comments on news group bulletin boards, which are in turn read by hundreds, maybe thousands, of people around the world. An inability to deliver excellence in goods and services will not be hidden for long. Please note this doesn't just refer to quality products delivered with a cheery "Thank You!" on the invoice. It extends to your ability to ship in a timely manner, your treatment of customer complaints, the quality of assistance you give when asked, and your respect for a customer's privacy.

And—unlike the brick-and-mortar place that may get away with lapses in service because it's the only one of its kind on the block—your online store will be painfully easy to ignore, even easier to forget. Worse yet, your competitors will be literally just a mouse click away.

Deb Steinberg, Nickers & Neighs
Offer extraordinary customer service—answer e-mail immediately, ship within hours, not days of order. I believe that one of the main keys to success in any business is not to meet your customers' expectations, but to exceed them. Every customer is special, and should feel that their business is important to you. If an item is out of stock, e-mail or phone the customer immediately, and let them make the decision to ship and back order, hold and ship complete, or cancel the item completely.

Sherry Peterson, Main St. Toys
We offer exceptional customer service. We feel that just because a person is shopping over the Internet, it doesn't mean that they don't want prompt,

friendly, personal service. We offer free gift-wrapping, personalize enclosure cards to include if the purchase is for a gift, and do everything we can to make sure their shopping experience with us is a good one.

Last Christmas we had a customer call from New York City (we are in a small town in central Kansas), and she wanted to order some toys for her niece's children. Her niece lives in a small town about fifteen miles from us and had given her aunt our toll-free phone number, along with a list of some toys that her children would like for Christmas. After discussing the toys and picking out about three toys for each of four children, the customer said, "Now, how much will it cost me to have them shipped to my niece?" I told her that my husband just happened to be going to that town that same afternoon, and he could gift wrap them and deliver them to her niece's home at no charge. She was delighted and I will bet that she will call us again this Christmas. That's shopping on the Internet, but with the addition of personal service. Good customer service is not that hard to do. It is offering your merchandise at a fair price, treating the customer like you would want to be treated, and giving them better service than they ever expected.

We also think it is important to make sure that all of us in the store know what is going on with customers who might be calling back about an order or a question, so that if the same person who helped them the first time isn't available, they don't have to start explaining from square one again. That is frustrating to me as a customer and I'm sure it is to others as well. We are a small store so we don't have so many employees to keep informed as larger companies do.

> By making customer service a priority, e-tailers can salvage at least 7.8 percent of abandoned online orders.
>
> *Source: Datamonitor (www.datamonitor.com)*

e-fact

Kevin Gorman, WebCyclery

In order to succeed with an online store, there has to be a reason for people to buy from you rather than your competition. There has to be some sort of value added to the product. In most cases, that "value-add" is going to be customer service. Online customer service is different from in brick-and-mortar stores, in that you rarely get any face-to-face contact. People like to know that their order is being taken care of by a real person. Responding quickly to e-mails and phone calls is an easy way of gaining trust, which helps convert visitors into customers. Confirmation e-mails and updates on back orders also helps. Great customer service also helps with word-of-mouth advertising, while poor customer service can destroy you.

Anna Burton, Stylocracy
[Good customer service] is essential, easy, and not expensive: friendly service, prompt replies, same-day order processing, gift-wrapping (… yes we can do orange paper and purple bow and whatever length of missive hand-inscribed on a nice, heavy card), flexibility (… yes, of course we can ship this now to your daughter in Halifax and send the invoice to a separate address and will e-mail you the tracking number and also send an e-mail to the daughter with the tracking number and we'll look into getting those vases with dancing elephants that you saw in Victoria …). Great customer service is one way in which you can beat the mammoth competitors, like Amazon.com. We've had gushing e-mails from those who loved the unexpectedly courteous, polite, prompt treatment. Our policy is just to treat others as we like to be treated. The customer wants to be treated like Julia Roberts walking into Holt Renfrew, not like somebody returning underwear at Kmart. So why not? Roll out the red carpet. Be nice, solicitous, and your customers will not only come back but will tell their friends about you too.

Chris Harrower, Choo Choo Barn
It's not that much different from running a physical store … the customer is the reason you are in business. Customer service is primary. The site must be designed so they can find what they are looking for quickly and easily, but also designed so the casual browser can locate something of interest quickly and easily.

Richard Flynn, Red Trumpet
Remember that your site is a customer-service addition, not a substitute. Make it easy for people to get in touch with you, and help them in every way you can. Why? Because customers who are frustrated still want to hear a human voice that is both knowledgeable and reassuring, and the best Web site in the world can't accomplish that. We've had customers return merchandise for reasons we consider absolutely ludicrous, or ask

questions that could earn them warm bunks at the nearest state facilities. But they're our customers, and after we've pulled our hair out in the privacy of the office, we'll almost always call them—yes, by telephone—and do anything reasonable to satisfy them.

Allow Real-Time Credit Card Transactions
Bodega Bob Homme, The Submarine Store
Our ability to execute instant transactions has been instrumental to our commercial success. If a business believes that it can survive on phone and "print this form and fax it" orders from the Web, it is sadly mistaken. We realized, when we did our initial market research, that our two primary competitors were thriving in spite of no online transactional ability. I believe that as soon as we went live with our Web site, many of our competitors' shoppers became our customers simply because we made it comfortable, easy, and secure for them to purchase at the moment their purchase decision was made! Clearly, I can't quantify that, but the anecdotal evidence gleaned from the customer feedback we received immediately after taking the store live, and to some degree even still, identifies the ability to execute online transactions from our site as a significant reason for purchasing from The Submarine Store.

Kevin Gorman, WebCyclery
To be taken seriously, an online store also needs to accept credit cards. Making people send a cheque to a post office box is a big mistake.

Provide Answers to Frequently Asked Questions
Christopher Mott, Mott's Miniatures
Product knowledge is king. We sell product because we know the product. We can answer questions about it and keep the answers to the questions on our site. Every time someone asks us a question about a particular product, we take the answer and put it on the Web site in the hope of keeping someone from calling in with that question again.

Let Customers Know What's Important to You
Lynn Moller, Lynn's Collectibles
Your customers need to know you. Find a way to convey your identity (because you are special), what is important to you, and that you enjoy

being in business. The Web can be a very cold, unfriendly place, which leads to suspicion and distrust. Having a relationship with the visitors to your site creates trust, an essential ingredient for e-commerce.

Know When to Apologize
Deb Steinberg, Nickers & Neighs

Know when to say, "I'm sorry, we screwed up. What can we do to make it up to you?" And if an apology is in order, it is much better to do it by phone, if possible. Keep some small items on hand to send as free gifts when you have not met your customers' expectations of service.

Stick to a Business You Know
Christopher Mott, Mott's Miniatures

Don't jump into an e-business because it sounds fun or sounds profitable. It should be something that you understand, are familiar with, or have some experience or expertise in. If you could not see yourself getting a job as a manager in a similar "real" business, don't go into that "e-business."

---

e-fact

The market for reverse logistics providers that manage returns for retail goods sold online will reach nearly US $7.5 billion by 2004, up from US $1.2 billion in 2000.

Source: International Data Corporation (www.idc.com)

Effective Marketing
Doug Young, Noggintops.com

Don't wait to be found ... Get found! Some people have the impression that the mere possession of an online store means that their products will be exposed to millions of consumers. In truth, your products will be accessible to millions of consumers, but that in itself has very little bearing on the number of consumers who actually see your product. I have heard the old "needle in a haystack" cliché applied here, but "needle in a needle stack" would be more accurate. Make that a needle in a mountain-sized needle stack. Your online store will just be one invisible electronic blip among millions of other electronic blips. Waiting for people to somehow stumble across your quaint little "backstreet" e-shop will leave you dismally disappointed ... and broke. You should have a plan for how you are going to market your e-store before you take it online.

Diane Morgan, Morgan Mailboxes & More

Once you have a site up and running, you need to promote, promote, and promote again. This should become part of your normal business tasks. I have joined thirty-five online craft malls that list my products or link back to my site. Not only does this increase my sales potential, but it broadens my visibility. The more I put my name and my URL out there, the more chances I have that new eyes will see it. Many sites have a links page—take the time to go to those links and post your information on them. Join digest groups, network groups, and organizations that are related to your business. Create a signature for your e-mail messages that includes your name and links to your Web site so every time you e-mail anyone, you've given yourself a free plug by including your Web address. All these steps are developing and building your network.

Bodega Bob Homme, The Submarine Store

Effective marketing has, perhaps, been the single most significant contributor to our success. And, in fact, it can be argued that the application of The Submarine Store's 100 percent Satisfaction Guarantee is as much a marketing strategy as it is a customer service strategy. We employ aggressive marketing strategies in a combination of venues, both electronic and traditional. Our electronic newsletter is an excellent advertising and promotional tool and clearly the one with the most immediate and significant effect. Our affiliate program is also quite significant. This program has been very successful in generating business from a variety of different types of Web sites, but primarily those associated in some way or another with the submarine community. We have several affiliates who aggressively promote their association with us. This results in an identifiable impact on our revenue as well as significant commission payouts to our affiliates. A significant portion of our visitor traffic is generated from the various search engines. We continuously monitor our placement among the big eight, adjusting our pages and resubmitting as necessary to ensure good placements. In addition, we closely monitor our server logs to detect any significant changes in search engine-generated traffic either by source (which engine) or the keywords that are bringing visitors to our site.

On the traditional side, we are active in the submarine community with donations of money and merchandise for resale or auction to charities, associations, restoration projects, and museums. (Hey, even the Smithsonian has some of our products on display!) We place print ads in a variety of publications including reunion programs and veteran association directories. We currently have on the planning table for next year billboards at targeted naval bases, an expansion of our presence in targeted glossy magazines and periodicals, and our first incursion into the realm of broadcast media.

Ron Mis, Galeton Gloves

I believe a key driver of success in operating an online store is driving qualified traffic to the site. If the company has an established customer base and is offering them online purchasing as a new channel, the customers are known and an analysis can be completed of the cost and benefit of driving existing customers to the Web site. But what about new customers? Hoping that high search engine rankings can be achieved and maintained, and that potential new customers will search for and find the company's products is not a great strategy. Traditional and electronic media will most likely be needed to promote the online store and drive qualified leads to view the company's online offering. The economics of using these promotional tools will vary dramatically for start-up and established companies. Established businesses already using print and other media to promote their products will likely find the incremental cost of driving sales leads to their Web site to be small and easily justified. Start-ups will face a much greater challenge, having to allocate the entire cost of their promotion to their initially low online order rates.

Kevin Gorman, WebCyclery

Anyone can have a great site, but the idea of "build it and they will come" no longer holds true. Finding potential customers is a time-consuming and costly process. This includes online marketing, such as getting links from related sites and manufacturers, search engine optimization, and participating in newsgroups, as well as traditional types of marketing, such as print advertising, sending out press releases, and word of mouth. Having and implementing a well-thought-out marketing strategy is a very big part of running an online store.

Listen to Your Customers

Rhonda Wells, Payless ShoeSource

Online, you can ask for your customers' feedback and they are more than willing to give you their point of view. Learning to ask, listen, and respond to your customers' feedback is critical.

Treat Customers as You Would Want to Be Treated
Richard Flynn, Red Trumpet
This does not mean that you have to give in to every whim or suggestion, but responding to concerns in a fair and professional way helps to maintain their respect and loyalty.

Regularly Update Your Web Site
Deb Steinberg, Nickers & Neighs
Change your front page often (at least monthly) to keep it fresh. Some customers will visit your site several times before they ever purchase anything.

Study Your Competition
Richard Snow, Pull Up Our Sox
Know all the competition—in a world where information is easily shared, it's very important for a business to make sure that they are offering the best possible value on products/services to their respective market niche. People can be very fickle, especially online where their identity can be virtually virtual. A nickel can be the difference between a loyal or a lost customer. Relationship building may be less important to the online shopper, otherwise they would probably be shopping offline. Reputation, on the other hand, is very important in distinguishing your store apart from others in the mind of the customer.

Sell Something People Want
Doug Young, Noggintops.com
Yeah, I know. You're thinking: "Duh!" But that obvious principle seems to be continually overlooked by people who just have faith that the Internet will bring droves of people willing to plunk down a credit card for a squirrel-powered blender. Now, granted, the Internet may be the greatest medium around for selling those hard-to-find or niche items (hats, in some ways, being among them), but "hard-to-find" does imply that someone is already looking for it, and "niche" implies that there is a sizable segment of people who will be interested in it. If you don't have firm (and reasonably objective) reasons for believing you will be able to find enough people who will buy your product in enough quantity to sustain your business, you shouldn't do it.

Don't Get Carried Away with Bells and Whistles

Rhonda Wells, Payless ShoeSource

When we first brought the site up, other online retailers that were a few years ahead of us were putting together new technologies and gimmicks like "dress-up dolls" and "instant chat," among others. Originally, I was very concerned that our site would launch without all the bells and whistles customers would expect, based on our benchmarking research of other significant retail sites. Regardless of this concern, payless.com launched as a very simple site with navigation that resembled our shopping experience in our stores (shop by gender and size, only show the customer what we have available to sell and ship that day, etc.). As we began planning for future enhancements and modifications to the site, we performed our benchmark analysis of other leading retail sites again. We quickly discovered that what was important on these sites just a few months earlier was no longer important enough to be called out on their home page. We found that content like "dress-up dolls" was now buried several layers down in their sites.

It is clear that new technology is exciting, but it may not be required on your site until after it has proved itself as a useful shopping tool for the customer and a profitable way to drive sales. The only way to know if the new technology is important to your customer is to first be intimate with your customer, versus intimate with technology and your site.

Christopher Mott, Mott's Miniatures

I hate going to a Web site only to be bombarded with banners and buttons for advertisers. Resist the temptation to "junk up" your Web site with this stuff. Keep your graphics and your colours simple. Some sites are really loaded down with high-resolution pictures, moving banners, and other images just because more people now have higher-speed modems, DSL, and cable connections. Just because you can do something does not mean that you should.

Chris Harrower, Choo Choo Barn

Don't be snowed by all the bells and whistles … if that flash animation slows things down for your prospective customer, or that panoramic image of your store takes fifteen minutes to download, they won't wait and they won't be back! Want a bulletin board, chat room, guest book, video clips, etc?

Great ... but they are secondary (if not tertiary) in importance to service for the customer.

Don't Try to Be Everything to Everybody
Rob Snell, ystore.com

One thing I learned very early on is that what works in my retail stores does not work the same on the Web. In my retail stores we carry a little bit of everything. We're in rural Mississippi. People expect us to be more like the general store of pet supplies, or pop culture, or role-playing games. On the Web, we've done better by focusing on doing a whole lot of one thing rather than being something for everyone.

Build Trust and Credibility
Kevin Gorman, WebCyclery

Once you have people coming to your site, you have to be able to convert them into customers. In order to increase your conversion rate, you need to have a site that instills confidence and trust. People are afraid of being cheated, especially since the transaction isn't face to face. Creating a feeling of trust can be difficult. It might be as simple as having your name and business address listed on your site, or it might be as complex as showing credentials, certifications, and awards from entities such as the Better Business Bureau, Gomez.com, or BizRate.com. An "About Us" page seems to help too. People like to feel that they are dealing with a real person and not just a number on an order.

Dave Mack, RadioShack Canada

Trust in the quality of your products. Trust in your returns policy. Trust in your pricing policies. Trust in your business ethics. Trust in your consistency. Trust in your ability to deliver. Trust in the information you provide. Trust in your responsiveness to their concerns. There is a *thin* line between success and failure ... that line is called "Trust." Earning trust is the foundation of a successful site; keeping it is vital to your survival. Never stop earning trust.

Internet users are up to four times more likely to shop and purchase online from Web sites that support their native language.

Source: International Data Corporation (www.idc.com)

e-fact

Have Clear Product Images and Descriptions

Deb Steinberg, Nickers & Neighs

Products should be photographed clearly and thorough descriptions written including measurements or size equivalents so customers can order your merchandise with confidence. Use a graphic compression service like GIF Wizard (www.gifwizard.com) to shrink graphics to a quick-loading size.

Bonnie Clewans, The Bead Gallery

Make sure the colours don't detract from the product. Some sites are so busy or dark that it is difficult to see the products they are selling.

Anna Burton, Stylocracy

The product you sell needs to be of first-rate quality and represented well and accurately on your Web site or you'll have disappointed customers and trouble with returns.

Communicate with Your Customers

Sherry Peterson, Main St. Toys

Answer e-mail questions from customers immediately upon receipt. As a customer, I would want to buy from someone who got back with me in a timely manner, and I know that our customers feel the same way. Many times we get two or three e-mails from a customer with various questions before they finally decide on an item and make a purchase. We continually get e-mail responses that say "thanks for your prompt reply." We have decided that some Internet shoppers probably e-mail several businesses with a question, but only hear back from a few. We e-mail the customer back, even if it is to say, "no, we don't have that item, but you might try…" and we give them phone numbers or Web sites of other businesses that might be able to help them. We feel that if we help them find what they are wanting, even if it is another store, they might remember us and try us next time they are shopping for a toy.

Richard Snow, Pull Up Our Sox

I've found that online shoppers really appreciate being kept informed about the status of their order. It all ties into our "hunter/gatherer" instincts. We like to be rewarded (almost immediately) for our efforts—many consider shopping to be "work." I am convinced that if there were some way in which the shopper could somehow watch their order being carefully prepared for shipment, they would be very interested. We only use shipping couriers who offer an online tracking system. This lets the customer check the precise location of their shipment—right to their door. Online customer service chat programs like www.liveperson.com have helped us bring our personal touch to the shopper.

Building Customer Loyalty
Sue Schwartz, YarnXpress.com
One of the contributors to YarnXpress's success is the interactive components of the site. It is important to build a site that brings the customers back. All things being equal, one needs to create an environment that piques the customers' curiosity and invites frequent visits. How one does this is as unique as the online shop.

Spend Your Advertising Dollars Wisely
Doug Young, Noggintops.com
The majority of the world's population does not care about your product. Ouch. That's a painful one, but you will be better off if you can come to terms with the truth of it. You are going to have to spend considerable resources—whether time or money—promoting your online store. No matter what you are selling, there are going to be people—a lot of them— who just are not going to buy. Good business sense dictates that every dollar you spend on advertising should bring a return in sales. Therefore, do not waste your money advertising to people who will not buy. Focus in on a segment of people who are likely to buy, then zoom in even further on the segment that is most likely to buy ... and buy, and buy. If you have an online sewing supply store, for example, you will get far more advertising bang for your buck by spending a few thousand dollars putting ads in a dozen sewing magazines than you would spending millions on a TV commercial during the Super Bowl.

Focus Your Product Line
Doug Young, Noggintops.com
This is important both at start-up and when you begin to grow. As an example, let's say you want to sell books online. You're all revved up and ready to show Amazon.com and Barnes & Noble what's what, so you begin assembling an inventory of titles from *Aardvarks for Fun and Profit* to *Zen Buddhism for Dummies*. Very quickly you discover that there are an awful

lot of book categories, so you decide to spend your inventory budget to stock four or five titles in each category. Predictably, your first prospective customer is disgusted to find you have only five mystery novels to choose from. Your second prospective customer is disappointed to find such a poor selection of self-help books. You get the picture. A far better strategy would be to focus on one specific type of book—preferably a type the well-established heavy hitters have been neglecting—and make yourself the best at that.

There are two very significant advantages to this. First, it enables you to gain an essential toehold in the market by setting you apart from competitors who already have the advantage of name recognition, market share, huge inventories, etc. You've got a fighting chance if you can get people thinking and saying, "Yep, they're small, but they've got the best selection of classic mystery novels anywhere, by golly." Second, it allows you to focus your advertising dollars on a narrower market. Look around and you can find a magazine, newsletter, and organization for most any area of interest. And if those exist, you can bet there are dozens of Web sites devoted to it too. Put your advertising dollars in those places and you will have a more cost-effective ad campaign than the "do-it-all" stores who have to advertise everywhere. This also makes it easier for you to develop advertising content because you'll need to speak to only one area of interest, rather than many. An often overlooked bonus of this niche marketing approach is that people with similar interests tend to hang out together and communicate a lot. Your potential for free word-of-mouth advertising is maximized … and nothing, but nothing, beats good old word of mouth.

Don't Accept Orders for Items You Don't Have in Stock

Sherry Peterson, Main St. Toys

We don't take an order on our Web site unless the item is in stock. We just feel that it is too risky to accept an order when the merchandise isn't sitting in our warehouse. On our Web site it says, "Oops, this item is temporarily out of stock. Please call us at our store for availability," and then lists our toll-free number. When they call us we can tell them when the item is expected in and we take their name and phone number or e-mail address and notify them when the item is back in stock. That is the simplest way for us to handle the situation at this time. It's easier than taking the order and charging their credit card for the item, and then having to issue a credit, in case the manufacturer can't get the merchandise to us for some reason.

Provide Useful Information on Your Web Site

Doug Young, Noggintops.com

These days, the launching of a new Web site will be greeted with roughly the same amount of fanfare as an announcement that your business has acquired a new electric pencil sharpener. The fact that you have a Web site isn't going to impress anyone (except maybe your mother). By now the average Internet shopper has seen and forgotten hundreds of Web sites. With that in mind, be very aware that people will be very unforgiving of Web sites that are uninformative. Many people like Internet shopping because it is easier to comparison shop. Web shoppers tend to be more information-oriented; they want to know the details. They're not just looking for the lowest prices, they're looking for value, and decisions about value demand information. A Web site that is nothing more than an electronic brochure replete with teaser lines and vague product descriptions will not be taken seriously. Server space is cheap, and there's no excuse for not providing all the information a customer could possibly want. Now, that doesn't mean you have to cram the full ingredients list of your vegetarian puppy snacks right on the home page. The beauty of a Web site is that you can structure information in an almost infinite number of layers, allowing the customer to dig as deeply as he or she wants. Every time you get a question from a customer, you ought to think about how you can put that information on the Web site. This is very important. I may be a neophyte e-merchant, but I am a veteran Web shopper. If I spend twenty minutes on a search engine looking for a product only to arrive at an anemic Web site that doesn't tell me what I need to know, I'm moving on.

Have a Toll-Free Number

Sherry Peterson, Main St. Toys

I think having a toll-free number helps our business. I know if I had a choice of calling two businesses who might have the same item, if one had a toll-free number and the other one didn't, I'd call the toll-free number first! Several of our suppliers give our toll-free numbers to people who call them asking for retailers also, which is a big help to us. Some of our suppliers also have Web sites where they will have a list of retailers' Web sites and phone numbers, so our toll-free number is listed there too.

Consistently Add More Value

Dave Mack, RadioShack Canada

Keep building and looking for new ways to add value. Provide more informational content, and better tools to help make the right decision, adding valuable features and services that make it more convenient to shop, like improved search tools, listing "essentials" to ensure they have everything they need, and product location tools to find the product in the closest store to them for immediate access to what they need.

Recognize the Importance of Shipping and Brokerage Fees

Anna Burton, Stylocracy

Consider shipping costs, since size and shape of packages make a big difference in terms of shipping costs and you're competing against businesses within the U.S. whose comparable shipping costs are much less. American businesses can deliver quicker and cheaper than you can. Also consider duty and brokerage fees you may incur when shipping to the U.S. At the moment there's no duty leveraged on shipments under $200 to the U.S., so you want to keep this in mind when determining the price points of your merchandise.

Find a Good Web Developer/Designer

Ray Ritchey, Childbook.com

It was important to get the software done for my custom Web site at a fair price. It was a trade-off between quality, price, and time. It's so easy to get a Web site that does not accomplish what you want it to do. Lots of designers love graphics, which get out of control. Or technical people who ignore the customer needs. It required a lot of interviewing to find somebody I trusted both to do a good job on the Web site, as well as the credit card processing.

Question #2:
What Was the Most Difficult Obstacle or Challenge You Faced When You Created Your Online Store?

Building Credibility

Doug Young, Noggintops.com

I think the single greatest challenge that a new online store faces is building credibility. This has always been the case, but it is perhaps even more true given the recent media storm of dot-com failures and Internet scams. Suppliers will be hesitant to extend lines of credit, and sometimes reluctant to supply you at all. It's a hassle and a risk to get involved with a business that's going to go down in flames in six months. Customers will be cautious (if not outright suspicious) at first, especially if you are a new name. They're wondering if you'll deliver the product in a reasonable time, if it will be what you say it is, and if they'll be treated fairly if there's a problem with the product. If it's a product that the customer is unfamiliar with, they'll be wondering if you really know anything about it yourself. The only solution for that is time or, I should say, time filled with your doing a bang-up job. Show that you can move the supplier's product and pay your bills and you will have all the credibility you need. Customers are a little harder to convince, and you should work harder at convincing them. Before you take your store online, make sure your business is ready to deliver products and customer service that will leave them saying "Wow!" or, if they're not the effusive type, "Yes, that was a most satisfying shopping experience and I would not hesitate to repeat it."

Managing Growth

Bodega Bob Homme, The Submarine Store

Our few thousand-dollar initial investment for start-up was commensurate with our expectations for the size of business we thought we would be operating. Then suddenly, BANG!, we're getting overwhelmed by sales volume, opportunities to bring new products to market, expectations from the submarine community for our participation in charitable events, and a hundred other money-burning situations. I mean, hey, the success was our own fault and, in hindsight, we should have anticipated it. We did the right things, good site, good products, good rollout marketing, good business processes, and frankly we expected to be successful. However, not as quickly as we were. The rate of growth was way beyond anything we could have projected. It came right out of the sun and we had to adapt and overcome quickly before it buried us.

Finally, our capacity and cash flow have caught up with the demands of the business volume. If I had it to do over again, though, I'd come in with a bigger cash reserve and possibly some pipeline to additional capital. Sometimes in the first few months Harry and I felt like that plate-spinning guy who used to appear on the Ed Sullivan show and keep about three dozen plates spinning all at once!

Integrating the Offline Business with the Online Business

Chris Harrower, Choo Choo Barn

Our most difficult challenge remains the same today as it was last year when the site went online: it's trying to interface our online store presence with our retail point-of-sale software. Due to an incredibly steep learning curve for our employees, we have been utilizing an older, DOS-based POS system (only now being upgraded to Windows). It required that everything on the site be created by hand, and there is no connection between physical inventory and online stock status, except for a manual system on a daily basis. It remains our number-one obstacle and requires, during busy seasons, several employees working on a daily basis to keep the site current.

Dave Mack, RadioShack Canada

Our most difficult hurdle was ensuring a solid consistency between online and offline customer experiences. Getting around the paradigm shift of communicating our brand value attributes from "bricks" to "clicks." We knew most consumers came to RadioShack for knowledgeable, helpful, and trustworthy staff. A convenient store where they could get all the "free" advice they needed and the products to make it all work in harmony. Nailing down all of those processes right up to developing online content that reflected a similarity to our in-store experience was critical to us. For example, we wanted to ensure that things such as online refunds could be easily handled in-store. We spent an unexpected amount of energy trying to create a consistency between our online and in-store experience and we are still not yet where we want to be.

Not Having Any Business Experience

Anna Burton, Stylocracy

At the beginning we didn't know what we were doing. I had a graduate degree in Greek Classics and no business experience at all! Nor did we have a clear idea of what was possible. E-business was new, the rate of growth of electronic commerce was entirely speculative. Happily, we couldn't afford to buy into all the hype and decided to keep a firm grip on our costs. A lot of our competition went out of business because they expected to grow at an unrealistic rate and spent accordingly. The government agencies that foster small businesses were a fantastic help. For example, the Saskatchewan Business Service Centre office in Saskatoon was great at tracking down information that I needed and pointing me in the right direction. There is support of this kind available across Canada. We've been around a while and marketing opportunities have even started to come to us without our having to chase them down: recently we were cited in *GQ* magazine and Oxygen Media ran a TV feature on us. That's gravy, of course. Most of the exposure we have had has been as a result of persistence.

Choosing a Web Designer
Deb Steinberg, Nickers & Neighs
It was hard wading through the presentations of Web designers, with quotes of $8,000 to $55,000, and separating the wheat from the chaff. We knew up front what features we wanted on our site, but at that time, there wasn't the plethora of e-commerce solution companies available [as there are today], and costs were higher.

> Western Europe and Japan will account for 47 percent of worldwide e-commerce by 2003.
>
> *Source: International Data Corporation (www.idc.com)*
>
> **e-fact**

Figuring Out What Prices to Charge
Richard Snow, Pull Up Our Sox
[It was hard to come up with] an accurate cost figure to base margin markup on. Since this is a new domain, I didn't really know what all the variable costs associated with selling online would be. Advertising, payment provider/merchant credit card, shipping and handling expenses all need to be factored into the cost of doing business. Our pricing takes all of these into careful consideration in order for us to be profitable.

Becoming Computer Literate
Tane Chan, The Wok Shop
I didn't know anything about computers (and I still don't)—I was intimidated by them. I didn't even know how to turn one on. Since I am computer illiterate and work full-time in my own brick-and-mortar store, an online store seemed impossible and very remote. I had absolutely no knowledge of computers, didn't even own one, didn't even want to learn to e-mail my children away at college because I was intimidated. My son

Mark is the reason my business went online. He started the whole online business from registering our name, www.wokshop.com, to being the Webmaster and doing all the technical aspects of the Web site. He hired a graphic designer who, with Mark, photographed all the items with a digital camera. I hired a recent college graduate that knew nothing about my products and instructed her to write the text according to how she would like to read it ... and would best describe the product to a customer that is interested in it but does not really know how to use it, or to describe the product in such a way that they should buy it because it is practical, different, necessary, and unusual. In other words, the text should answer her curiosity. My job, emphatically emphasized by my son, was to become computer knowledgeable, otherwise the world would pass me by. He bought me the simplest user-friendly computer, an iMac, and encouraged me to learn on my own ... hands on.

Technical Execution
Ron Mis, Galeton Gloves
I've created more than one store at this point, so the obstacles or challenges have changed. But in the beginning I think it was just comprehending how B2B e-commerce would work. It wasn't really happening yet, and everybody was theorizing all kinds of cool and powerful marketing methods, but the basic methods of how it would work weren't clear to me. What wasn't an obstacle was putting up a site. So I did that, and then accumulated data (from the site and from talking to others involved in e-commerce) to begin putting my own theories together. By the time I got to the second and third sites, I had a better grasp of how I thought B2B e-commerce can function, but the technical issues of creating the site became more challenging, so I guess it's kind of shifted. Today I have a much clearer idea of what I want, and probably a harder time getting it technically executed.

Managing Inventory
Sherry Peterson, Main St. Toys
Our biggest obstacle was not knowing what our volume of business would be. It was hard to know how much inventory to have on hand when we first went online. It's still a challenge, but we are learning how to gauge our ordering process better.

Kim Michaux, One of a Kind Kid.com

After getting started, my biggest challenge has been where to store all the inventory—it has taken over my house! I'm not quite to the point where I feel comfortable renting warehouse space.

Building a Market Presence

Sue Schwartz, YarnXpress.com

It was and still is building a presence in my particular market. I, like the many hundreds of thousands of small businesses, am looking for ways to stand apart from the other similar online vendors. At this point in YarnXpress's evolution, I am beginning the process of creative destruction—taking apart things that could be done better, looking for ways to convey our vision in a more unique mode, and expanding the customer base and inventory. I think, in retrospect, the most important challenge was defining what we were not. Keeping the financial plan firm in the first year was a pivotal key to our growth.

Meeting an Aggressive Time Frame

Rhonda Wells, Payless ShoeSource

Our most difficult challenge was our aggressive time frame. We had been challenged by our senior management staff to put together a team of partners in late February of 1999 and have our site launched by May 28, 1999. This date was important as it was the date of our Board of Directors' meeting and we wanted the Board of Directors to be our first customers. This gave us only three months to put together a team composed of effectively four subteams representing all areas of the business: (1) a business team (marketing, merchandising, fulfillment, customer service, financial planning, legal, etc.); (2) an internal information systems team to build all the interfaces to the legacy systems and ensure we launched fully integrated; (3) a technology team (IBM Global Services) to install and develop the site on the IBM Net.Commerce engine; and (4) a design team (Organic) to design the look and feel of the site along with the navigation and functional design.

Realizing That Success Won't Come Overnight

Deb Steinberg, Nickers & Neighs

We built our online store in 1997 and went live in early 1998. At that time, dot-com ads were still a rarity, and the Web wasn't yet a part of everyday life. I certainly didn't realize that the old adage "it takes three to five years to build a business" would apply to my new nifty-swifty Web business!

Finding the Right Software Package

Jason Friedman, J&R Music and Computer World

The most difficult obstacle is finding the right software package that can really do what the salespeople say it can do. Everything looks great in a demo. It takes weeks, if not months, to first research who all the players are in your market niche (this was an even harder challenge four years ago when the Web was less categorized than it is today), then call them all in for demos, then take it upon yourself to write out apples-to-apples comparisons of how each vendor hit the core topics that concern you. The fun isn't over there. Then there's price and negotiating mutually profitable partnerships. This whole process is tedious and frustrating, and before you think you have it nailed, your top-choice vendor goes out of business or is bought by one of your competitors.

Constantly Outgrowing Our Online Store Technology

Christopher Mott, Mott's Miniatures

I have gone through about five different programs to build and design my site and the online catalogue. The current application, number five, is not even a year old and I have been looking to replace it for two months. I realized that it would not meet our needs for longer than eighteen months about seven months after I bought it.... The small start-up company will probably have to design, and redesign, and redesign their site several times. These are growing pains. The pain subsides, but the time and money they consume are real. There are a lot of inexpensive ways to get started with online selling. You can rent stores from Yahoo!, Amazon, and others. That is fine for small operations, but keep your eye on the future. As you start to grow, a small portal that limits you to a few hundred items can eventually hurt you. You outgrow it one day but now you have a large following of customers going to that other portal and no way to bring them forward. You could be stuck running two sites or risk losing part of your customer base.

e-fact

Businesses worldwide could save an aggregate US $2.3 trillion a year by using the Internet to purchase supplies and resources.

Source: The Aberdeen Group (www.aberdeen.com)

Working with the Technology
Rhonda Wells, Payless ShoeSource

A significant hurdle for the business team and the internal information systems team was the technology. To ensure that our focus was on the Payless customer, our business team was pulled from the internal core business teams and effectively had no experience with online selling. Our information systems team had the challenge of understanding how our existing legacy systems could merge with the latest e-commerce technologies to develop an online site. I remember having a conversation with our lead information systems partner and she told me that her team had learned ten new [computer] languages in three months (I've lost count of how many new languages they have learned over the last eighteen months.) In light of our aggressive plan and our steep learning curve, we are all very proud that [our teams] were able to work together, take ownership and accountability for what had to be done, become a student of the business, and execute.

Trying to Replace the Tangible Shopping Experience
Richard Snow, Pull Up Our Sox

[One of our biggest challenges was] creating images and product descriptions that could sufficiently replace the need for a shopper to see and touch what they are buying (as with shopping offline). I feel that this is more of an issue when selling products with subtle attribute variations, such as clothing, whereas books and CDs don't vary, leaving little to the shopper's imagination.

Marketing
Kevin Gorman, WebCyclery

Marketing was and still is the greatest obstacle. Expending time and money into marketing can be a scary thing. It's hard to quantify results, but without it, there aren't many results at all.

Finding Customers
Diane Morgan, Morgan Mailboxes & More

By far, the most difficult challenge is to find your customer base. You have the Web site, you've done the promotion, but you still need more traffic. I sat down, really analyzed my product, and asked myself some very important questions. Who is my customer, where is my customer, and how do I reach that customer? This holds true for offline marketing strategies, as well. For an example, I thought a whole new customer base for my hand-painted mailboxes might be the real estate industry. I spent two weeks hoofing to real estates agencies in my local area and also contacted online brokers, and I carved another new niche for my product. The brokers give a mailbox to their clients as a housewarming gift and this has proved to be quite successful. The worst thing that can happen is they might say no, but you'll never know if you don't attempt it.

Achieving Synergy Between the Web Site and Our Brick-and-Mortar Stores

Rhonda Wells, Payless ShoeSource

I had only been given two rules when I was assigned the job of putting together an Internet presence for Payless ShoeSource: (1) build on our core competencies, don't build a site that is uniquely different from our business today; and (2) do not jeopardize the core business. Our teams have stayed very focused on both of these goals throughout the continued development of the site. Our initiative, immediately after launch, was to build synergy with our 26,000 store associates. I went on the road for six weeks and met with our store operations partners across the United States to share the site with them, answer any questions about the site or the Internet they had, and train them on the site functionality. Today, our store associates will tell you that the online store is the biggest customer satisfaction tool Payless ShoeSource has given them in the last several years. The online store carries all current product in all available sizes. Our inventory position allows the store associate to meet out-of-stock or out-of-season customer requests online. Achieving the goal of customer satisfaction and associate satisfaction was a significant challenge and Payless.com and Payless ShoeSource did extraordinarily well. Our customer is never asked to choose between the online store and the brick-and-mortar store. We sell our site in our stores and our stores on our site.

Technical/Software Bugs

Lynn Moller, Lynn's Collectibles

I was surprised by how unreliable the Web technology was in 1999. Underestimating the technology issues led to some embarrassment. Imagine inviting potential suppliers and partners to your Web store and finding out it had mysteriously disappeared from the Web. Customers will find unplanned paths through the site and lots of software bugs. Every problem is an opportunity to demonstrate that you are customer focused. I initially rewarded customers that let me know about problems with free memberships, discounts, and even free products. When multiple customers were impacted, I tripled the value of the monthly contest. You need to let customers know you care about service with a meaningful response. Most of these early customers have become my best and most loyal customers. It took six to eight months to get most of the bugs out of Lynn's Collectibles Web site. A turning point in reliability was implementing a new process of making all changes on a development site and including vigorous testing before the live site was updated.

Time Management
Kim Michaux, One of a Kind Kid.com
This is truly a full-time business—the advantage to being online is that your hours are flexible. The disadvantage is that you feel like you're always working and just squeezing in your family sometimes!

Question #3:
What Lessons Have You Learned as a Result of Setting Up Your Internet Business?

The Old Rules of Marketing Still Apply
Ron Mis, Galeton Gloves
E-commerce is still governed by the same rules of marketing that apply in offline channels, so don't think that you can get away from all of the marketing issues (e.g., Who is your target market? What are their purchasing criteria? How do you identify and contact them? How does your offer compare to competing offers?, etc.) just because you're selling online.

Customers Often Have Unrealistic Expectations
Christopher Mott, Mott's Miniatures
Big companies like Amazon.com are changing the face of mail order. It used to be that when you ordered a product from a mail order catalogue, you sent your order in and six to eight weeks later it would arrive. Now giants like Amazon.com have spoiled people. My wife can place an order for a book on Tuesday morning and the damn thing will arrive in the mail on Wednesday or Thursday. And now everyone thinks that all Internet

companies have huge warehouses, with twenty-four-hour staffs, and get orders whipped out within seconds of placing their order. I have had people call me on Monday morning telling me that they placed an order at 10 p.m. on Saturday and requested next-day air, and their package was not delivered on Sunday. What do you say to someone like that? How do you answer them without laughing? I think some folks watched too many Road Runner cartoons where the Coyote would drop an order in the mailbox and two seconds later an Acme delivery truck would pull up alongside the road. People really have some misguided expectations of e-commerce. Be aware of it and be prepared to deal with it.

It Costs More and Takes Longer than You Think It Will
Kim Michaux, One of a Kind Kid.com
There are so many expenses I didn't expect, like warehouse expense, a faster Internet connection (when you are on most of the day, speed is essential!), and part-time help. Be prepared for unexpected expenses, like warehousing, software to track inventory, etc., camera to photograph merchandise, shelving or racks for your inventory. It also takes more time than you think it will. There is far more to operating a business than simply photographing items and putting them online. Promoting your site takes days and it is neverending. People won't even know you exist if you don't promote.

Have a Business Plan
Kevin Gorman, WebCyclery
One of the lessons that I learned is, as with any type of business, that having a business plan is crucial. Without having a business plan, going down a wrong path becomes very easy. As wrong as projections and assumptions may be, having a plan keeps you on track at the very least.

Senior Management Support Is Crucial
Rhonda Wells, Payless ShoeSource
Senior management support is absolutely critical. There is no way to really understand the hurdles in an environment that is new and unknown. We had strong, educated points of view, but no means to provide statistical data to support these. If you try to develop a site with "Monday morning quarterbacks," it will not work. The teams will not be dedicated because the company is not dedicated. It is truly an example

of "the shadow of the leader" theory. I've heard many horror stories about lack of senior management support. In the case of Payless ShoeSource, this was never a problem.

Be Careful!

Anna Burton, Stylocracy

Some early mistakes taught me to do my homework and to test ideas cheaply before investing heavily in them. We lost money on an expensive ad in the *New Yorker* magazine and a listing on LuxuryFinder.com (no longer exists). Research every decision thoroughly even if, on the face of it, it seems like a good idea. Find a business in an area you enjoy and in which you have a flare, but at the end of the day, be governed by your head rather than your heart.

Keep Total Control of Your Web Site Development

Jason Friedman, J&R Music and Computer World

Outsourcing is frustrating and expensive. The programmers translating your business into computer code on the other side of town, or sometimes the other part of the world, are usually not more talented than someone you can (and should) hire yourself. Plus, they inevitably (somewhere around 98 percent of the time) code the processes incorrectly, but close enough to the spec so that you still have to pay them twice to fix it.

Invest in Building Business Capacity Before You Need It

Bodega Bob Homme, The Submarine Store

The data management, transactional infrastructure, product acquisition, order fulfillment, and customer service modules for online businesses must be robust and effective, and ours are. Maybe I'd better explain that. What I mean is that each of these components must be well defined, functional, and scaled correctly for the business. I can't stress enough the value of testing each of these before taking the Web business live! These should be developed with one's initial projections in mind, but also, as we learned somewhat painfully at the start, with a margin for growth. We critically analyze the market and the existing capacities of our business. This must be an ongoing process. In our case, we expected to be successful, but the magnitude of our success way outstripped even our most optimistic projections. That sent us to battle stations for a while in a frantic effort to upgrade our business infrastructure to keep up with the rate of growth.

Now, however, we're a little saltier. Before we introduce new products or site features, we take the time to build the capacity of our business first. To be perfectly honest, and many of your readers will be able to identify with this, the enthusiasm of bringing a new product or idea to market tends to generate a momentum of enthusiasm and energy all its own. The tendency is to launch and then address the additional burdens placed on the delivery or administrative infrastructure at some later time. But you have to resist the sense of urgency. Thankfully, we learned this lesson early on with minimal damage!

You Need to Be a Mind Reader
Richard Snow, Pull Up Our Sox
I try and predict what the target customer is looking for or wondering about and make the link to that information as obvious as possible. Shoppers enjoy a site that is both logical to navigate and interesting to browse through. When designing your site, you need to be a bit of a mind reader.

Smaller Is Better
Rob Snell, ystore.com
Not only is it okay for people to know that you're a little guy, it's actually an advantage. People like dealing with the owner of a business, especially when you run a professional operation. If you order from Amazon.com, what are the odds that you'll get a personal note from Jeff Bezos? If you order from our company, you deal with the owners.

Keep It Simple!
Chris Harrower, Choo Choo Barn
We've all heard the "KISS" principle, and it applies in e-commerce more than anywhere else. People don't want to wade through page after page of how great you are, how you are the only, the best, the finest, the fastest, and other superlatives. They want to buy what they came for and move

along! By all means, add your information, but don't be hurt if very few people actually read about how wonderful you are.

You Have to Work Hard to Drive Traffic to Your Web Site
Diane Morgan, Morgan Mailboxes & More

Just because you built it doesn't mean that they will come. You have to constantly promote your Web address. Advertise the Web site address everywhere: return address labels, your chequing account address, business cards, flyers, ads, product tags, letterhead, e-mail signature, etc. Always carry business cards for distribution.

Make Backups of Your Web Site and Databases
Christopher Mott, Mott's Miniatures

In June 1999 the server that my Web site resides on, which was being co-located by my ISP at a national data centre, experienced "thermal damage" (it caught on fire). And the wet-behind-the-ears tech at the data centre destroyed their only backup of my database. Fortunately, I had a copy that was only a few days old. It took a full seven days to get back up and running. The only other backup we had was from several months prior. I shudder at the thought of having to re-enter months of inventory updates and site changes.

Success Requires Careful Integration of New Business Models with Old Ones
Rhonda Wells, Payless ShoeSource

To launch a site is really the easy part. The tough part is understanding how the new business model will survive and be cohesive with your current business model. For example, when we started, we had a world-class distribution centre. However, it was a distribution centre, not a warehouse. We had to learn how to warehouse product to be able to guarantee fulfillment of orders and we had to learn how to pick individual orders versus fill orders that would flow to our over 4,600 stores on a routine basis. It required building new core competencies while leveraging the existing ones. When you're operating within areas like fulfillment and merchandising, where we are considered experts, it is most difficult to remember to challenge "how we've always done it" with "how should it be done for the online store." Building partners across the entire organization is what made us successful in building new processes and core competencies.

Web Site Design Is an Evolving Process
Richard Flynn, Red Trumpet

Be ready and willing to throw away everything you've done and start from scratch. Graphic designers inevitably get tired of looking at work they did months ago; programmers learn and change, and eventually notice that there's a better, faster, and cleaner way of coding everything they coded last year. Just like any software project, your site will have a Release 2.0. Besides keeping your staff happy, a fresh look and new features will keep your customers interested too.

Don't Underestimate the Importance of Word of Mouth
Diane Morgan, Morgan Mailboxes & More

Always remember your customer is the top priority. You have spent a lot of time, money, and energy to get that customer to come through your front door. Repeat customers and word of mouth are extremely important to a small business. I want a happy customer who has a pleasant shopping experience with me so they will come back, and tell their friends about my site.

Sherry Peterson, Main St. Toys

Word of mouth is still a good way to increase your volume of business. We got a phone order from a lady in a Colorado. After she placed her order, she asked me where we were located and when I told her Kansas she said, "You're kidding! The person who told me you had this toy and gave me your phone number was in Italy!" She had been in a chat room discussing a certain toy and someone in Italy who had ordered one recommended us.

Michelle Donahue-Arpas, Genius Babies!

We've watched a number of the "big boys" go under. They spent on average hundreds of dollars in marketing for each customer who visited their site. They offered products with deep discounts, free shipping, coupons, discounts, etc. We offer fair prices, with great customer service—personalized free gift wrapping and handwritten cards—the little things. Our best marketing has all been free … by word of mouth, from our happy customers.

Protect Yourself Against Fraud

Bonnie Clewans, The Bead Gallery

Make sure you have a system for verifying addresses and preventing credit card fraud. I was a victim and I learned so much from this one incident. The banks and credit card processors have a lot of small print and basically the merchant winds up footing the bill for the fraud.

Christopher Mott, Mott's Miniatures

Protect yourself by establishing a set of policies for the handling of on-line transactions, post them on your site, and make sure to link to them from every page of your site and from the checkout pages of your shopping basket. Most of your transactions are going to be credit cards, and credit card companies take care of their cardholders first, so you are in the position of being found guilty and having to prove your innocence when a customer submits a chargeback request to their bank. If you don't know what a chargeback is, just open an online business and you soon will. It is when a credit card customer disputes the charge on their card, and it can be a lot of paperwork. The merchant is at a disadvantage under current laws because the agreement you sign with the bank says that you have to get a signature on the draft. Without that signature you have to prove that you did not charge the customer's card without their authorization. Keep printed records of everything, and get tracking numbers on packages and signatures on deliveries. Have orders called in on an 800 number so you get a record of their call. In some cases your order policies will have to build as you go, learning by circumstances when your policies don't cover a specific instance and then updating your policies to cover it in the future. And establish "Terms of Use" for your site that include the acceptance by your customer of your ordering policies, even if they place their order by means other than the shopping basket.

Your Customer Base May Surprise You!

Anna Burton, Stylocracy

The demographics of our customers are different than I thought. We operate out of a remote part of Saskatchewan and I figured we'd be selling to people like myself who can't get what they want locally and turn to the Internet to shop. To our surprise, most of our customers are people in New York or Los Angeles who could get what we sell downtown, but haven't the time or inclination and find it simpler online. I had no idea that so little of my customer base (or even visitors to the site) would be Canadian. Given that we ship most orders to the U.S., I've had to change somewhat my criteria of what to stock and am now careful to take size into consideration when deciding. Big, expensive-to-ship products are hard to sell at competitive prices when your American competition can ship much more cheaply.

Don't Force Your Customers to Buy Online

Dave Mack, RadioShack Canada

If you're a "clicks" and "bricks" retailer, don't try to force your customers to buy online. When we were first developing our site, we were told, "You're prices online should be cheaper than your stores, otherwise they won't buy online." Many would use "below the line" tactics to capture profit through inflated delivery fees. That was never our intent. We never believed in forcing our customers to shop online; we always believed, even when it wasn't a popular opinion to have, that we would support the customer in whatever method of shopping they preferred. It was the customer's choice to pick and our job to deliver the very best experience regardless of how the customer chose to shop. That's why we have always had one of the lowest, if not the lowest, delivery charges in the industry.

Complete Technology Solutions Are Few and Far Between

Rhonda Wells, Payless ShoeSource

The infrastructure can make or break your business model. There are no "end-to-end" solutions in this technology. What this means is that you have one piece of software as an engine, another for back-end tracking, another for personalization, another for … We brought up the site on the Net.Commerce engine, which allowed us to bring up a very basic selling site, but we had very limited ability to know and understand the activity on our site. To make this happen, we now have thirteen packages that hang off of this engine. Each one of these packages will upgrade yearly and the integration to the other packages will all create significant jeopardy in the success of the upgrade. This dynamic could mean you would spend your entire information systems resource time upgrading packages versus improving the site to meet customer expectations. Infrastructure and marketing costs are keeping many online initiatives from being able to reach profitability. Today, there are few answers in this area. It is such a widespread and known problem that many vendors are working toward more end-to-end solutions.

E-Commerce Requires a Lot of Commitment and Hard Work

Doug Young, Noggintops.com

I am often approached by people wanting to start a little e-store "on the side" for extra income, or as a career that would allow a lot of free time and flexibility. First off, there is no such thing as a Web site that maintains itself, improves itself, and promotes itself. All of those things are an ongoing necessity and require a tremendous amount of time. I can count on one finger the number of weeks I worked less than sixty hours in the past year. A seventy-hour week is common, eighty to ninety not unheard of. Now, I'm not saying that's a good thing or that's how it should be ... in fact I'm rather hoping that will change in the near future. The point is starting an online store and nurturing it to self-sufficiency, then profitability, is no walk in the park. Second, a half-hearted online store is usually seen as such by customers, either immediately due to second-rate Web site qualities, or after two or three visits in which nothing on the Web site ever changes, leaving them wondering if there really is anyone "in there."

Deb Steinberg, Nickers & Neighs

The most important lesson I learned is that the Internet is not like the Kevin Costner movie *Field of Dreams* and the quote "If you build it, they will come." Putting a store on the Web is no different from putting it on a street corner! It requires the same amount of nurturing, marketing, advertising, and time to grow and succeed.

Sue Schwartz, YarnXpress.com

Owning and operating a business is a very time-consuming task. A company is only as good as the service it provides. There is no such thing as "fast money" and the hours are ridiculously long. One must be prepared to sacrifice much to build a successful online business, or any business for that fact!

Customers Value Their Anonymity

Lynn Moller, Lynn's Collectibles

I tried to increase the relationship with my customers by sending them a membership card and brochure in the regular mail, thinking that something physical would make Lynn's Collectibles more real. I discovered that Internet customers really value their anonymity. I could contact them by e-mail, but not by regular mail. It was like standing too close to someone that you are talking to. I had violated their personal space. I lost many customers on this innocent regular mail campaign.

Plan Ahead on Everything
Chris Harrower, Choo Choo Barn

Take the time to walk through your entire process and see where it might break down (because those "might"s will become "will"s once you go live). Have a plan for any eventuality ... The Boy Scouts are right: Be prepared.

Marketing and Technical Staff Need to Respect Each Other's Roles
Jason Friedman, J&R Music and Computer World

Let the technical people do their jobs and the marketing/business development people do theirs. You can't be in worse shape than when you put too much faith in your technical lead, and next thing you know he is negotiating contracts with your vendors, or vice versa, when a business development person starts taking on deals that are technically unfeasible.

Implement a Flexible Search Tool
Richard Flynn, Red Trumpet

One of the best features of any site is a flexible search tool. Go beyond simple word searches to provide searches by field, price range, selection, and anything else you can think of—all while maintaining some order of simplicity. We revamped our search tools after learning that more than 80 percent of our users find their purchases by searching rather than browsing. You need to be flexible enough to listen to people, and then implement changes based on feedback.

Don't Overinvest
Ron Mis, Galeton Gloves

Look at all of the business-to-consumer businesses that have flamed out, many after burning through hundreds of millions of dollars. Incredible! How many companies do that when selling through traditional channels? A smarter course can be to take it slow, do some tests, figure out what works, and then increase your spending. Let the other guy go out of business from charging ahead too fast. Use your cash wisely because it's valuable stuff.

Assume Your Customers Are Internet Novices

Doug Young, Noggintops.com

Never assume people entering your online store will be Web-proficient. The Internet is such a fascinating phenomenon, has so many uses, and has caused such a stir that many people who have previously had no need of or interest in computers are wading into it. Your Web site must be excruciatingly easy to navigate. All relevant information must be "hit-you-in-the-face" easy to find. Using my store as an example, one of the most important pieces of information a hat store needs to make available is a size chart, so we put a big old button marked "Sizing Info" on every single page of the Web site. Good enough, right? Nope. Just about every day someone e-mailed to ask for sizing instructions. It got to be so routine that I made up a form e-mail to send in response to the question. Then it finally soaked in. If people have to ask that regularly, it ain't obvious enough. We added a text link that said "Click here to find your size!" in bright red letters directly under each hat. E-mail inquiries about size dropped off immediately. I shudder to think about the number of people who didn't bother to e-mail for instructions and just left in frustration. Find the most novice Internet users you can to test your Web design ... and learn from them.

> Seventy-nine percent of online consumers focus on convenience when buying on the Internet, while 32 percent value price savings.
>
> *Source: GartnerG2 (www.gartnerg2.com)*

e-fact

Read the Fine Print

Diane Morgan, Morgan Mailboxes & More

Learn to read the small print in any contractual agreement that you encounter on the Internet. If it seems too good to be true, you know it is. I print out all contracts, thoroughly read them, highlight items I'm unsure of, ask questions and more questions until I'm satisfied. I have no clue who the person on the other end of this computer is, you can't make personal judgments by sight, so investigate for your own safety.

Try It Yourself Before Outsourcing

Kevin Gorman, WebCyclery

When WebCyclery first went online, we hired an advertising agency to help us. We wanted help with usability, but at that time we didn't really know it. After spending thousands and thousands of dollars, all that we ended up with was business cards and a disdain for advertising agencies. After that we brought everything in-house. I learned how to use graphics programs, I read books on usability and design, I joined related discussion groups. I became an expert on usability, design and graphics, and advertising. Now I make sure to familiarize myself with anything before I outsource it.

Choose Your Web Developer/Web Designer Carefully

Doug Young, Noggintops.com

The Internet is absolutely filled with well-meaning Web designers and ambitious sales representatives who will try to sell you services that you don't need. Would-be e-merchants are easily misled because they are more naïve (I was, still am in some cases) and they are usually desperate to "get it going" either in terms of getting the store online or increasing sales. There are a lot of self-proclaimed "Web developers" out there offering their services. I recently spoke to an entrepreneur who was ready to plunk down several thousand dollars for some Web developer to build him an "online store." Examination of the design revealed that the Web site was going to be little more than a glorified electronic brochure with poorly designed navigation and no order management functions. Ordering was to take place via a primitive form page where the customer would manually type in the order and e-mail it.

After bursting his bubble by telling him his store would be approximately five years out of date, I happily informed him that for less than $1,000 he could buy a number of storefront software packages that would allow him to build a store with minimal Web design skills and that would already have integrated into it features like a shopping cart, online ordering and credit card verification capability, shipping and tax calculation, automatic e-mail order confirmation, customer database, product database with inventory tracking, search feature, and a host of other online store basics. He walked away looking as though he had been snatched from the jaws of a lion. I'm sure the Web developer was very disappointed. (I'm smiling even now to think of it.) To my knowledge, there are no laws requiring Web developers to practise within their range of competence, so it's going to be up to you to make sure you don't fall victim to "e-malpractice." If you're going to use the services of other professionals, make sure you check them out very carefully. Demand references and follow up on them. Make the developer prove they've built online stores that work. Building a Web site is something that a lot of thirteen-year-olds can do these days. Building an e-commerce-enabled Web site is something else altogether and requires that the developer be intimately familiar with customer behaviour, customer service, and retail business functions.

Not Everyone Is Comfortable Ordering Online

Sherry Peterson, Main St. Toys

Even though we have a secure shopping cart system, we still have customers call and give us the order over the phone. Sometimes they don't feel comfortable giving their credit card number over the Internet, or sometimes they don't understand the ordering process because they are new users, so they would rather call us. That's fine with us, we are happy to help them either way. That's where that personal customer service comes into play again!

Stick to the Products You Know

Christopher Mott, Mott's Miniatures

In a virtual store, there is no limit to the number of products you can display, unlike in a real store where you are limited by shelf space. And with manufacturers and distributors offering drop-shipping services, it can be very tempting to try to set up your own Amazon.com and try to sell everything to everyone. But, just as with a "real" store, you need to establish in your business plan exactly what it is you want to accomplish with the business—what the focus of its products and services is going to be—and then stay focused. Resist the temptation to display products on your site just because you can. If it is not something that you would put on the shelves of your real store, don't put it on your Web site. I have been tempted more than once to expand my selection into trains. I have wanted to sell trains for fifteen years, and every so often I get a little itch and order some catalogues from distributors and go through them. But after the blood returns to my brain, I realize that I don't know anything about trains. I haven't touched a model train since I was a boy. And I couldn't answer even the most rudimentary question about trains if my life depended on it. I have put some gift items on my site, but they don't sell because they are not what people are coming to my site to buy.

Don't Go Live During the Busiest Time of the Year
Chris Harrower, Choo Choo Barn
Our store went online during the month of October, and we spent the Christmas holidays being very thankful that we had had the intervening month to work on system processes that we had missed in our planning.

Know Whom You're Competing Against
Deb Steinberg, Nickers & Neighs
Know your competition, and answer for yourself why your customer should buy from you instead of them. Ask yourself how you are different from your competitors, and what you do better. When I wrote my business plan, I researched all the online and catalogue competitors, even making purchases to determine service levels and shipping times. Before I could really believe that my business could be successful, I had to know what I could do better than my competitors, and how my business would be different. Over the last few years, the number of Web stores competing for my customers has increased tremendously, and with each new competitor, I do enough research to determine that we still do it "best." However, "best" doesn't mean cheapest, it means the entire shopping experience, including shipping costs, quality of merchandise, pricing, shipping time, etc.

Treat Customer Feedback Seriously
Jason Friedman, J&R Music and Computer World
Have someone at the top closely monitor customer feedback. At JandR.com, this is me. When you send mail to "Webmaster," it goes directly into my mailbox. I read every single piece of feedback our customers have about our site. I use this to judge when a feature on our site needs fixing and send it off to quality control appropriately, and generally gauge demand for more features to keep customers happy and coming back. The reason I say it should be read by someone on top is because it is all too easy to delete feedback e-mail from customers, and I don't trust anyone else for making sure that every single concern gets addressed, no matter how tedious it is to follow up to make sure it gets done.

Be Wary of Search Engine Optimization Companies

Doug Young, Noggintops.com

There are a fair number of ill-meaning scam artists seeking to blatantly rip you off and, again, we highly enthusiastic and hungry entrepreneurs are easy targets. One of the biggest scams right now is in the area of so-called search engine optimization. Within twenty-four hours of going online, you will receive a host of offers to register you with all the major search engines and a thousand minor search engines for just $19.95 or some such bargain price (been there, done that). Some make more extravagant claims about actually boosting your position in search engine results ... for more money, of course (been there, done that, too). Most of these services use automated submission software that is greatly despised by search engine companies because it clogs up their system. Most search engines make a concerted effort to negate these services, successfully I might add, judging by the huge number of people who have found these services to be utterly worthless. Use of these services can even delay your search engine registration because the search engine may respond to your automated submission attempt by purposely excluding your Web site for a time.

While there are a limited number of firms who have demonstrated they can optimize search engine placement, they do their work on a case-by-case basis and thus are very expensive. You must be certain that search engine placement is important in reaching your market before investing in their services. Though a little tedious, search engine registration is quite simple and is better done manually. Unfortunately, this lesson cost me a bit of money and two or three precious months of search engine invisibility.

You Can Sell Online from Anywhere!

Sherry Peterson, Main St. Toys

The customer usually doesn't care where we are located as long as they can get the item they want by the time they need it. As I said before, we are located in the Midwest, but most of our orders come from larger cities all over the country. I've decided that there are more people who don't want to fight the traffic and fight the crowds to do their shopping. They can also search on the Net to find hard-to-find items and have them shipped much easier than running all over town and still not finding what they want.

Be Careful with Banner Advertising
Doug Young, Noggintops.com
Another form of scam is the peddling of overpriced banner ads on Web sites with trumped-up traffic claims. Even if the Web site appears to be reaching your desired target market, be very cautious. Demand references and, when checking them, get very specific about results they have received. If you do decide to proceed with paid advertising on a Web site, try to get a one- or two-month cancellable contract rather than a whole year's worth. That way you can pull out and cut your losses if it isn't doing anything for you.

Keep Reinventing Your Web Site
Lynn Moller, Lynn's Collectibles
A lesson that I fortunately learned early on is to keep reinventing your site. If you are not happy, change it. It is not likely everything will be perfect the first time. I still continue to find ways to simplify navigation through the site; the less clicks the better. While not quite statistically correct, think of each click causing half of your remaining visitors to leave. I found this to be correct in the first three to four clicks.

Know Your Customer
Deb Steinberg, Nickers & Neighs
Know your customer, what they want, and provide it. Do your homework regarding your target market, know the demographics, and continuously refine your product offerings until they can't resist making a purchase. Know when to "bite the bullet" and mark things down—blow items out, and learn from the experience.

Be Prepared to Sell Small-Ticket Items
Sherry Peterson, Main St. Toys
We ship lots of small items and I guess I assumed that most people would only purchase larger items over the Internet. One of our first Internet sales was a $5.99 Koosh ball. The customer was in New York City and she knew exactly what she wanted. It was easier for her to do a search on the Internet and find us, call on our toll-free number, and have it shipped than to get in her car and drive around looking for the ball.

Put Customers' Needs First

Chris Harrower, Choo Choo Barn

Be flexible and give the customers what they want, not what you want, or what you think they want. When we first went live, I had spent a month or so creating this wonderful JavaScript that would pop up a picture of any item in a small window on people's computers, allowing them to click to see any item, but removing the necessity of having pictures on each catalogue page, thereby slowing the load time of that page considerably. Well, that JavaScript was wonderful and powerful, and didn't work on the computers of about 15 percent of our customers! While 15 percent may not seem like a big problem, even one unhappy customer can hurt your business. In the end, the JavaScript was thrown away and a simpler solution was put in place to meet our customers' needs.

Question #4:
What Key Piece(s) of Advice Would You Offer Someone Who Is Thinking of Setting Up an Online Store?

Be Patient

Anna Burton, Stylocracy

Patience is a valuable virtue here. Starting such a business is extremely time consuming and the payoff is delayed. With perseverance and shrewd decision making, you can slowly build your online presence, but don't be driven by the "If I build it they will come" mentality, even if you think you've got a brilliant idea for an Internet business. Keep your costs down as much as possible: begin by investing what you can in a good Web site.

Lynn Moller, Lynn's Collectibles

It is important to be patient about success. It takes time to build long-lasting relationships, the foundation of a successful business. I am privileged to have supportive suppliers, a gifted graphics designer, a responsive hosting company, and wonderful customers. The people in your life determine your success; treat them well.

Find a Knowledgeable Web Developer/Web Designer

Sherry Peterson, Main St. Toys

Find that key person who is knowledgeable about the Web and Web site design. It will cost you to hire someone with the expertise you need, but in the long run I think it is essential to having a successful Internet business. I know there are computer programs out there that let you design your own Web site, but if you want a professional-looking site that is functional, it takes a lot of knowledge that the average person doesn't have. We are a small company, but that doesn't mean that we can't be professional in how we do business. Most businesses start small and if they do things in a professional manner, they grow into larger companies.

Don't Let Your Web Designer Control You

Chris Harrower, Choo Choo Barn

Do the necessary research and find a good local company if you don't have the time to learn how to make your own Web pages. If you do hire an outside company to do your work, make sure you are happy with it! Make your Web site reflect your company, not the design company! There are a lot of designers out there (not all designers, but there are a lot) who want to make themselves look good, not make you look good. (I know ... I used to be one of those. I was more interested in making sure people knew what I could do than in what worked for the company I was supposed to be representing.)

Don't Be Afraid of Failure

Bodega Bob Homme, The Submarine Store

Every successful entrepreneur has some (usually very entertaining) story of a venture that failed. We submariners who served during the Cold War used to have a saying when we played tag with the Soviet boats. "Sometimes you get the Bear, sometimes the Bear gets you!" When the bear gets you, get the damage under control, return to port, put everything back in order, and get the heck back out there and do it again! You will never be able to hit a home run unless you step up to the plate and swing at a pitch. And the more times you are at bat, the greater your number of chances to knock one out of the park!

Research Your Online Business Carefully

Sue Schwartz, YarnXpress.com

I would suggest that anyone who is considering an online store carefully research the demand prior to building the business. An online shop needs to offer something different than the retail brick-and-mortars do. I would never advise someone to build an online store just to build one. The expectation that you build it and the dollars roll in is just not true.

Marketing strategies need to be explored and implemented. You need to understand your target audience.

Some people believe that an online business is easier than a brick-and-mortar establishment. I would encourage anyone who subscribes to this belief to revisit the research.

> Forty-eight percent of Canadian parents admit their kids have at least some influence on the purchase of new technology for the household.
>
> *Source: Ipsos-Reid (www.ipsos-reid.com)*
>
> **e-fact**

E-Commerce Works Best When It Complements Your Core Business
Dave Mack, RadioShack Canada

If your goal for an online store is simply to deliver incremental profits to your core business, there may be more effective ways to do that. If your goal is to use your online store to complement your core in-store business and extend your brand presence to the online world, there is no better way to do it.

Make Customer Satisfaction Your Number-One Priority
Rhonda Wells, Payless ShoeSource

I would have to reiterate that the key advice is to know your customer and set realistic strategies to meet the customers' needs. Keep your customers' satisfaction as the first and last question of every decision. You can have a great site that is "overbuilt," but you won't have a chance at profitability.

You Have to Be Responsive to Your Customers
Tane Chan, The Wok Shop

Be prepared to spend hours (if you are a small business) on the computer answering inquiries with a personal touch and acknowledging orders immediately, then shipping out orders the same day or the next day. Online customers are ordering online because they want prompt service—you must acknowledge their order immediately and status of shipping.

Previous Retail or Catalogue Experience Gives You an Advantage
Rob Snell, ystore.com

If you already have a "real store" or a mail order company, you're already 50 percent of the way to being e-commerce ready. If you have a credit card processing account, access to UPS or FedEx shipping, and you sell a product that has ever been sold by catalogue, you have the seeds of what it takes to grow a successful e-commerce operation. Most of the people I talk to are new entrepreneurs who know that they want to sell their stuff online, but they don't know how to set up an account with a distributor or get a line of credit at the bank. If you already have the "business" stuff down, the e-commerce part isn't as hard as you think. Successful catalogue and mail order companies can transition to the Web because they already have the fulfillment and customer service parts down, and this is a killer for fast-growing mom-and-pops. I see so many of the new Yahoo! Stores I work with hit a choke point around $10,000 a month in sales. They have too many orders for one person to handle, but not enough profit to hire a staff. And there's another choke point around $50,000–$60,000 a month where they need a computer person and a phone system and all of this in-frastructure, and they're not sure if they want to outlay the capital to grow the company to another profitable level. Having a good-looking, fast-loading, e-commerce-enabled Web site is the first leg of a very long jour-ney. I cringe when I see an Internet service provider say, "Build a complete e-store in thirteen minutes!" I understand the marketing, but the last thing we need are 500,000 more bad e-commerce sites. It's the commerce part of e-commerce [that's important]. It's almost like saying, get your MBA in minutes by buying these eighty-five textbooks. Just because someone has the tools doesn't mean they know how to use them.

Be Realistic with Your Expectations

Deb Steinberg, Nickers & Neighs
Examine your motives and expectations and determine that they are hon-est and realistic.

Richard Flynn, Red Trumpet
If you are hoping to make a quick buck, forget it. We are very fortunate that our team consists of music lovers first, which helps us relate better to our customers. To make a million overnight, you have to be both good and lucky. Best to focus on being good—the part you can actually control.

Bonnie Clewans, The Bead Gallery
E-commerce takes time to develop. Don't expect to go online and start getting thousands of orders. It takes hard work to market your business on a budget.

Your Web Site Is a Tool

Christopher Mott, Mott's Miniatures

Your Web site is not a business, it is a tool. Do not think that you can open a Web site and make money. You still have to run a business. Back in 1995 I built Web sites for other companies as a way of supplementing my income. I even tried opening my own Web design company. What I soon discovered was that there were a lot of people out there who thought that owning an Internet business was like some kind of magic. That a Web site could just make money all day and all night and the owner of a Web site could sit on an island in the Bahamas and sip drinks with little paper umbrellas in them. These were people who had no clue what it is to actually own or run a business. I think this has best been represented by the number of virtual companies who close or sell off.

Make Sure You Really Want to Do This

Diane Morgan, Morgan Mailboxes & More

Make sure this is really what you want to do. You have to be completely dedicated and have drive, ambition, motivation, and perserverance to get your business running successfully and to maintain it. The e-commerce world is no longer a nine-to-five job. It's really twenty-four hours, seven days a week.

Kim Michaux, One of a Kind Kid.com

Make sure you have the passion for what you're doing—you're going to spend a lot of hours doing it! You need the passion to keep you going on the bad days.

Make Sure That You Have Products in Inventory

Bonnie Clewans, The Bead Gallery

Turnaround time is extremely important for online shoppers. I have had people ask about setting up a Web site where they would take orders and only then would they try to obtain the merchandise. I strongly advise against this, as my biggest concern for all of us doing e-business is reputation and honesty. I have many repeat customers who gladly accept my suggestion for a substitution if a specific item is out of stock. Almost all my orders go out within forty-eight hours and they are shipped complete.

Selling Online Is Harder than You Think
Richard Snow, Pull Up Our Sox

At first I thought that selling online would be a piece of cake—design a Web site, get a domain name, list my products, sit back, relax, and the orders (and money) will start rolling in! In reality, all of this is true with the exception of the sitting back and relaxing part. I have been keeping very busy with pursuing valuable advertising opportunities, close communication with shoppers and suppliers, keeping Web site content up to date, etc., etc.

Don't Go Overboard with Technology
Doug Young, Noggintops.com

Technology is a tool, it is not itself the solution. Technology will not sell your product. Your ability to communicate meaningful content to the consumer is what will sell your product. That fact should be the guiding force as you design and build your online store. Web site construction is a technical thing; Web site design is not. The person responsible for the layout of your store, the part that the customer sees and interacts with, should be someone who is extremely customer-oriented. He or she should also be intimately familiar with how your particular product is best presented to the customer. If you're hiring a professional Web developer, don't count on them to know how to sell your product and service your customer.

e-fact

Forty-one percent of online consumers have wanted to return a product purchased from an online shopping site, but decided it was just too much hassle to do so.

Source: PricewaterhouseCoopers (www.pwcglobal.com)

New technologies and Web site enhancements appear every day. Before you hastily add them to your online store, you should give some thought as to whether it will really add to the customer's shopping experience on your Web site. For example, I recently visited an online store that had one of those chat windows you could use to talk to a live sales representative. I clicked on it and received a friendly message saying someone would be available to assist me in a moment. So I waited … and waited … and waited. Out of curiosity, I quickly fired off an e-mail of the question while dialing the customer service phone number. After just a few seconds on hold, I spoke with someone who answered my question. Less than an hour later, I received an e-mail response answering my question. Not too bad. The online chat window? I finally got bored waiting and terminated the session. Maybe it was just an off day. Maybe they were having some technical difficulties (the bane of online existence). In any case, my immediate perception was that they had employed a technology that they were not able to use effectively. To their credit, they had effective alternative avenues for customer assistance, but the risk of turning people off by showcasing an ineffective one is not worth it, in my opinion, no matter how cool it seems to be. I want to make it clear that I'm not bashing live chat windows. If you have the personnel to employ them effectively, I have no doubt that they can be a great asset. The same can be said for 3-D graphics, video, audio, and animations. They may have their place, but you need to make sure that it genuinely adds to the quality of the shopping experience before you add it to your Web site. An online store should not be just a collection of whiz-bang technologies. It should be a cohesive unit that guides the customer to the product and to the sale.

An Online Business Must Be Run like Any Successful Brick-and-Mortar Business

Jason Friedman, J&R Music and Computer World
J&R's philosophy is to always keep the customer happy, concentrate on customer satisfaction, smooth fulfillment, competitive pricing, and constant inventory replenishment. These are principles that must be followed whether you are talking about setting up a brick-and-mortar or online storefront.

Business Skills Are Essential

Bodega Bob Homme, The Submarine Store
Too often Web entrepreneurs focus on the "e" in e-business. Focus on the business! Knowing about the Web or how to build a Web site or any of the myriad processes and functions of the Web is not going to make your business successful. This knowledge may be a component of your potential success, but business is about business, not the venue in which it is conducted, not the supporting processes. Business! If you have only a passing understanding of good business practices, team up with or hire someone who does. Conversely, if you know your business but are unfamiliar with its execution on the Web, team up with or hire someone who does. In short,

critically analyze your strengths, compare them to those required by your venture, be humble enough to identify the areas that are insufficient in your skill or knowledge inventory, and be smart enough to team up with or hire others with the skill set necessary to ensure your success.

Choose Your Technical Platform Carefully
Richard Flynn, Red Trumpet

Build your Web site on a stable and secure technical platform. Downtime, slow response time, and security failures devastate the credibility of an e-commerce presence. Customers appreciate sites that run crisply and are always available. Factors contributing to the reliability of your site include the server hardware, operating system, Internet connection, Web server software, and programming environment.

Create a Business Plan
Kevin Gorman, WebCyclery

Create a business plan. It's one of the hardest things you will do, but it is also the most important. Going through the process of creating a business plan makes you really think about what you want and how you are going to get it. It is an extremely useful tool, something that you will be able to use to help you find your way when things don't go the way you expected.

Ray Ritchey, Childbook.com

Do a business plan and figure out your customers' needs and what you can do to satisfy them better than your competition. Is this a sustainable advantage? What can be done to make it so? Do a worst-case cash flow projection.

Question #5:
What Is the Best Feature You've Built into Your Online Store?

Synergies with Our Retail Stores
Rhonda Wells, Payless ShoeSource

The simplistic, yet synergistic, shopping experience that mirrors our customers' shopping experience in our stores. This feature has engaged 26,000 store associates in selling our site in our stores and has drawn countless positive e-mails from our customers. The customer really appreciates not having to figure out how to work our site; they simply want to buy our great value, fashion, and quality footwear.

A Monthly Contest

Deb Steinberg, Nickers & Neighs

We have a horse trivia game that is challenging and fun. We select a winner each month and give away a nice prize. Many people visit our site every month just to get their name on the list for the prize!

Kevin Gorman, WebCyclery

The best feature that we have on our site is our contest/newsletter. We let people sign up to win a monthly giveaway. In doing so they can sign up for our newsletter, which allows us to continue to market to them and keep them as a customer.

Twenty percent of all Canadian families with home Internet access have computers that have been networked to others within the home.

Source: Ipsos-Reid (www.ipsos-reid.com)

e-fact

Myself

Sue Schwartz, YarnXpress.com

YarnXpress.com is a reflection of my love of knitting and yarn. It is a creative place that people can visit and become part of an active and creative community.

Personal Service

Tane Chan, The Wok Shop

E-mailing each and every customer thanking them for their business and asking them about the particular product(s) they bought. This is so personal and each customer takes it very personally and even acknowledges this gesture with much appreciation. This is what I mean when I said to be prepared to spend hours on the computer ... whether your message is brief or long, it makes a difference.

My approach to a successful online business may not apply to other businesses. My line of products are "ethnic" or special and not available in most regions of the United States (my main business), so I really have to describe the product very clearly and briefly and the photo has to be very clear. Prospective customers cannot just walk into a department store or specialty store in their area and see the item. My customers are really depending on my text, copy, description, and photo to sell them and then my own input as if I am conversing with them in the physical store. Many of my customers are purchasing my products without ever seeing them or touching them, and they really don't know what to expect. They have put their trust in me to deliver exactly as described and satisfaction guaranteed, and I do. After ten months of a Web site and five months of online ordering, I have yet to have a disappointed or dissatisfied customer. In fact, all the customers that have taken the time to comment on our Web site, products, service, prices, etc., have given us an "excellent" rating and I have met many new "friends" through cyberspace.

My online small business is run like my brick-and-mortar business ... good, knowledgeable, prompt, honest, friendly service ... I do through e-mail and cyberspace what I normally do in the store. I e-mail my customers as if I am talking to them in the store. I even recommend items and advise them on use, etc. I correct or suggest online orders because from experience I know what goes with what and they appreciate and thank me so much. I either call them or e-mail my suggestions or corrections. Since their orders are being shipped, I save them time, hassle, returns, and money. About 25 percent of my customers do not order online, but they visit the site, do their homework, and call in their order because they don't feel comfortable releasing their credit card number online, and some customers call in their orders because they have questions. So, as I mentioned earlier, I do sell a different type of product, which requires a different approach and selling technique and I have found that this very personalized approach is what works for me.

I would consider our online business a success and I look forward to improving it and adding more items. I listen to my customers and know that if one customer is asking about an item not featured, other customers will too.

Our Ship-to-Store and Find-It in Store Features
Dave Mack, RadioShack Canada
I believe we have been true innovators in our online store with these two unique features:

1. *Ship-to-store:* As a FREE DELIVERY service, customers can have their online order shipped to their local RadioShack store for pickup. We simply add their order to the next shipment headed for the corporate RadioShack store of their choice. Our customers benefit from free delivery and helpful advice when they arrive to pick it up. RadioShack benefits from the additional foot traffic into our stores as well as the opportunity to suggest some essential add-ons that the customer may have not included in their original order.

2. *Find-it in store:* Since we added this feature over a year ago, it has been an instant success with our customers and our stores. In an effort to further use our online store to complement our brick-and-mortar stores, we offer customers the ability to instantly confirm the availability of a product in any of our 500 corporate RadioShack stores. Customers love the convenience of ensuring the product is in stock before driving to the store and they can get it "today." Our stores love the additional sales this feature has generated and the satisfying customer experience it creates in store.

Our Submarine Community Centre
Bodega Bob Homme, The Submarine Store
There we provide our shipmates and their families with discussion forums, a newsletter, electronic postcards, reunion announcements, shipmate locators, a news clipping service, original articles, a calendar of events in the submarine community, a Web directory, as well as topical chat rooms—all of these are submarine-oriented, of course. Granted, they all serve to drive traffic to our site, but their development and maintenance are a marketing expense. We derive no direct revenue from their existence and, according to the feedback we receive, this area of our site is extremely well received and greatly appreciated by the community we serve.

Real-Time Inventory
Richard Flynn, Red Trumpet
In a business like ours, when items go out of stock, they can be gone forever, so accurate inventory is vitally important. Having to tell customers who placed an order that items are unavailable is embarrassing and diminishes credibility. We've employed complex inventory tracking that combines ordering, shipping, receiving, and the shopping cart system on

our site to produce a constantly up-to-date count of units on hand for any item. Once an item is no longer available, it vanishes from the site immediately. This has proven to be one of our greatest assets. (As an aside, this was also a lesson we learned, since we had to take a complete inventory about a dozen times before the site was up and running! Needless to say, it convinced us of the value of real-time inventory tracking.)

---

e-fact

Seventy percent of just over 1,000 Canadian Internet users responding to an online poll said they prefer to do their holiday shopping on dot-ca (.ca) Web sites rather than dot-com (.com) sites.

Source: Canadian Internet Registration Authority (www.cira.ca)

Richard Snow, Pull Up Our Sox

Our inventory level indicator provides the shopper with a warning if they are trying to order more of an item than is currently in stock. This reduces the likelihood of the shopper having to wait or us having to issue a refund (transaction cost involved) for out-of-stock items. This feature helps us to automatically set up an accurate shopper's expectation that they will get exactly what was ordered in the time frame advertised.

Our Product Knowledge

Christopher Mott, Mott's Miniatures

I think the best feature the site has is the knowledge of the owners of the business. In my case, it is our knowledge of the products we sell, fifty years' worth in three generations. The Internet is the most effective tool we have for communicating that knowledge to customers. An example is the amount of product description we give our products. We sell dollhouses, which come in either a do-it-yourself kit or finished, or anywhere in between. The product I sell is not the kind of product that is sold in every store in America, or is something that everyone understands. It is not like a vacuum cleaner that you can get anywhere. There are all kinds of houses. We sell kits that start at $40 and finished mansions that can reach $20,000. If you are going to sell one of the more expensive houses, say a kit that costs $500 or $1,000, you have to explain to people how that kit is different from a kit that costs $40, and how what we sell is different from a $20 plastic dollhouse you get at Toys "R" Us. It is especially important when they are buying it over the Internet and can't walk into a local showroom and touch it like a vacuum cleaner. This is a pretty obscure product. Some products have one- or two-page descriptions. We describe in as much detail as possible what a customer gets, what they don't get, and what they will end up with. We have fifty years' experience running a retail store and helping people find the product they are looking for. We have managed to take that experience and translate it into a tool that sells products twenty-four hours a day, in every country on the planet.

Selling Brand Names and Our Web Site Design

Anna Burton, Stylocracy

One of the primary ways our Web site is "found" is through search engines and this has been a real bonus for us as far as marketing goes. Because we sell name-brand items that people are familiar with and are looking for, we are found when people look for these things through search engines. If you want a tea kettle by well-known architect Frank Gehry, type the key words ("tea," "kettle," "Frank Gehry") into Google and we will be listed. If we sold generic or little-known tea kettles, no one would find us this way and the search engines would be of no use for us. I'm not necessarily advocating name-brands, just something that lends itself well to being found by a search engine.

Also, we're "sticky," that is, most who visit the Web site stay for a while and have a good look around before exiting. We've been pleased by these high statistics and think they are the result of the design of our Web site, which is interesting, pleasant, smart, easy to navigate, and our content is an added attraction. The things we sell are beautiful in and of themselves and certainly help bring up the tone of the entire package. A significant number of the people who visit us each day do so because they've bookmarked us. There will be many out there trying to capture the same niche and you need to set yourself apart from them, in part by the presentation of yourself. If you're a mom-and-pop cookie cutter site, you won't be memorable and are less likely to have your visitors return.

Having a good Web site is essential to your credibility and it will help with the marketing of your Web site. It will help you gain listings in directories where people will come across your Web site. We got for free a very valuable listing on Style 365.com, and being listed next to Tiffany & Co., The Gap, the Sharper Image, and Dean & Deluca helps our credibility immensely. These links also help to improve your standing in search engines. We are taking part in a program at Visa.com in which they list us as a recommended merchant and we offer a coupon discount to those using their Visa card. This fell in our lap and I suspect it wouldn't have if we didn't look professional and have some appeal. Participating in Visa's program has given us great exposure and again, great credibility to be alongside marthastewart.com and Cooking.com.

The "About Us" Section
Sherry Peterson, Main St. Toys

A feature that I like about our catalogue is a section that's titled "About Us" and shows a photo of the four people who own the store. It also tells about where we are located and what our mission statement is, so if people don't want to do business with a machine, it makes it feel a little more personal. I wondered if people really went to that section of the catalogue, but I just had a customer last week ask me what my name was again, and she said, "I'm in your catalogue and I'm looking at your picture."

User-Friendliness
Doug Young, Noggintops.com

We worked hard to make navigation around the Web site easy, both in terms of finding something and getting back to where you were. We provide multiple avenues for getting questions answered: a Frequently Asked Questions (FAQ) button, links to our e-mail on every page, and easy-to-find telephone numbers. You want people wondering about how many of your products they should buy, not about what your shipping rates are, what your return policy is, how to contact you, etc. We excluded features and "window trappings" that don't add to the functionality of the Web site.

Elaborate backgrounds may be pretty and animated juggling monkeys may be cute, but they also slow down the speed of the Web site. Many people still have relatively slow Internet connections, and many people shop online in a hurry (i.e., over their lunch break). In any case, nobody likes to navigate around a slow Web site.

We organized our products into categories and put the information and pictures in layers. We provide small (fast-loading) "thumbnail" pictures of each hat along with a brief description so that customers can quickly decide which hats they might want to look at in more detail. When they see something that piques their interest, they can click on the thumbnail and see a large picture with a detailed product description. If they want more detail, they can click on that picture to see a really big picture with multiple angles, colour choices, etc. Some Web sites just cram a bunch of product descriptions and large pictures all on one page, which makes a slow-loading page and requires the customer to waste time looking at things they might not be interested in, which increases the risk that they will leave before finding what they want. When leaving your store is as easy as one finger movement, you don't want to make your customers impatient. The arrogant belief that your products are "worth waiting for" will be a costly one.

Educational Resources

Jason Friedman, J&R Music and Computer World

From day one, back in 1996, we had a JavaScript-based online technical glossary. In other words, in the description of a computer, the term "100BaseTX" will be hyperlinked, and when clicked on will pop up a small window explaining the term. When an average user wants to buy his first computer, knows how much he wants to spend, and sees that features like this can make a computer more expensive, he wants to know what it means. Most sites take it for granted that customers understand the jargon as well as the people writing the copy. This is obviously not true—just ask a customer in any computer store who you see hiding in the corner, scared to ask what he thinks might be an obvious question. This initial feature is indicative of the hundreds of other features we have put in place in the following four years.

> Only one in four Web sites meets minimum standards for Internet users with disabilities.
>
> *Source: Forrester Research (www.forrester.com)*

e-fact

Our site is geared toward being the computers, electronics, and music site for everybody. Most of the items we sell are highly technical. People know they want them, but have a hard time distinguishing one Greek-sounding feature from the next. We have an entire team dedicated to distilling this information for the customer in the form of Buyer's Guides, in-depth product reviews, carefully plain-English written product descriptions, and standardized product specification sheets so customers can compare most of our catalogue of 400,000 products side by side, apples to apples. We also offer unique exclusive multimedia content so the customer can actually watch a homegrown infomercial on a product and never feel that they are missing anything by not coming down to the store. The only thing our site is missing at this point is the ability for the customer to physically pick up and touch the product via virtual reality. Rest assured, we're working on it.

Online Credit Card Processing

Diane Morgan, Morgan Mailboxes & More

The best feature I added to my site was merchant account and shopping cart features. I spent about six months researching different merchant account services that would be best for my business needs. My sales increased dramatically when I offered credit card services. I think this served two purposes. This provided legitimacy, credibility, and professionalism to my business from the customer's point of view. The convenience of on-line payment increases the chances of the customer purchasing your product. A chance of a completed sale decreases dramatically once the customer leaves your "store," so you have to make it as easy and convenient as you can. When I first started the Web site, I didn't have a real order form system or a merchant account. The customer had to either e-mail, fax, or phone in an order and then send a cheque for payment. I've found that if the customer doesn't order at that first initial sit-down at the computer and has to do "more work" on their end, there's a good possibility you've lost that sale.

Question #6:
Has Your Venture into Online Retailing Met Your Expectations?

Sherry Peterson, Main St. Toys

Yes and no. When we first went online, I think we all thought we were going to be flooded with orders immediately and we were sort of disappointed that we weren't. Then after we talked and sort of re-evaluated things, we decided that it's not good to grow too fast and that it would have probably been too much for a small company like us to handle. (I might say at this point our corporation is made up of my husband and me and our daughter and her husband. She and I own the majority of the stock, do the buying, and manage the store and the catalogue.) Now that our catalogue has been online for about three years and has grown steadily, it has allowed us to learn more about e-tailing as we have grown and made changes along the way. Maybe sure and steady does win the race after all! Our online catalogue has been a scary but exciting venture. I'm in my early fifties, so a few years ago if someone had told me I was going to have a catalogue on the Net, I would have said they were crazy, but it's just been a wonderful experience. I am by no means a computer whiz and have learned so much in the last four years, it's incredible. Every day I'm amazed by something that happens in a day's work and I can't wait to go to work to see what the day will bring.

Kevin Gorman, WebCyclery

Yes and no. From a financial standpoint, it has not. When I started, I thought that I would be making millions of dollars, and would have trouble keeping up with demand. Of course, that didn't happen, but we do continue to grow and that's exciting. What I've learned has far surpassed my expectations. I started this business because I like bikes and took an HTML class in college. What I've learned in the past two years is more than I learned in college and would make me an extremely valuable asset to any company.

Richard Snow, Pull Up Our Sox

I am pleased to say that online retailing has enabled us to share our winning fashion retail experience with a much broader and diverse market as well as sufficiently meeting our financial expectations. We have shipped products to Asia, Europe, and the U.S. There are no borders on the World Wide Web! Landlord/tenant rules governing specialty retailers in malls, for example, simply don't apply here—it's completely OUR show! Several of our long-standing offline customers have tried shopping at our online store and have commented on the convenience it offers. People are glad to hear that we offer an online shopping option (whether they use it or not). Our suppliers are anxious to make sure that their product lines are represented online too. This is a win-win for everybody. Our revenue figures are well within the industry standard—with our online store sales approaching 10 percent that of our brick-and-mortar store sales.

Richard Flynn, Red Trumpet

As relative newcomers in the field of online retailing, we weren't entirely sure what to expect when we launched our site. We've experienced a strong but inconsistent rise in sales that surprises us on some days and disappoints on others. This is partially due to our minimalist approach to marketing: we've actually publicized our site more slowly than we could have. We want to be certain before we entice people to spend all of their money at our store that our fulfillment process is solid and there are no delays under high load. In some ways, achieving terrific customer satisfaction (which we had even before launching our site) is a bar we've raised very high for ourselves: it means that everything we do must meet the same high standards people have come to expect from our company. I have found this venture into e-commerce very fulfilling from a professional standpoint. After fifteen years of inconsistent challenges in the corporate world, I was becoming too complacent and taking too few risks. In fact, the risks are vitally important to me as a business owner since I have learned much more from failures than successes. Red Trumpet has provided an opportunity to put together a team of players that share my enthusiasm, dedication, and willingness to take risks—careful, thoughtful, researched risks—that are essential in the new business climate. And though we enjoy the challenges and risks of our business model, we also remember that our business is based on turning a profit, which we have done every quarter since inception.

Anna Burton, Stylocracy
Our expectations were fairly modest: we hoped that in time it would provide an extra income and flexible working hours for me, a stay-at-home mom with small children. We've been happy with consistent and steady growth, even during the economic downturn and are very pleased that we quadrupled our number of sales during the 2001 Christmas season.

Ray Ritchey, Childbook.com
It's been a lot slower than I thought on the growth. Cash flow is a headache, as is importing items from overseas. Having a business with inventory is a headache. You try to guess what the customer will buy, and if you guess too high, you have a lot of money sitting there on a shelf doing nothing. If you guess too low, you have unhappy customers with items on back order.

Bonnie Clewans, The Bead Gallery
When I started online five years ago, I would get an order about once a week. After I started marketing my site, orders started arriving almost

daily and now I get several orders per day. The online orders are larger than my walk-in business and I am competing with large mail-order businesses. I have received orders from all over the world and developed relationships with customers from practically all fifty states. Customers enjoy our online help as well as personalized service. I looked at my competitors and decided to offer whatever service they did not.

Lynn Moller, Lynn's Collectibles
Yes! I am privileged with a large quantity of happy and loyal, repeat customers. I have found a way to help people and I can see my way to making a positive income in the near future. Winning the Open Directory (www.dmoz.org) cool site award was a nice recent surprise.

Dave Mack, RadioShack Canada
The goal of our online store was to complement our brick-and-mortar business and use our online site to drive additional traffic into these stores. It has accomplished both very well and we are very pleased with the results we have seen so far.

An online store can complement many small businesses and extend their brand presence in a very cost-effective way. If business owners have clear expectations of what they want their online store to do for them and don't allow themselves to get caught up in the hype and hundreds of optional enhancements that only offer marginal returns, this can truly be a great investment.

Deb Steinberg, Nickers & Neighs
My initial expectations were naïve and unrealistic. However, as reality set in, I was able to temper and adjust my expectations. At this point I can say that my business is growing very nicely, and we have a large number of repeat customers. We are beginning to experience some name and brand recognition within our target market, and have achieved a 100 percent increase in sales over 1999.

Chris Harrower, Choo Choo Barn
Oh, yeah! The leadership of the company had met early on in the process and said that if we reached a certain dollar amount in the first year of this process, we would be happy, but that we understand that it may take

several years to reach that lofty goal (like any new start-up). Well, in the first year online, we hit a sales volume that was seven times the initial projection and there seems to be no limit where it will go from here!

Kim Michaux, One of a Kind Kid.com

It has been great! I love it. I am able to stay home with my children, work flexible hours. The downside is that I feel like I'm always working. It's hard to get away for weekends and I've yet to figure out how to go away for a week. But that isn't any different from a non-Web-based business. I think opening an online store is the best of everything. The flexible hours are wonderful for moms—just have to give up some sleep! If you're thinking about starting an online business, go for it! If I can do this, anyone can. It is a lot of hard work, but in exchange, you get a flexible schedule and your own business.

Rhonda Wells, Payless ShoeSource

Absolutely. Our expectations were pretty simple: (1) build on our core competencies, while building synergy with our stores; (2) do not jeopardize the core business, let the customer shop and buy our great product anywhere, anytime.

Diane Morgan, Morgan Mailboxes & More

My online experience has more than met my expectations. It took me two years to get where I am today, but I have a full-time, successful online business and I have hired my first part-time employee to help keep up with the demand in orders. Not only do I have steady growth in sales, I now have businesses contacting me who are interested in my products.

Bodega Bob Homme, The Submarine Store

The only thing I can compare it to is the time when I was a little boy, about five, and my twelve-year-old neighbour got a go-cart for his birthday. One day he, some of his older friends, and his dad were out in the pasture field riding it and they offered to let me take it for a spin. I can't imagine what they were thinking, but, man, was I excited as they strapped me into that baby! I hit the gas, took off, and was so freaked by the ride (my first), and the speed (seemed like about Mach 2), and the noise (the engine sits right behind your head when you're only about four feet tall) that all I could do was hang on breathlessly and try to avoid the creek, the large rocks, the cows, and the people, while trying not to tip over or drive over the rather steep bordering hillside. I was too petrified to take my foot off the gas, so there I was, a five-year-old strapped to an out-of-control cruise missile, zipping around at full speed, scaring the hell out of the livestock, the observers, and myself! I couldn't get the situation under enough control to realize that I had to take my foot off the accelerator. All I could concentrate on was doing my best not to hit anything. Well, thankfully, the thing finally ran out of gas and I coasted to a stop, pale, shaking, breathless, wide-eyed, and with my foot still rigid against the accelerator.

The Submarine Store has certainly not run out of gas! In fact we're still growing at a rate far beyond our projections, but we've finally managed to get this baby under control.

Tane Chan, The Wok Shop
Yes … but it has consumed my evenings and nights because I am a mom-and-pop business with no pop (I'm a widow). Since I started e-mailing each and every customer, whether the message is long or short, I spend a minimum of four hours every night on my computer. The results are so incredible. The responses from customers are so gratifying, it's all worthwhile.

Christopher Mott, Mott's Miniatures
It has actually surpassed my expectations. When I took over the company in the mid-1980s, I noticed that a lot of customers we had were out-of-town or foreign visitors who did not have shops like mine near them and asked if we would ship to them. It was something that was done only on a limited basis before I took over. But my feeling was, what the heck. If I've got it, I'll put it in a box and send it to you. I built up the mail order as time went on, but then we lost our tourist location, a spot we had been at for thirty-four years. We had to move and we lost that constant flow of tourists. Now we had to pay to advertise to find customers. By 1994, I was on the verge of shutting down our mail order operations because it was too expensive to advertise, print catalogues, and own an 800 number for the dwindling orders we were receiving.

E-mail is the most widely used application on the Internet and the first thing people use when they go online.

Source: Yankee Group Survey of Online Households (www.yankeegroup.com)

e-fact

I had been looking for a way to reach out to people electronically through these new online services, AOL and CompuServe, but they were terribly expensive. I considered a CD catalogue or even trying to create my own "bulletin board" (remember those!) where people could download price lists and small pictures. To make a long story short, I found the "My Space" on AOL and put up a page. In 1995, we had our worst mail order year, every month was down from the prior year, but I decided to give the Internet one more year. The requests for catalogues and products continued to grow and more and more people were calling about product they had seen on our Web pages. By 1996, we had our own www and a secure order form. By 1998, we had our first shopping cart. Internet sales have been growing at the average rate of 96 percent per year over the last four years and are expected to remain at this level for the next three to five years. I kick myself every day when I think of the domain names I could have owned back then. Who knew! Now my company is bursting at the seams. Last November I was thinking about advertising on Yahoo! and my wife said absolutely not, we can barely keep up with the orders we have. She was right.

Doug Young, Noggintops.com
I would say that on the whole my online store experience is meeting my expectations. Perhaps that is due to the fact that I tried to keep my expectations on a realistic level to begin with. I envisioned that sales would follow a slow, steady growth curve, and so they have, for the most part. There have been some sudden large spurts as a result of some fortuitous publicity, but mostly it has been a lot of hard work and constantly, constantly, prospecting for customers. Anyone thinking an online store is going to be an easy way to get rich quickly is going to be very disappointed. I can tell you it has not been a case of simply sitting back and watching the orders magically roll in. We feel like we earn every single order. Apparently our customers feel we are earning them, too, as they are showing a level of customer loyalty and repeat purchases that has—happily— gone beyond our expectations. As I keep telling myself, "It's the customer, stupid!" I would have to say we're right where we want to be and looking forward to more of that slow, steady growth.

Jason Friedman, J&R Music and Computer World
Yes and no. I have done many things with the site that I have wanted to, but by the same token, there have been many things that I have wanted to

do since 1996, and because of time, resources, and technological limitations, have still been unable to do.

Sue Schwartz, YarnXpress.com
YarnXpress.com has surpassed my expectations and fulfilled some of my dreams. I did not expect the revenue that a fully automated shopping cart offers. Going from the inefficient mode of accepting cheques to the real-time processing of credit cards gave us access to a cash flow that enabled us to grow within the first couple of months online.

We have now grown to a point that our orders will be filled by a fulfillment centre in another state. A new member of the YarnXpress.com staff will maintain the Regional Events information portion of the site. Our sample knitters and crocheters have increased threefold. And we have had the unsurpassed pleasure of assisting some very talented knit and crochet designers enter the market. I am thrilled with our growth and sometimes overwhelmed with the future!!!

Epilogue

"Internet technology, in ways too diverse to mention, has already made a massive contribution to business internationally. It will make an even greater impact in the coming years."

—*The Sunday Herald,* January 27, 2002

After we finished the first edition of this book, the retail dot-com collapse began in full swing. All around us, day by day, came word of yet another online retailer shutting down—pet supply stores, online furniture stores, bookstores, hockey supply stores, camera stores. You name it, they tried to sell it, and they failed—miserably. The fact is they didn't sell, and they went out of business.

A sense of gloom pervaded the Internet toward the end of 2000, and permeated the world of technology right through to 2002. Web site after Web site put up notices announcing they had gone out of business. Newspapers and magazines were full of stories about the collapse of online retailers. Many people concluded that there was no future in e-commerce.

Is E-Business Dead?

Was it all but a dream? Well, if your impression of e-commerce comes from the stock market and the dot-com hysteria of the dot-com years, you might think so. The dot-com collapse might convince you there is no future for retail on the Internet.

Business-to-consumer e-commerce in the United States is projected to reach US $227.7 billion by 2005.

Source: GartnerG2 (www.gartnerg2.com)

e-fact

There is another way to think about this state of affairs, though. We should all be delighted that so many of the early Internet retailers and dot-com start-ups quickly met the great liquidator in the sky. After all, everyone now knows that plenty of these early pioneers were built on shaky foundations: business plans that didn't make sense, inadequate financing, unrealistic expectations, poor management, or a lack of understanding of markets.

Then there was the fact that the hysteria simply led to a situation in which greed took over and all common sense was thrown out the window. Quite simply, a dot-com start-up became a way for lots of people to make lots of money without any real substance to the deals at hand. They ended up where they deserved to be, and plenty of people were happy to see them go. After all, the collapse helps to return the world of the Internet and e-commerce to sanity—and allows folks like you to get on with the job of figuring out how you might be able to sell things online.

E-Biz Is Not Dead!

Our attitude is that far from being dead, e-business is thriving. Get beyond the dot-com hype and you can find countless people (as we did in Chapter 8) who have been successful at selling online, building successful businesses, winning customers, making a profit, extending their reach to global markets, and having fun!

The number of Canadians shopping online will reach 7.2 million by 2005.

Source: Forrester Research (www.forrester.com)

e-fact

Quite evidently, as more and more people use the Internet in every aspect of their lives, it has come to play a huge role in our consumer behaviour. It has become a sales channel—not one that replaces traditional sales channels—but one that augments them.

For small businesses in particular, having an online store can help you generate sales from people who would never have found you if it weren't for the Internet. For example, take a look at the Web site of Barnstable Bat Co. (www.barnstablebat.com), a company that makes wooden baseball bats. Since creating a Web site a few years ago, the owner has seen sales increase by 35 percent, and online sales now account for 20 percent of the 12,000 bats the company sells each year. Barnstable even made a sale to the Slovenian national baseball team, a sale that wouldn't have been possible had the team not found the store on the Web.

The point is, there are many, many more examples of companies like Barnstable Bat Co. that have found success with online retailing. Unfortunately, they tend to be obscured by all the stories of companies that have failed on the Web.

---

e-fact

The number of Internet users around the world will reach 943 million by 2005.

Source: International Data Corporation (www.idc.com)

Far from being over, e-commerce is just getting started as an industry. And the fact is, those individuals who learn to work with the Web, understand it, experiment with it, and integrate it into their existing lines of businesses will be able to take advantage of all the exciting opportunities that e-commerce provides, which leads to the final question. Can you do it? Can you sell online?

Of course you can! And when you do, we'd love to hear from you!

Jim and Rick

jcarroll@jimcarroll.com / rickb@rickbroadhead.com

APPENDIX:
Financial Institution/Merchant Acquirer—Contact Directory

Name of FI	Merchant Acquirer	Department	Telephone Number	Web Address
Scotiabank	The Bank of Nova Scotia	Merchant Services	1-800-265-5158	www.scotiabank.ca
CIBC Canada Inc.	Global Payments	Merchant Help Desk	1-800-263-2970	www.globalpay.com
Visa Desjardins	Visa Desjardins	Merchant Services	1-888-285-0015	www.desjardins.com
Laurentian Bank of Canada	Laurentian Bank of Canada	Visa Merchant Services	1-514-284-5842	www.laurebtianbank.com
RBC Financial Group	Moneris Solutions	Merchant Services	1-800-268-8644	www.moneris.com
TDCanada Trust	TDCanada Trust	Merchant Sales and Service	1-800-363-1163	www.tdcanadatrust.com
Van City	Vancouver City Savings Credit Union	Merchant Services	1-604-877-7582	www.vancity.com

INDEX